P9-DMY-922

THE
NEW
FATHER

A DAD'S GUIDE
TO THE FIRST YEAR

Oooglie ooglie googlie googlie...
Who is this person? Where's the one with the milk??
SIPRESS

THE
NEW
FATHER

3rd EDITION

A DAD'S GUIDE
TO THE FIRST YEAR

ARMIN A. BROTT

Abbeville Press Publishers
New York · London

For Zoë, Talya, and Tirzah, who teach me every day
what fatherhood is all about

EDITOR: Jacqueline Decter
DESIGNER: Celia Fuller
PRODUCTION EDITOR: Nicole Lanctot
PRODUCTION MANAGER: Louise Kurtz

Text copyright © 2015, 2004, 1997 Armin A. Brott. Compilation—including selection of text and images—copyright © 2015, 2004, 1997 Abbeville Press. All rights reserved under international copyright conventions. No part of this book may be reproduced or utilized in any form or by any means, electronic or mechanical, including photocopying, recording, or by any information storage and retrieval system, without permission in writing from the publisher. Inquiries should be addressed to Abbeville Press, 655 Third Avenue, New York, NY 10017. The text of this book was set in Kepler Std. Printed and bound in the United States of America.

Third paperback edition
10   9   8   7   6
ISBN 978-0-7892-1177-4

Cover photograph by Geoff Spear. For cartoon credits, see page 334.

Library of Congress Cataloging-in-Publication Data
  Brott, Armin A.
  The new father : a dad's guide to the first year / by Armin A. Brott. —,
Third edition.
      pages cm.—(New father series)
  Summary: "An essential handbook for first-year fathers with a
  month-to-month guide to baby's development"—Provided by publisher.
  ISBN 978-0-7892-1176-7 (hardcover)—ISBN 978-0-7892-1177-4 (paperback)
  1. Infants. 2. Infants—Care. 3. Father and infant. I. Title.
  HQ774.B777 2015
  649'.122—dc23
                    2015005705

For bulk and premium sales and for text adoption procedures, write to Customer Service Manager, Abbeville Press, 655 Third Avenue, New York, NY 10017, or call 1-800-ARTBOOK.

Visit Abbeville Press online at www.abbeville.com.

Contents

Introduction

Nobody really knows how or when it started, but one of the most widespread—and most cherished—myths about child-rearing is that women are naturally more nurturing than men, that they are instinctively better at the parenting thing, and that men are nearly incompetent.

The facts, however, tell a very different story. A significant amount of research has proven that men are inherently just as nurturing and responsive to their children's needs as women. What too many men (and women) don't realize is that to the extent that women are "better" parents, it's simply because they've had more practice. In fact, the single most important factor in determining the depth of long-term father-child relationships is opportunity.

Basically, it comes down to this: "Having children makes you no more a parent than having a piano makes you a pianist," writes author Michael Levine in *Lessons at the Halfway Point.*

Men and women parent differently in a wide variety of ways:

- Dads tend to play more with their children than mothers do, and that play tends to be more rough-and-tumble and more unpredictable than mothers'. In other words, dads are more likely than moms to become human jungle gyms.
- Dads tend to emphasize independence more than moms and give children more freedom to explore. If a baby is struggling to grab a toy that's just out of reach, mothers are more likely to move the toy closer, while dads are more likely to wait a little longer, seeing whether the baby will be able to get it. Moms are more likely to pick up a toddler who's fallen, while dads are more likely to encourage the child to get up on his own.
- Dads tend to use more complex speech patterns than mothers, who tend to simplify what they're saying and slow it down. Dads also tend to ask their

babies more open-ended questions (who, what, where, when, why) than moms, an approach that helps kids expand their vocabulary.

- Dads tend to think more about how a child will fare in the world as he or she grows; moms tend to think more about the child's emotional development. When reacting to a test score, for example, a dad might be concerned about how the score will affect the child's future plans and ability to be self-sufficient, while a mom is more likely to be concerned about how the score makes the child feel.
- Dads tend to represent the outside world while mothers represent the home. You can see this almost anyplace where parents are out with their babies: dads tend to hold their children face out, while mothers hold them face in.

Please keep in mind here that I'm talking about general *tendencies*. Plenty of moms wrestle with their kids and use big words, and many dads rush to pick up fallen toddlers and hold their babies facing inward. The point is that they parent differently—not better or worse, just differently. And children benefit greatly from having plenty of exposure to both styles.

It shouldn't come as any surprise, then, that fathers have very different needs from mothers when it comes to parenting information and resources. But more than a decade into the twenty-first century, the vast majority of books, videos, seminars, and magazine articles on raising kids are still aimed primarily at women and focus on helping them acquire the skills they need to be better parents. Fathers have been essentially ignored—until now.

HOW THIS BOOK IS DIFFERENT

Because babies develop so quickly, most resources aimed at parents of infants (babies from birth through twelve months) are broken down by month and focus mostly on how babies develop during this period. That's pretty important stuff, so we spend a little time covering similar territory. However, the primary focus of *The New Father: A Dad's Guide to the First Year* is on how *dads* change, grow, and develop over the first twelve months of fatherhood. That's an approach that has rarely, if ever, been tried.

Going from *man* to *father* is one of the most dramatic changes you'll ever experience. It'll force you to rethink who you are, what you do, and what it means to be a man. Your relationships—with your partner, your parents, your friends, your coworkers—will change forever as you begin to reevaluate what's important to you and reorder your priorities. Some parts of the man-to-father transition are sudden: one day it's just you and your partner, the next day you've got a baby. But for the most part, fatherhood is a gradual, ever-changing process that will last your entire lifetime. Most of us develop and change along fairly predictable lines, but the journey is always a little different for everyone.

The first year may be the most important one in your development as a father. It's the time when you start forming those all-important parent-child bonds and start laying the foundation of your lifelong relationship with each other. It's also especially interesting because the growth and development you experience during these first twelve months is kind of a condensed version of what you'll go through over the rest of your life as a parent.

Each of the chapters is divided into several major sections:

What's Going On with the Baby

This short section is designed to give you an overview of the four major areas of your baby's development: physical, intellectual, verbal, and emotional/social. A lot of what you're going to experience as a father is directly related to, or in response to, your children. So knowing the basics of your baby's growth will help put your own growth into better perspective. Please remember, however, that babies develop at different rates, and that the range of "normal" behavior is very wide. If your baby isn't doing the things covered in the predicted month, don't worry. But if he's more than a few months behind, check with your pediatrician.

What You're Going Through

Because the things new dads think, worry, panic, dream, and rejoice about have largely been ignored in parenting books, many men think the feelings and concerns they have are abnormal. In this section we dig deep into what new fathers go through and the ways they grow and develop—emotionally and psychologically—over the course of their fatherhood. You're a lot more normal than you think.

But wait, there's more . . .

What's Going On with Your Partner

One of the most important parts of being a good dad is being a good spouse. That's why I'm including special sections in the first several chapters that deal with your partner's physical, emotional, and psychological recovery and specific ways you can help.

You and Your Baby

This section gives you all the tools you need to understand and create the deepest, closest possible relationship with your child—even if you have only half an hour a day to spend with her. In this section we cover topics as diverse as play, music, reading, discipline, and temperament.

Family Matters

A number of the chapters feature a "Family Matters" section in which we discuss a variety of issues that will have a major impact not only on you but also on your family as a whole. Topics include dealing with crying, postpartum depression (which men get too!), childproofing, family finances, and finding appropriate child care. Many chapters also include a special "You and Your Partner" section that focuses on specific topics that may affect your relationship with the mother of your children.

WHY GET INVOLVED?

First, because it's good for your kids, your partner, and even yourself:
- For your baby. Numerous studies have shown that the more involved dads are with their infants, the better they perform on all sorts of intelligence tests. Babies who are deprived of quality time with their fathers in the first year of life often have problems forming stable relationships later in life. Apparently, not having a dad around makes it hard for children to develop the kinds of behavior that other children value. In addition, the more actively involved dads are with their babies, the more physically coordinated they are. They also feel more comfortable around strangers and handle stressful situations better.
- For your partner and your marriage. Division-of-labor issues are one of the top causes of marital stress. The more involved you are and the more emotionally supportive, the happier your partner will be and the better she'll perform her parenting duties. Men whose partners are happy in their relationships tend to be happier themselves. And men who are happy in their relationships are generally more involved as dads. It just never ends—and there's no reason why it should.
- For you. As we'll discuss throughout this book, being an involved father will affect you in a number of ways. You'll learn to feel, express, and manage emotions (positive, negative, and everything in between) you never knew you had. You'll be more empathetic and better able to see things from others' perspectives. Plus, dads who are actively involved with their children tend to be mentally and physically healthier and are more likely to advance in their careers. It can also change the way you think about yourself. "Fathering often helps men to clarify their values and to set priorities," writes my colleague Ross Parke, one of the pioneers in fatherhood research. "It may enhance their self-esteem if they

manage its demands and responsibilities well, or alternatively, it may be unsettling and depressing by revealing their limitations and weaknesses. Fathers can learn from their children and be matured by them."

A NOTE ON TERMINOLOGY

He, She, It

In the not-so-distant past (and the present, too, really) parenting books, in which the parent is assumed to be the mother, almost always referred to the baby as "he." While there's an argument to be made that in English the male pronoun is sort of a generic term, as the father of three girls, I wanted to see at least an occasional "she," just to let me know that what I was reading might actually apply to my children. But as a writer, I find that phrases like "his or her," "he or she," and especially "s/he" make for cumbersome reading and awkward sentences and I really don't like using "they" as a singular. "It" doesn't seem like the right word to use when talking about a human being, and those manufactured gender-neutral pronouns (such as "ni," "nirs," "xe," and "xyrs") aren't yet ready for prime time. The solution? I'm simply going to alternate between "he" and "she" one chapter at a time. Except in a few specific cases (circumcision, for example), the terms are interchangeable.

Your Partner in Parenting

In much the same way that calling all babies "he" discounts the experience of all the "shes" out there, calling all mothers "wives" essentially denies the existence of the many, many other women who have children: girlfriends, lovers, live-in companions, fiancées, and so on. So, to keep from making any kind of statement about the importance (or lack of importance, depending on how you feel) of marriage, I refer to the mother of your child as "your partner," just as I did in *The Expectant Father: The Ultimate Guide for Dads-to-Be*.

IF SOME OF THIS SOUNDS A LITTLE FAMILIAR…

If you read *The Expectant Father* (and if you didn't, it's not too late), you may notice that there's a little bit of overlap between the end of that book and the early part of this book. I assure you that this repetition of material is less the result of laziness on my part than of the necessity born of having to cover several of the same important topics in both books. After all, the birth that ends a pregnancy is the same one that launches a childhood.

WHAT THIS BOOK ISN'T

While there's no doubt that this book is filled with information you can't get any-where else, it is not intended to take the place of your pediatrician, financial planner, or lawyer. Naturally, I wouldn't suggest that you do anything I wouldn't do (or haven't done already). Still, before blindly following my advice, please save us both a lot of unnecessary worry, and check with an appropriate professional.

① Congratulations, You're a Dad!

WEEK

WHAT'S GOING ON WITH THE BABY

Physically

- Although most of your newborn's physical capabilities are run by a series of reflexes (see pages 60–61), she does have some control over her tiny body.
- She can focus her eyes—for a few seconds, at least—on an object held 8–12 inches from her face, and she may be able to move her head from side to side.
- She probably won't eat much for the first 24 hours, but after that, she'll want 7–8 feedings each day. In between all those meals, she'll try to suck on anything that comes near her mouth.
- At around 40 breaths and 120 heartbeats/minute, her metabolism is zipping along about twice as fast as yours.
- Her intestines are moving even faster: she'll urinate as many as 18 times and move those brand-new bowels 4–7 times every 24 hours.
- To help her recover from all that activity, she'll spend 80–90 percent of her time asleep, taking as many as 8 naps a day. Some babies, though, sleep as few as 8 hours.

Intellectually

- Right from birth, your baby is capable of making a number of intellectual decisions.
- If she hears a sound, she can tell whether it's coming from the right, the left, straight ahead, or even behind.
- She can distinguish between sweet and sour (preferring sweet, like most of us).

- She also has a highly developed sense of smell. Before the end of this week, she'll be able to tell the difference between a pad sprinkled with her own mother's milk and one from another nursing mother.
- Although her eyes may seem to work independently of each other, she likes looking at things, preferring simple patterns to complex ones and the borders of objects (such as your jaw or hairline) to the inner details (mouth and nose).
- She can't, however, differentiate herself from the other objects in her world. If she grasps your hand, for example, her little brain doesn't know whether she's holding her own hand or yours—or, for that matter, that those things on the ends of her arms even belong to her.

Verbally

- At this point, most of the vocal sounds your baby produces will be cries or animal-like grunts, snorts, and squeaks.

Emotionally/Socially

- Although she's alert and comfortable for only 30 or so minutes out of every 4 hours, your baby comes prewired to connect with you. Within a few hours (or days at most), she'll follow your gaze and try to mimic your facial expressions. And she prefers looking at a drawing of a face to one with the features scrambled.
- When she hears a voice or other noise—especially your partner's or yours (although it could also be a faucet dripping or a heavy metal band)—she may become quiet and try to focus.
- She's capable of showing excitement and distress, and will probably quiet down when you pick her up. She's also capable of expressing empathy for others (we'll talk more about that in later chapters).

WHAT'S GOING ON WITH YOUR PARTNER

Physically

- Vaginal discharge (called *lochia*) that will gradually change from bloody to pink to brown to yellow over the next six weeks or so.
- Major discomfort if there is an episiotomy or C-section incision (the pain will disappear over the next six weeks).
- Constipation.

- Breast discomfort—starting on about the third day after the birth (when her breasts become engorged with milk), and as soon as she starts breastfeeding, her nipples will probably be sore for about two weeks.
- Gradual weight loss.
- Exhaustion—especially if her labor was long and difficult.
- Continued contractions, especially while breastfeeding, but disappearing gradually over the next several days.
- Hair loss. Most women stop losing hair while they're pregnant, but when the pregnancy's over, so are all those great-hair days.

Emotionally

- Relief that it's finally over.
- Excitement, depression, or both (see pages 59, 62–63).
- Worry about how she'll perform as a mother, and whether she'll be able to breastfeed. But as her confidence builds over the next few weeks, those worries should disappear.
- A deep need to get to know the baby.
- Impatience at her lack of mobility.
- Decreased sex drive, assuming she had any left before the baby came.

WHAT YOU'RE GOING THROUGH

Congratulations, You're a Dad!

Well, the pregnancy you and your partner have shared for the past nine months is over, and although it may not have hit you yet, you've got a family now, which means all sorts of new responsibilities, pressures, and expectations to live up to. For some new fathers, this seemingly basic epiphany comes early, before they leave the hospital. For others, reality may not sink in for a few days. But whenever it hits, you'll always remember being there for the birth of your baby as one of the great moments of your life.

Right now, though, you may be feeling a little helpless and overwhelmed. But if you're like most guys I've spoken with over the years, you'll also experience at least some of the following feelings immediately after the birth:

- love
- excitement, almost like being intoxicated
- the desire to hold and touch and rock and kiss the baby

- an even stronger desire to simply stare dumbfounded at the baby
- accomplishment, pride, and disbelief
- virility and self-worth
- a powerful connection to your baby and partner
- the need to count toes and fingers to make sure everything's where it's supposed to be
- curiosity about whether the baby's features are more like yours or your partner's

Back in the 1970s, Dr. Martin Greenberg did a study of fathers who were present for their child's delivery (which was relatively rare then). The men in his study had many of the above feelings, and Greenberg coined a term, *engrossment*, to describe "a father's sense of absorption, preoccupation, and interest in his baby."

What triggers engrossment in men? Exactly the same thing that prompts similar nurturing feelings in women: early contact with their infants. So take a deep breath and do what feels most natural to you—chances are it'll be exactly the right thing.

The truth is—and there's a lot of research to back me up on this—that from the instant their children are born, fathers are just as caring, interested, and involved with their infants as mothers are, and they hold, touch, kiss, rock, and coo at their new babies at least as frequently as mothers do.

Comparing How You Imagined the Birth Would Go with How It Went

Let's face it: every expecting couple secretly (or not so secretly) hopes for a pain-free, twenty-minute labor, and very few people ever really plan for a horrible birth experience. Even in childbirth education classes, if the instructor talks at all about the unpleasant things that can happen, she usually refers to them as "contingencies"—a word that makes it seem as though everything is still under control.

If your partner's labor and delivery went according to plan, chances are you're delighted with the way things turned out, and you're oohing and ahhing over your baby. But if there were any problems—induced labor, an emergency C-section, a threat to your partner's or your baby's life—your whole impression of the birth process may have changed. It's not unusual in these cases to blame the baby for causing your partner so much physical pain and you so much psychological agony. It can happen easily, without your really being aware of it.

So pay close attention during the first few weeks to how you're feeling about your baby. If you find yourself angry or resentful of her, or thinking or saying things—even in jest—such as "All the pain is the baby's fault," or (as I did) "The

baby had jammed herself in there sideways and refused to come out," try to remember that no matter how brilliant and talented you think your baby is, she was a completely passive player in the entire process. Giving in to the temptation to blame your baby for anything at this point can seriously interfere with your future relationship together.

The Brief "Is This Really My Baby?" Phase

The first thing I did after each of my daughters was born was count their arms, legs, fingers, and toes. Once all limbs and extremities were accounted for, I quickly looked them over to see whether they had "my" nose or chin.

Later on, I felt a little guilty about that—after all, shouldn't I have been hugging and kissing my daughters instead of giving them a full-body inspection? Maybe, but as it turns out, that's what almost all new dads do within the first few minutes after the birth of their babies: immediately look for physical similarities—as if to prove to themselves that the baby is truly theirs. This happens for a reason: for most of us—regardless of how many prenatal doctor appointments we went to, how many times we heard the baby's heartbeat or saw her squirm around on an ultrasound, and how many times we felt her kick—the baby isn't completely "real" until after the birth, when we finally have a chance to meet each other face to face. "Seeing the infant emerge from his mate's body through vaginal or cesarean birth is a powerful experience for each father," writes researcher Pamela Jordan. "Birth proved that this infant had been the growth within the mother's abdomen."

As it turns out, only one of my daughters has "my" chin, and it's looking like none of them will have to suffer through life with my nose (and the accompanying sinus problems). When the first two were born, I remember being very disappointed that neither of them had the Brott family webbed toes (it isn't all that noticeable, but it helps my swimming immeasurably). But you can't imagine my delight when I found a little webbing between the youngest one's toes (she's also the only one of the three who's shown a serious interest in swimming).

Now, Wait a Minute—This Isn't What I Was Expecting at All

Babies hardly ever look exactly as you imagined they would before they were born. And being disappointed about a nose, a chin, or even some toes is something you'll get over soon enough—especially when you discover in a few weeks that the baby does have something of yours (they always do).

But what if the baby has a penis or a vagina when you were expecting the opposite? Getting a boy when you expected a girl, or vice versa, can be a real shock. A team of Swedish researchers found that fathers are generally more satisfied with their roles when their babies—boys or girls—are the sex they'd hoped for. But if the fantasy doesn't materialize, regret can settle in and interfere with your accepting and loving your baby. In fact, children who aren't the sex their parents wanted have worse relationships with their parents in childhood than preferred-sex kids. That seems to be especially true for kids whose parents had wanted a boy but got a girl.

YOU AND YOUR PARTNER

Her Emotional and Physical Recovery after a C-Section

Having an unplanned C-section can trigger a whole host of conflicting emotions in your partner. She, like you, may feel greatly relieved that the pain is over and the baby is safe. At the same time, it's very natural for her to second-guess herself and the decisions she made, to start wondering whether there was anything she could have done to avoid the operation, or to believe she's failed because she didn't deliver vaginally. These feelings are especially common when the C-section

Coping with a Special-Needs Child

We all expect a perfect baby, but unfortunately not everyone gets one. In recent years, technology has made it easier for expectant parents to avoid having—or at least to prepare themselves for—a disabled child.

But prepared or not, parents of disabled children still have plenty of adjusting to do. For some fathers, having a disabled child is similar to having a miscarriage—there's a mourning for the child who might have been. Some feel shock, anger, disbelief, or denial. They may blame themselves and see the child as a kind of punishment, or they may blame their partner. Others feel ambivalent and may even secretly wish that the child had died.

Having a child with a disability can be particularly tough for highly educated or intellectual couples who had great expectations for their baby, expectations the baby may never be able to live up to. Interestingly, moms and dads react somewhat differently. Moms tend to be more concerned about the emotional strain of having to care for the child, while dads are more concerned with the costs of providing care and with the baby's ability to be a leader and her potential for academic success. Having a child with a disability can undermine a father's feelings of masculinity and his confidence in himself.

According to researcher Michael Lamb, couples who are in better marriages and who have more social support have an easier time coming to terms with their disabled child. He also found that acceptance of the disabled child by the father's parents has a big influence on the father's acceptance of the child. Oddly, boys with intellectual disabilities seem to have a more negative impact on marriages than girls. This may reflect fathers' and mothers' greater expectations for their sons (and, sadly, lower ones for their daughters).

was performed because labor "failed to progress" (meaning that the cervix wasn't dilating as quickly as the doctors thought it should).

If you sense that your partner is experiencing any of these negative emotions, it's important for you to counter them immediately. She really needs to know that *no one* could have done more, or been stronger or braver than she was; that she didn't give in to the pain too soon; that she tried everything humanly possible to jump-start a stalled labor; that another few hours of labor that wasn't going anywhere wouldn't have done anyone any good; and that the decision she made (or at least agreed to) was the best one—both for the baby and for herself.

Some of these thoughts might seem obvious—so obvious that you might think they don't need to be said at all. But they do—especially by you. You were there with her, and you know better than anyone else exactly what she went through. So being comforted and praised by you will mean a lot more to her than hearing the same words from a well-meaning nurse or doctor.

Having a baby isn't a competition, although some people make it into one. (Hearing a bunch of new moms talk about their labor redefines the concept of macho. "I had a 17-hour labor." "Well, mine was 22 hours—and I did it without any drugs." "Oh, yeah, mine was . . .")

As far as her physical recovery goes, keep the following in mind while you're at the hospital. We'll talk more about at-home recovery a little later in this chapter.

- Your partner's incision will be tender or downright painful for at least several days. Fortunately, she'll most likely be receiving some intravenous (IV) pain medication.
- The nursing staff will visit quite frequently to make sure that your partner's uterus is getting firm and returning to its proper place, to see whether she's producing enough urine, and to check her bandages.
- Your partner will have an IV until her bowels start functioning again (usually one to three days after delivery). After the IV is removed, she'll start on a liquid diet, then add a few soft foods, and finally return to her normal diet.
- Your partner will need to get up and move around. Even though a C-section is major abdominal surgery, fewer than twenty-four hours after the delivery the nurses will probably encourage—and help—your partner to get out of bed and take a couple of rather painful-looking steps.
- Before your partner leaves the hospital, the sutures or staples will be removed. Yes, staples. Until I heard the clink as the doctor dropped them into a jar, I'd just assumed that my wife had been sewn up after her C-section. In some cases, the surgeon may use dissolvable stitches, glue, or tape to close the incision.

YOU AND YOUR BABY

First Impressions

Before I became a father, I'm quite sure that I believed that my children—even right after their birth—would be stunningly gorgeous. Well, chalk up another victory for the ad execs. The fact is that in most cases, babies look a little strange. If your baby was born vaginally, the trip through the birth canal may have made her look like she just got beat up—cone headed, mushed, and bruised. She came out covered in white cheesy-looking stuff, her eyes may be swollen and cross-eyed, and her hairy back and shoulders might have you worrying about what'll happen when the moon is full.

Take it easy. Within a few weeks her nose will pop out, and her head will get rounder (C-section babies usually look a little better). The cheesy stuff is called *vernix*, and it's a natural moisturizer that protects the baby's skin while she's in the womb. The puffy eyes are most likely the result of the antibiotic ointment the medical staff put in her eyes after birth to prevent infection, and that fuzz on her back is called *lanugo*, and it'll fall out pretty soon.

But for a lot of new dads, the biggest shock is the condition of their babies' skin—all those splotches (especially on the neck and the eyelids), strange-looking birthmarks, and tiny zits can be a little disconcerting. But before you grab your cell phone and call a dermatologist, take a minute and read about some of the more common, and perfectly normal, conditions:

- Acne. These cute little pimples are usually confined to the baby's face and are either the result of your partner's hormones continuing to swim through the baby's system or of her underdeveloped pores. Either way, don't squeeze, poke, pick at, or scrub these pimples. Just wash them with water a few times a day, pat them dry, and they'll go away in a few months.

- Blisters. Pictures taken of babies in utero have shown that long before birth they frequently suck their thumbs—or any other part of their body they can reach. Sometimes they suck so hard, they raise blisters.

- Jaundice. If your baby's skin and/or the whites of her eyes seem a little yellow, she may have jaundice. This condition is the result of the baby's liver being unable to adequately process *bilirubin*, a yellowish by-product of red blood cells. It affects about 25 percent of newborns (and a higher percentage of preemies), appears within the first five days of life, and is usually gone a few days later.

- Splotches, blotches, and birthmarks. They can be white, purple, brown, or even yellow with white bumps in the center, and they can appear on the face, legs, arms, and back. In most cases, they'll go away on their own if you just leave them alone. But if you're really worried, check with your pediatrician.

- Cradle cap (or, more informally, "cradle crap"). Also called *seborrheic dermatitis*, this stuff looks like flaky, yellowish, sometimes greasy dandruff. It usually shows up on the head, but it can also work its way into baby's eyebrows. It's not a serious condition and will bother you much more than it does the baby. It's also not contagious, and regular shampooing with a baby shampoo may help it go away.

Let the Tests Begin

Your baby's first few minutes outside the womb are going to be a time of intense physical and emotional release for you and your partner. She may want to try nursing the baby (although it's going to be mostly for bonding purposes; most newborns aren't hungry for at least the first twelve hours or so), and you'll probably want to stroke her brand-new skin and marvel at her tiny fingernails. But depending on the hospital and the conditions of the birth, your baby's first few minutes could be spent being poked and prodded by doctors and nurses instead of being held and cuddled by you.

One minute after she's born, your baby will be examined to give the medical staff a quick take on her overall condition. (You may have thought that the first test your child would really have to worry about passing would be the SAT, or maybe the exam they give kids before they get accepted into exclusive preschools. But oh, no—it starts waaaay sooner than that.) The Apgar test (named after anesthesiologist Virginia Apgar, who first started using the test in the early 1950s) measures your baby's Appearance (skin color), Pulse, Grimace (reflexes), Activity, and Respiration. The nurse or midwife will chart your baby's Apgar score at one minute and five minutes after birth. The score sheet looks something like the chart on the next page. Keep in mind that the scores are used by the medical staff to help them determine how much intervention (if any) the baby needs. Although the scores have absolutely nothing to do with IQ or future earning power, and college admissions committees never ask for them, they do give new parents a handy (but completely useless) way of comparing their children.

The theoretical maximum score is 10, but anything between 7 and 10 at one minute is a sign of good health. Almost no baby gets a 10 (unless she's the child of someone on the medical team) because most of them are born with slightly blue toes and fingers. This means that the baby needs only routine care. A baby who scores 4–6 may require some medical intervention such as oxygen or suction to remove mucus from the throat or lungs. A score of less than 4 may indicate the need for resuscitation. However, a low score could be the result of pain medication given to the mother or of the baby being born prematurely. The test will be done again at five minutes after birth to assess the effectiveness of the interventions. If the score is still low, the test will be repeated at five-minute intervals.

At the same time as the tests are going on, your baby will be weighed, measured, given ID and security bracelets, bathed, diapered, footprinted, have some antibiotic ointment applied to her eyes, get a quick injection of Vitamin K (to prevent bleeding and help her blood clot properly), and be wrapped in a blanket. She may even get her first picture taken. If your baby was delivered by C-section,

APGAR TEST	2 POINTS	1 POINT	0 POINTS
A-Appearance	The entire body is pink from head to toe	Body is pink but arms and/or legs may be bluish	Body is entirely blue, pale, or gray
P-Pulse and heart rate	Above 100 beats per minute	Fewer than 100 beats per minute	Not detectible
G-Grimace (reflexes)	Loud cry when reflexes are stimulated	Moderate crying or whimpering when reflexes are stimulated	No response
A-Activity	Lots of movement of the arms or legs	Some movement of the arms and legs	No move-ment at all
R-Respiration	Big breaths and lots of crying mean those little lungs are working well	Slow, weak, or irregular breaths	No breathing

or if there were any other complications, she'll have her little lungs suctioned before returning for the rest of the cleanup routine.

Quality Time Starts Now

Most hospitals now encourage "rooming in"—keeping the baby in the same room as the new mom and dad. Some don't have nurseries at all, except the ones for babies with serious health problems. Others still have nurseries but offer unlimited access for the parents.

If your hospital does have a nursery, you may want to take advantage of it. You may be tempted to have the baby room with your partner, but depending on how the birth went, she might really need to rest. Ask the nursing staff to bring the baby to your partner at feeding times. You, on the other hand, can spend as much time as you want with the baby. Of course, if your partner would prefer to have the baby nearby—plenty of new moms want exactly that—don't bother arguing with her.

And while we're on the subject of rest, you may have to get tough with the staff to make sure your partner gets enough. The nurses will tell her that she needs to sleep as much as possible, but if you don't ask them to give her a break, they'll be in every hour or two to check her vital signs.

The Placenta

For some reason, before my first child was born I'd never really thought very much about the placenta, which had been my daughter's life-support system for a lot of the pregnancy. But whether you think about it or not, it's still there—and it has to come out.

After the baby is born, your partner will continue to have mild contractions for anywhere from five minutes to about an hour until the placenta is delivered. The strange thing about this stage of the delivery is that neither you nor your partner will probably even know it's happening—you'll be much too involved with your new baby and with each other.

Once the placenta is out, however, you need to decide what to do with it. In this country most people never even see it, and those who do just leave it at the hospital (where it will either be destroyed or, more likely, sold to a cosmetics company—honest). But in many other cultures, the placenta is considered to have a permanent, almost magical bond with the child it nourished in the womb, and disposal is handled with a great deal more reverence. Some have special rituals and believe that if the placenta isn't properly buried, the child—or the parents, or even the entire village—will suffer some terrible consequences.

In rural Peru, for example, the father is required to go to a far-off location and bury the placenta deep enough so that no animals or people will accidentally discover it. Otherwise, it might become "jealous" of the attention paid to the baby and take revenge by causing an epidemic.

In some South American Indian cultures, they believe that a child's life can be influenced by objects that are buried with its placenta. Boys' placentas are

Newborn Screenings

If you thought the testing was over with the Apgar test, think again. Even the healthiest-looking babies sometimes have invisible disorders that, if undetected, could stunt their physical and intellectual growth, lead to permanent brain or organ damage, and even cause death. Caught early, most of these disorders can be controlled or even cured. For that reason, your baby will be tested for a number of conditions before you're allowed to take her home.

There are three types of tests: blood, hearing, and heart.

BLOOD TESTS

In the U.S., about 19,000 babies have a treatable condition that could be picked up by a screening test. Several organizations have pushed for a Recommended

frequently buried with a shovel or a pick, and girls' are buried with a loom or a hoe. In the Philippines, some bury the placenta with books as a way of ensuring intelligence.

But placentas are not always buried. In ancient Egypt, pharaohs' placentas were wrapped in special containers to keep them from harm. Traditional Vietnamese medicine uses placentas to combat sterility and senility, and in India, touching a placenta is supposed to help a childless woman conceive a healthy baby of her own. And in China, some believe that breastfeeding mothers can improve the quality of their milk by drinking a broth made of boiled placenta.

This sort of placenta usage isn't limited to non-Western cultures. Even today, in France and other countries, placentas are found in a variety of products, including cosmetics and medicines. And some people even believe that eating some of the placenta (called *placentophagy*) may help a new mom increase her milk supply and reduce her pain and the risk of developing postpartum depression. There's no solid scientific proof behind any of that. But one thing is for sure, if your partner chooses to do this, she should stick to her own. Yumm.

Whatever you and your partner decide to do, it's probably best to keep it a secret—at least from the hospital staff. Some states try to regulate what you can do with a placenta and may even prohibit you from taking it home (although if you really want to, you can probably find a sympathetic nurse who will pack it in a Tupperware container for you). My oldest's placenta stayed at the hospital, but we stored the younger ones' in the freezer for a year before burying them and planting trees on top.

Universal Screening Panel (RUSP) that would require routine testing for more than fifty conditions. But for now, each state sets its own standards and depending on where you live, the actual number of required tests ranges from four to more than forty. (Babysfirsttest.org has a complete listing of the screenings required by your state at www.babysfirsttest.org/newborn-screening/states.) The good news is that all of those tests can be done from the same sample, a few drops of blood taken from your baby's heel immediately after the birth.

HEARING TESTS

About 1 in 1,000 healthy babies and 2 in 100 in intensive care units have hearing loss. If the loss is caught during newborn screenings, babies can be fitted with hearing aids that can help prevent speech and language problems. If it's not caught early, it might not be evident until age two or three and will be far harder to deal with. The tests are safe, quick, and painless; in fact, babies usually sleep right through them.

HEART TESTS

About 9 in 1,000 babies are born with some kind of congenital heart disease. Doctors use a non-invasive test called *pulse oximetry* to check your baby's heart rate and the levels of oxygen in her blood. The goal is to flag a group of heart conditions called Critical Congenital Heart Disease (CCHD), which can include abnormal heart rhythms and potentially dangerous structural problems. Caught early, many CCHDs can be treated and babies can lead relatively normal lives.

GETTING TO KNOW YOU

"Most people make babies out to be very complicated," says comedian Dave Barry, "but the truth is they have only three moods: Mood One: Just about to cry. Mood Two: Crying. Mood Three: Just finished crying. Your job, as a parent, is to keep the baby in Mood Three as much as possible." With just a few days of fatherhood under your belt, you may be inclined to go along with Barry's summary. But the real truth is that babies' moods are a bit more subtle.

Babies actually have six clearly defined behavioral states that are apparent within just a few minutes after their birth. In my first few weeks of fatherhood, I found that learning about these six states—which were explained to me by Dr. Marshall Klaus, coauthor of *The Amazing Newborn*—was absolutely critical to my getting to know my babies. Here's a summary of the six states, based on Dr. Klaus's book.

QUIET ALERT

Within the first hour of life, most healthy infants have a period of quiet alertness that lasts an average of forty minutes, and during her first week, she'll spend about 10 percent of any twenty-four-hour period in this state. Babies in quiet alert mode rarely move—all their energy is channeled into seeing, hearing, and absorbing information about their new world. They can (and do) follow objects with their eyes and may even imitate your facial expressions. That's when it'll first hit you that there's a real person inside that tiny body.

ACTIVE ALERT

In the active alert state, the baby will make small sounds and move her arms, head, body, face, and eyes frequently and actively. Her movements usually come in short bursts—a few seconds of thrashing around every minute or two. Some researchers say these movements are designed to give parents subtle clues about what the baby wants and needs. Others say they're just interesting to watch, and therefore promote parent-infant interaction. Either way, the active alert state is a great time to do physical things with your baby—we'll talk about what, exactly, that means in the "You and Your Baby" sections throughout the rest of this book.

CRYING

Crying is a perfectly natural—and for some, all-too-frequent—state (for more on this, see pages 66–70). Your infant's eyes may be open or closed, her face red, and her arms and legs moving vigorously. (Don't be surprised if you don't see any tears: newborns' tear ducts often don't function for the first week or two after delivery. When the tears finally do kick in, though, they'll break your heart.)

Often just picking her up and walking around with her will stop the crying. Interestingly, researchers used to think that babies were soothed by being held or rocked in the upright position. It turns out, though, that what makes them stop crying is not being upright, but the movement that gets them there.

Keep in mind, too, that crying is not a bad thing—it not only allows the baby to communicate but is also a good workout. So if your efforts to calm aren't immediately successful (and the baby isn't hungry or stewing in a dirty diaper), don't worry; chances are she'll settle down by herself in a few minutes.

DROWSINESS

Drowsiness is a transition state that occurs as the baby is waking up or falling asleep. There may still be some movement, but the eyes will often look dull or unfocused. Leave her alone to drift off to sleep or move into one of the alert stages.

QUIET SLEEP

During quiet sleep, the baby's face is relaxed and her eyelids are closed and still. Her body is almost completely motionless, with only tiny, almost imperceptible mouth movements.

When your baby is in this state, you may be alarmed at the lack of movement and be afraid she has stopped breathing. If so, lean as close as you can and listen for her breath. Otherwise, gently put a hand on her stomach (she should be sleeping on her back—for information on why this is so important, see page 104) and feel it rise and fall. Try to resist the urge to wake the baby up—in fact, do *not* wake up a sleeping baby unless your pediatrician has told you otherwise. Instead, use the time to post the latest pics or catch a few Zs yourself.

ACTIVE SLEEP

Eyes are usually closed, but may occasionally flicker open. The baby may also smile or frown, make sucking or chewing movements, and even whimper or twitch—just as adults do in their active sleep state.

Half of a baby's sleep time is spent in quiet sleep, the other half in active sleep, with the two states alternating in thirty-minute shifts. So if your sleeping baby starts to stir, makes a few crying noises, or seems to be waking up unhappy, wait a few seconds before you pick her up to feed, change, or hold. Left alone, she may well slip back into the quiet sleep state.

Newborn babies are capable of a lot more than crying, sleeping, filling their diapers, and looking around. Just a few hours out of the womb, they are already trying to communicate with those around them.

Marshall Klaus told me about playing a game with an eight-hour-old girl in which he asked one colleague (who was a stranger to the baby) to stick out her tongue slowly while holding the baby. After a few seconds, the baby imitated the woman. Then Dr. Klaus took the baby and passed her around to twelve other doctors and nurses who were participating in the game, all of whom were told not to stick their tongues out. When the baby finally came back to the first doctor, the baby—without any prompting—immediately stuck out her tongue again. Even at just a few hours old, she had apparently remembered her "friend."

Interacting with Your Baby

Although it may be tempting just to sit and stare at your baby, marveling at every little thing she does, you'll need to do a lot more than that if you're really going to develop a relationship with her. Here are some of the best ways to get to know your baby:

- Hold her. Newborns love to be held and carried around. If you can, take off your shirt—skin-to-skin contact helps warm the baby, and you'll love it too. It's perfectly fine for you to lie down on your back and let the baby nap face down on your chest. But remember, this is the only time that she should sleep on her tummy.
- Talk to her. No, she can't understand a word you're saying. In fact, she barely even knows you exist. But talk to her anyway—explain everything you're doing, tell her what's happening in the news, and so forth—it will help her get to know the rhythm of the language.
- Change her. It doesn't sound like much fun, but diaper changing is a highly underrated bonding experience—a great time to interact with the baby one-on-one, to rub her soft belly, tickle her knees, and kiss her tiny fingers. For at

least the first month or so, she needs to be changed every two hours—a baby's supersensitive skin shouldn't soak in human waste—so there are plenty of opportunities. See "Diaper Changing 101" on pages 30–31.

- Keep her clean—but not too clean. You may take a shower every day, but until your baby starts crawling, she's unlikely to do anything that would get her terribly dirty, so there's no real need to bathe her more than once or twice a week— any more than that could unnecessarily dry her skin. Two small exceptions: it's okay to wash the baby's face every day using plain water, and carefully clean everything covered up by her diapers every time you change her. When you're cleaning your baby's head, pay close attention to the soft spots on the top; sometimes you can see them beat in time with the baby's pulse. These soft spots (called *fontanels*) have a purpose—to allow the baby's skull to make it through the birth canal without breaking—and the skin covering them is pretty sturdy, so there's no reason to worry about harming the baby when washing the area.

A Note on Diapers

It seems as though you can hardly do anything anymore without having to make choices—do you want the Tastes Great kind of beer or the Less Filling kind? Do you want toothpaste with tartar control or with peroxide and baking soda? Fortunately, most of the choices we make are pretty easy. But some come with their very own built-in political controversy: Death penalty or life in prison? Paper or plastic? Well, now that you're a parent, you can add "Disposable diapers or cloth?" to your list. Let's take a quick look at the pros and cons of each kind:

- **Disposables.** Americans throw away something like eighteen billion disposable diapers a year, enough to constitute more than 1 percent of the nation's landfills. They're made of plastic and will stay in their present form for about five hundred years. "Biodegradable" disposables are available in some places, but since these diapers are buried under tons of other garbage, they're deprived of the oxygen and sun they need to decompose. As a result, they may take just as long to break down.

   On the other hand, disposables are a lot more convenient. If you're traveling, you can just toss the dirty ones away instead of having to carry them around with you. And even if you're not traveling, they're very easy to use, which is probably why about 90 percent of parents (and about 100 percent of hospitals) use disposables.

   Disposable diapers for newborns are inexpensive. However, as your baby and her diapers get bigger, the number per package goes down while the cost per package stays about the same. Since you'll be going through about a dozen diapers a day, this option can get pretty pricey. But if you keep your eyes out for

Diaper Changing 101

By the time your baby gets potty-trained, you'll have changed about 10,000 diapers (more for boys than for girls, and way, way more for twins), so the faster and more efficiently you learn to get the job done, the less time you'll spend doing it. Here's the short course:

1. Get everything you need ready *before* you start: fresh diapers, water, towels, and a new outfit (mostly for the baby, but you might need one too, if things get messy enough). Stay away from commercial baby wipes for the first few weeks. Even the ones that are alcohol-free contain too many chemicals for brand-new skin. Use wet washcloths (room temperature is fine) or cotton balls instead. If you're planning to be away from the house at any point during this period, bring along some moistened disposable washcloths in a resealable plastic bag.

2. Find yourself a nice, flat place to do the job. Changing tables—or any other sturdy table—are great. Some changing tables come with straps for holding the baby secure, but don't rely on them—make sure you keep at least one hand on your baby at all times. Newborns are surprisingly strong—and clever too—and she'll pick the precise second you choose to turn around to propel herself over the edge. The floor is probably the safest spot, since there's no possibility of the baby falling, but it can be hard on the back (yours).

3. Undress the baby enough to free her legs. Be sure to take off her socks, if any. Babies love to kick their legs while they're being changed and have an uncanny ability to drag their feet through their own poop.

4. Lay the baby face-up on the changing surface. Some babies absolutely love having their diapers changed and are perfectly calm throughout the whole process. Others will kick and squirm and bounce and scream. If your baby is less than thrilled to be there, hanging a mobile right above the changing surface might provide enough distraction for you to do what you need to do. In the early days and weeks of parenthood, you and your partner might want to do some of your diaper changing as a team, one of you getting the supplies, entertaining the baby, and maybe holding those flailing legs, while the other does the actual cleaning.

5. Open a clean diaper and place it underneath the baby. Then unfasten the old one, gently lift the baby up by her ankles, and pull the dirty diaper out. Be sure to immediately cover the baby's genitals with a towel or cloth diaper. This isn't for modesty purposes; it's to keep you dry when the sudden rush of fresh air on your baby's crotch causes him or her to spray you.

6. Clean the bottom and genitals well—if there's a clean spot on the old diaper, use that to make a first pass. For girls, wipe from top to bottom to minimize the possibility of infection-causing bacteria getting into the vagina. For boys, clean under the scrotum. Keep a gentle but firm grip on your baby's ankles until you're through with step 8. With your free hand move the soiled diaper out of the way.

7. Apply diaper rash cream, but only if you really need to. Skip the lotions for the first few weeks (again, too harsh), and never, ever use baby powder that contains talc. Besides being a carcinogen, it can damage the lungs if inhaled. If you happen to have been raised in a family that doesn't think a baby is properly changed unless her bottom is covered in white powder, consider a nontoxic alternative containing cornstarch or natural, clay-based ingredients.

8. Fasten the diaper—snugly but still loose enough so it doesn't pinch the skin. And fold down the front edge so it doesn't rub against the cord stump. If the baby pees or poops into the new, clean diaper (which they love to do), repeat steps 4, 5, and 6.

9. Wash up—your hands and the baby's feet, if necessary. I've found that keeping a bottle of Purell or other cleanser is great if you aren't near running water.

10. Get the baby dressed.

Changing diapers is an acquired skill; it won't take long before you'll be able to do it with your eyes closed (although you probably shouldn't). In the meantime, even if you don't do it right, baby stool washes right off your hands—but not off your clothes, so quickly rinse off anything that gets hit.

coupons or shop at warehouse stores, you can save a lot. In addition, places like Toys Я Us, Walgreens, and other drugstore chains have generic or house brands that are a lot cheaper and usually just as good.

On the downside, disposables are so effective in absorbing moisture that kids who wear them stay comfortable longer and tend to be potty-trained later. (The average child who wears disposables is in them for 36–40 months, compared to 24–30 months for kids in cloth diapers.) Disposable-wearing kids are also more likely to get diaper rash because even though the moisture gets absorbed, the bacteria and ammonia that cause the rash stay inside.

- **Cloth.** These diapers are a lot easier on babies' brand-new, sensitive skin—no harsh chemicals or plastics. One of the traditional arguments against cloth diapers is that they aren't as convenient as disposables, and to some extent that's still true. You'll go through more cloth diapers in a day than you would with disposables, plus, if you're out of the house you'll have to schlep dirty ones with you until you get home, and if you run out, you'll have a tougher time finding extras. Still, there have been some important changes in the past few years. Today, for example, cloth diapers come in all sorts of styles: hourglass shaped, ones with elastic around the legs for better seal, Velcro closures instead of pins, special liners to make cleanup easier, and more.

  At the same time, although they're all natural, they still have a carbon footprint. Cloth diapers are made of cotton, which is taxing on farmland. And in order to sterilize cloth diapers properly, diaper services wash them seven times in near-boiling water, consuming huge amounts of power, water, and detergents. The diapers are then delivered all over town in trucks that fill the air with toxic pollutants. The pro-disposable lobby says that using diaper services consumes more fuel and causes as much air pollution as disposable diapers do. Seems like a bit of a stretch to me.

  If you're thinking about going cloth, use a diaper service. Over the long term, it may be more expensive than buying your own diapers and washing them yourself, but most new parents I've spoken with would rather spend their free time napping or hanging out together than doing laundry. Costs vary greatly around the country. If you sign up with a diaper service, you'll start with about eighty diapers per week. If you're buying your own, start with around forty.

  Even if you decide against using cloth diapers for the baby, buy a dozen anyway—they're great for drying baby bottoms on changing tables and for draping over your shoulder to protect your clothes when your baby spits up.

- **Other Options.** Overall it's a tough choice, and it's all yours. But I suggest that you do a combination of the two: use cloth diapers during the day and when you're at home, disposables at night and whenever you go out. Alternatively,

What's *Really* Going On Inside Those Diapers?

- **Meconium.** That's the word for those greenish black, sticky, tarry bowel movements that may have you worrying that there's something wrong with your baby's intestines. By about the fourth day of age, as your baby starts breast- or bottle-feeding, the meconium will be replaced with a much more pleasant-looking concoction. Breastfed babies usually fill their diapers with seedy, Dijon mustard–colored stool that doesn't smell all that bad. Formula-fed babies produce a more pasty substance that can smell like milk gone sour. Occasional changes in color and consistency are normal for both.

- **Early puberty?** It's not uncommon for boys' and girls' genitals and nipples to be swollen for the first few days after birth. There may even be a few drops of milk. Girls sometimes also have a whitish discharge and even some tiny streaks of blood from the vagina. Again, nothing to worry about. This has to do with the high levels of hormones the baby got from your partner, and all these symptoms will clear up within a week or two after delivery.

- **The umbilical cord stump.** Your baby's umbilical cord stump will drop off anywhere from one to three weeks after she's born. Folding down the front of the diaper exposes the stump to more air and speeds up the falling-off process. Until then, limit your baby-washing efforts to sponge baths. Other than keeping the stump clean and dry, there's no need to do anything special to take care of it. You can clean any drainage on or around the cord by gently wiping it off with a cotton swab or wet washcloth. When it does fall off, a small amount of bleeding is normal.

if you're not worried about spending a little extra money, there are a few eco-friendly options out there, including those that use cotton, cornstarch, and/or wood pulp to absorb liquid instead of gels, and some that are compostable or flushable (or have disposable inserts that are). All are widely available online or in brick-and-mortar stores.

Dads in the NICU

If your baby was born before about 32 weeks and had a very low birth weight, or if you had multiples, she (or they) will have to spend some time in the neo-natal (or newborn) intensive care unit (NICU, pronounced "Nick-U"). In the case of healthy-but-small babies, there's not a lot to worry about—they're called "growers and feeders" and just have to bulk up to four or five pounds before you can take them home. But not all babies in the NICU are healthy.

Watching your child struggle to hold on to life can be a frightening and humbling experience. (Even looking at a preemie can be scary. Depending on how premature the baby is, the eyes may still be fused shut, the skin may be translucent and reddish, and she may look more like a fetus than a baby. Over time, though, she'll gradually look more and more "normal.") A lot of dads I talked to told me that the feeling of helplessness was overwhelming. Not only were they powerless to help their child, but they often felt left out or ignored by the medical staff, who focused almost exclusively on the mother. For that reason, most new dads who have children in the NICU are generally left to come up with coping strategies on their own. Here are some that worked for many of the dads in my research:

- Try not to take it personally. The truth is that although it might feel like you're being left out, the staff's primary concern is to save your baby's life—and it should be yours too. And if the staff is focusing on your partner more than on you, that's because it's important that the baby eat, and her mother's milk is the best medicine.

- Don't be afraid to ask questions. You have a right to know exactly what's going on with your child every step of the way. A lot of men find that understanding the procedures, the reasons, the odds of success, what's normal, and what's not—is incredibly helpful, not only with coping with the situation, but also with bonding with their baby.

- Ask about kangaroo care. In Colombia, the mortality rate for premature infants was as high as 70 percent as recently as the 1980s. But a few doctors decided to try something different: they placed the tiny babies, wearing only a cap and a diaper, on a parent's bare chest, skin to skin, for several hours a day. The results were amazing. To start with, the mortality rate dropped to 30 percent. In studies in the United States and other countries, human kangaroo babies slept better, were taken off respirators sooner, cried less and were alert more, were better able to regulate their body temperature, gained more weight, and came home earlier. There were benefits for the parents as well: dads and moms who held their babies like this felt more confident in their parenting abilities and better able to do something productive for their babies. And breastfeeding moms who did kangaroo care were able to produce more milk. Unfortunately, not all hospitals allow kangaroo care (sometimes also called skin-to-skin care). If yours doesn't, ask the nursing staff whether you and your partner can do it anyway. If they need any convincing, show them this section.

- Be a little bit selfish. Sounds horrible, but it's not as bad as you think. The point is that you're not going to be much use to anyone—baby or partner—if you're

Not Your Father's NICU—and That's a Good Thing

Babies born before the 37th week of pregnancy are considered premature, and premature babies have increased risk of complications—and the earlier the baby is born, the higher that risk. Just thirty years ago or so, the "edge of viability" was 27 weeks, meaning that the chances of saving a baby were less than 50-50. Today, thanks to incredible advances in technology, it's possible to save babies as young as 23 weeks. But there's a lot of debate in the medical community about the ethics of saving babies that young. At least half of babies born before 26 weeks will have some kind of disability. About half the time, the disability is relatively minor: vision problems, asthma, behavior problems, and learning disabilities. The rest of the disabilities are severe: blindness, cerebral palsy, deafness, and significant cognitive impairment.

The higher the baby's gestational age, the greater the chances of survival and the lower the chance of major or minor long-term consequences. At 26 weeks, the baby has a 75–80 percent chance of making it, and at 28 weeks, the odds are 85–90 percent in favor.

Back to the technology. When babies are born too soon, they're simply not ripe yet. Their organs—especially the lungs—aren't developed. Their immune system isn't strong enough to fight off infections, they don't absorb nutrients from food and can't regulate their body temperature as well as babies just a few weeks or months older, and their immature circulation system can't always get enough oxygen to the brain. But a new breed of heart-lung machines help babies breathe, and new temperature-regulation systems can cool the baby's head, which can reduce the damage that would have been caused by oxygen deprivation.

walking around like a zombie because you haven't slept in forty-eight hours. You're in a really tough spot. Mom and baby need you to be there and to be strong for them. Plus, you've got your own stress, worry, and fears to deal with. So if you need to find a couch and take a nap, do it. And if you need to go for a run or play basketball or do something else to blow off steam, do it. Your whole family will be better off in the long run.

- Be emotionally strong too. You and your partner may have very different ways of coping with your baby's illness. A lot of men, for example, are fascinated by the technology and find that focusing on that helps them cope. Others only feel safe expressing anger. Women, though, tend to just go straight to the emotions—particularly sadness and sorrow. Some women get upset at what they interpret as their partner's "insensitivity" (which generally means that they aren't expressing their emotions in a very feminine way). If this happens, talk to her about what you're feeling. She needs to know you care.

- Connect with other parents. Many hospitals have moved from *open ward* NICUs, where several babies share one large room, to putting the babies in private or semi-private rooms. The idea is to give parents more privacy and to give the babies a quieter environment. But some unforeseen consequences have come up. First, parents in private rooms have fewer chances to connect with other parents who may be going through the same things at the same time. That support network can be extremely helpful in reducing parents' stress. Second, recent studies are finding that babies who were in quiet, private NICUs have poorer language skills at age two than those who were in open wards.

Once it's okay for you to touch your baby, don't waste a second. Babies who had daily ten-minute sessions of neck, shoulder, back, and leg massage and five minutes a day of gentle limb flexing grew almost 50 percent more than those who didn't get the massage—even though calorie intake for the two groups was the same, according to Dr. Tiffany Field, the director of the Touch Research Institute at the University of Miami School of Medicine. Hospital stays were shortened by almost a week, and the bills were correspondingly lower as well. On their first birthdays, formerly premature babies who'd been massaged were bigger and better developed than similarly premature kids who didn't get massaged. Pretty neat, eh? If you're interested in trying this, take a look at the instructions on pages 85–88.

FAMILY MATTERS

Coming Home

Boy, has your life changed. You're still your partner's lover and friend, just as you were a few weeks ago, but now, of course, you're also a father. You may be worried about how you're going to juggle all your various roles, but for the next few days the most important thing you can do is be a solid support person to your partner. Besides her physical recovery (which we'll talk more about below), she's going to need time to get to know the baby and to learn how to breastfeed. Your first days as a dad will be awfully busy—mine sure were: cooking, shopping, doing laundry, fixing up the baby's room, getting the word out, screening phone calls and visitors, and making sure my wife got plenty of rest.

Recovery

As far as the baby is concerned, there's not much to do in the beginning besides feeding, changing, and admiring her. But your partner is a different story. Despite whatever you've heard about women giving birth in the fields and returning to work a few minutes later, that's not the way things usually happen. Having a baby is a major shock—physically and emotionally—to a woman's system. And, contrary to popular belief, recovering from a vaginal birth isn't necessarily any shorter or easier than recovering from a C-section. In fact, a lot of women I've spoken with who've delivered both ways say that recovering from the C-section is actually easier.

Physically, whatever kind of delivery your partner has, she'll need some time—probably more than either of you think—to recover fully. Fatigue, breast soreness, and lingering uterine contractions may continue for months, and vaginal discomfort, bleeding, hemorrhoids, poor appetite, constipation, increased perspiration, acne, hand numbness or tingling, dizziness, and hot flashes may continue for weeks after delivery. In addition, between 10 and 40 percent of women feel pain during sexual intercourse (which they won't get around to for a few months anyway, so don't even bother thinking about it), have respiratory infections, and lose hair for three to six months.

Emotionally, your partner isn't much better off. She's likely to be a little impatient at her lack of mobility, and while she's undoubtedly relieved that the pregnancy is over and excited to be a mother, she'll probably experience the "baby blues" and may even suffer from postpartum depression (see pages 59, 62–63). Now that the baby is really here, she may feel a lot of pressure to assume her new role as mother and to breastfeed properly. That's an awful lot to ask. Fortunately, as she and the baby get to know each other, her confidence will grow, and a lot of her anxieties should disappear. Here are some things you can do to help your partner through the recovery process and to start parenting for both of you off on the right foot:

- Help your partner resist the urge to do too much too soon.
- Take over the household chores, or ask someone else to help. And if the house is a mess, don't blame each other.
- Be flexible. Expecting to maintain your normal, prefatherhood schedule is a complete fantasy, especially for the first few weeks after the birth.
- Be patient with yourself, your partner, and the baby. You're all new at this.
- Be sensitive to your partner's emotions. Her emotional recovery can take just as long as her physical one, if not longer.
- Get some time alone with the baby. You can do this while your partner is sleeping or, if you have to, while you send her out for a walk.

37

- Control the visiting hours and the number of people who can come at any given time. Dealing with visitors takes a lot more energy than you might think. And being poked, prodded, and passed around won't make the baby very happy. Also, for the first month or so, ask anyone who wants to touch the baby to wash his or her hands first (warm water and regular soap are fine—stay away from antibacterial soaps). Babies' immune systems aren't ready to handle the day-to-day germs we deal with.
- Keep your sense of humor.

YOU AND YOUR BABY

Within a few minutes after we'd brought our first daughter home from the hospital, my wife and I looked at each other and almost simultaneously asked, "Well, now what are we supposed to do?"

The things I mentioned back on pages 28–29—holding, talking, changing, bathing—are even more important now that you're home than they were at the hospital. In addition, there are a few things you need to know about at this stage:

- Dressing your newborn. This isn't going to be easy: her head seems too big to go through the appropriate openings in her shirts, and her arms are so bunched up that they may refuse to come out of the sleeves. Doing the following should make getting dressed a little easier for everyone involved:
  - Roll up the sleeves, then reach through and gently pull your baby's hands through—it's a lot easier than trying to shove from the other side.
  - Buy pants or overalls whose legs snap open. Some manufacturers make baby clothes that are absolutely beautiful but impossible to put on or take off. The snap-open legs also make diaper changing much easier—you don't have to remove the whole outfit to access the diaper.
  - Forget the clothes and keep her in nightgowns, but make sure you get the kind with elastic at the bottom and not string, which can be a choking hazard. You'll have to go back to real clothes with separate legs if you're putting the baby into a car seat or stroller.
  - If she can't walk, she doesn't need shoes. It's not only a waste of money, but confining your baby's feet in a hard pair of shoes all day long can actually damage her bones.
- Mani and pedi. Your baby's flailing arms and amazingly sharp fingernails are a bad combination, particularly around her eyes and face. Some clothes come with extra-long sleeves that can be folded over to keep the baby from scratching her face. But you should still learn how to do manicures.

Pets

Don't expect your pet to be as excited as you are about the birth of your baby. Many dogs and cats do not appreciate their new (lower) status in your house. To minimize the trauma for your pet (and to minimize the chance your pet will do something to harm the baby), try to get your pet used to the baby as early as possible.

You can do this even before the baby comes home by putting a blanket in the baby's bassinet in the hospital, then rushing it home to your pet. It'll give Rover or Fluffy a few days (or hours, at least) to get used to the little interloper's smell.

"Homewrecker!"

- First, collect all your supplies: blunt-tipped scissors and a nail file (regular nail clippers are too big).
- Make sure your baby is fast asleep—trimming grain-of-rice-sized nails when she's awake is going to be nearly impossible.
- Then, take one finger and gently pry it away from the fist. Push back on the pad of the finger so the nail sticks out a little bit more.

- Trim the nail by cutting straight across.
- File the entire edge of the nail, especially the corners.
- Repeat with all ten fingers.

When you get more comfortable with this process, you'll probably come up with a routine of your own. I've found, for example, that cuticle scissors work a lot better than ordinary baby-nail-trimming scissors. And I like to trim all the nails on one hand and then go back and do the filing. A few of the new dads I've interviewed have admitted that they'd occasionally bitten their baby's nails. Hey, if it works and it's not dangerous, knock yourself out.

Because your baby's fingernails grow so quickly, you'll be doing this every two or three days. Toenails are a different story—you won't need to trim them more than once or twice a month.

Have Some Fun

During the first few weeks, forget about football and chess. But try to spend at least twenty minutes a day (in five-minute installments) doing something with the baby one-on-one. Chatting, reading aloud, rocking, making faces, experimenting with her reflexes (see pages 60–61), or even simply catching her gaze and looking into her eyes are great activities. Here are a couple of ground rules:

- Take your cues from the baby. If she cries, looks away from you, or seems bored, stop what you're doing. Too much playing can overstimulate your child and make her fussy or irritable, so limit play sessions to five minutes or so.
- Schedule your fun. The best time for physical play is when the baby is in the active alert state; playing with toys or books is fine during the quiet alert state (see page 26). Also, choose a time when you can devote your full attention to the baby—no phone calls, social media, or other distractions.
- Be encouraging. Use lots of smiles and laughter as well as verbal encouragement. Although the baby can't understand the words, she definitely understands the feelings. Even at only a few days old, she'll want to please you, and lots of reinforcement will help build her self-confidence.
- Be gentle. Sudden movements, bright lights, and loud noises (especially sneezes, slamming doors, car alarms, and obnoxious cell phone rings) can scare her.
- Watch her head. Because babies' heads are relatively enormous (one-quarter of their body size at birth versus one-seventh by the time they're adults), and their neck muscles aren't yet well developed, their heads tend to be pretty floppy for the first few months. Be sure to support the head from behind at all times, and avoid sudden or jerky motions. Never shake your child. This can make her little

Different Isn't Bad, It's Just Different

From the moment their children are born, men and women have very different ways of handling them. Men tend to stress the physical and high-energy, women the social and emotional. Your baby will catch on to these differences within weeks, and she'll start reacting to you and your partner very differently. When she's hungry, she'll be more easily soothed by your partner (if she's breastfeeding), but she'll be happier to see you if she wants some physical stimulation. Don't let anyone tell you that the "guy things" you do are somehow not as important as the "girl things" your partner may do (or want you to do). Ultimately your baby needs both kinds of interactions, and it's a waste of time to try to compare or rate them. Just be gentle.

brain rattle around inside her skull, causing bruises or permanent injuries. And never throw the baby up in the air. Yes, your father may have done it to you, but he shouldn't have. It looks like fun but can be extremely dangerous.

Feeding Your Baby: Breast versus Bottle

It may seem hard to believe, but as recently as a few decades ago, breastfeeding was out of style and most new moms were given a wide variety of reasons (by their doctors, of course) not to. But today you'd be hard pressed to find anyone in the medical community who doesn't agree that breastfeeding is just about the best thing you can do for your child. Here's why:

FOR THE BABY

- Breast milk provides exactly the right balance of nutrients your newborn needs. It also contains several essential fatty acids that are not found in baby formula.
- Breast milk adapts, as if by magic, to your baby's changing nutritional needs. None of my children had a single sip of anything but breast milk for at least the first six months of life (and, unless your doctor tells you otherwise, neither should yours), and they're all wonderfully healthy.
- Breastfeeding greatly reduces the chance that your baby will develop food allergies. If either of your families has a history of food allergies, you should withhold solid foods for at least six months.
- Breastfed babies are less prone to obesity in adulthood than formula-fed babies. This may be because with the breast it's the baby—not the parent—who decides when to quit eating.

Just Because You Don't Have Breasts Doesn't Mean You Can't Help Breastfeed

Sounds strange, but you play a critical role in determining whether, how long, and how well your partner will breastfeed. Several studies have shown that women nurse longer and enjoy it more when their partners learn about breastfeeding (which you'll do as you read these pages), support them, and have confidence in their ability. Here are a few ways you can stay involved:

- Help your partner find the most comfortable position and position the baby. In the early days of breastfeeding, she may need to try three or four positions at every meal.
- Make sure she's got a big glass of water nearby—and that she actually drinks it. Breastfeeding can be very dehydrating.
- Encourage her every chance you get. Tell her what a great job she's doing, and be sympathetic but supportive when she gets frustrated.
- Sit next to your partner while she nurses and read her the latest comments people have posted about how beautiful your baby is.
- Bring the baby to your partner for those night feedings (for the first week or two; we'll talk more about middle-of-the-night feedings later).
- Do as much of the burping and diaper changing as you can.
- Gently stroke the baby's skin while she's feeding. But keep your hands off her head. Stroking the back of the head can sometimes trigger a pullback reflex,

- Breastfed babies have a greatly reduced risk of developing respiratory and gastrointestinal illness, ear infections, asthma, and some childhood cancers. It may also lower the risk of SIDS.
- Breastfeeding is thought to transmit to the infant the mother's immunity to certain diseases.

FOR YOU AND YOUR PARTNER

- It's convenient—no preparation, no heating, no bottles or dishes to wash. Plus, breastfed babies are a lot easier to travel with—no need to find clean water for mixing powder, nothing to refrigerate.
- It's free. Formula can be pretty pricey.
- It gives your partner a wonderful opportunity to bond with the baby. In addition, breastfeeding will help her lose weight and get her uterus back into shape and may reduce her risk of both ovarian and breast cancers.

and if the baby has a mouth full of breast and nipple at the time, your wife won't enjoy the experience.

- Let her set the tone outside. Some women are perfectly fine about lifting their shirts in public; others are incredibly shy. Don't put any pressure on her either way, regardless of how you feel.

- In most cases, there's always as much as the baby needs, and never any waste.
- Your baby's diapers won't stink. It's true. Breastfed babies produce poop that—especially when compared to formula poop—doesn't smell half bad.
- You may end up getting more rest. If your partner is nursing, you won't have to get up in the middle of the night to prepare formula (although you still may need to get up to bring the baby to your partner).

What If Your Partner Doesn't Breastfeed?

FORMULA

You can use powdered, full-strength liquid, or liquid concentrate (which you have to add water to). But when you start checking formula prices, your partner may decide to keep breastfeeding a while longer. All three options are basically the same in terms of their nutritional value. The only issues are price (powder is

Just Because Your Partner Has Breasts Doesn't Mean She Knows How to Use Them

As natural as breastfeeding appears to be, your partner and the baby may need anywhere from a few days to a few weeks to get the hang of it. The baby won't immediately know how to latch on to the breast properly, and your partner—especially if she's never done this before—won't know exactly what to do either. This initial period, in which cracked and even bloody nipples are not uncommon, may be quite painful for your partner. And with the baby feeding six or seven times a day for 10–15 minutes on each breast, it may take as long as two weeks for your partner's nipples to get sufficiently toughened up.

Surprisingly, she won't begin producing any real milk until two to five days after the baby is born. But there's no need to worry that the baby isn't getting enough food. Babies don't eat much the first 24–48 hours, and any sucking they do is almost purely for practice. Whatever nutritional needs your baby has will be fully satisfied by the tiny amounts of *colostrum* your partner produces. (Colostrum is a kind of premilk that helps the baby's immature digestive system get warmed up for the task of digesting real milk later.)

Overall, the first few weeks of breastfeeding can be stressful and often frustrating for your partner—so much so that she may be tempted to throw in the towel. Even if this happens, don't give in to the temptation to suggest switching to bottles. Instead, try some of the things on pages 65–66 and encourage her to keep trying. She may find it hard to believe right now, but there's an excellent chance that in a week or two she and the baby will have settled into a comfortable rhythm, and she'll hardly remember all the troubles she had. At the same time, you might ask your pediatrician for the name of a local lactation consultant (what a job!). We'll talk more about breastfeeding-related issues in the next chapter.

usually the cheapest, since you can whip up a pitcher in the morning and keep it in the fridge for the day) and convenience (full-strength liquid is the easiest—and most expensive).

If you're going the formula route, you may wonder how much to feed the baby. The easy answer is, "As much as she wants." If she's hungry, food will be the only thing that will soothe her. When she's had enough, she'll stop sucking or clamp her mouth shut. As a general guideline, though, you'll want to give your baby 2–2.5 ounces of formula per pound of body-weight every day. Then divide that into 6–8 feedings. Remember, every baby is different, so you'll have to do a little experimenting before you find the right amount.

Despite what your mother may have told you, there's no need to sterilize bottles or nipples. Just wash them thoroughly with warm, soapy water and rinse carefully. If a nipple is torn, hard, stiff, cracked, or deformed in any way, replace it right away.

JUICE

If you and your partner decide not to breastfeed or your pediatrician has told you to supplement breastfeeding with a bottle, don't fill it with juice. Children who drink large quantities of fruit juice—especially apple juice—suffer from frequent diarrhea, and in the worst cases may fail to grow and develop normally. The problem is that babies love juice so much that, if you give them all they want, they'll fill up their tiny stomachs with it, leaving no room for the more nutritious foods they need. Even worse, if your baby gets too used to juice, there's a chance that she may flat-out refuse formula or milk. The American Dietetic Association recommends that parents refrain from giving their babies juice until they're at least six months old, and then restrict juice intake until age two.

WATER, SUGAR WATER, ELECTROLYTE DRINKS, COW'S MILK, AND GOAT'S MILK

The short answer is that unless your doctor specifically tells you that your baby needs any of these, stay away from them.

For Boys Only

I'm assuming that by now, you and your partner have already made your decision about whether or not to circumcise your son. Whatever your choice—and whether the procedure is done in the hospital or is part of a religious ritual—your son's penis requires some special care.

THE CIRCUMCISED PENIS

The penis will be red and sore for a few days after the circumcision. Until it's fully healed, you'll need to protect the newly exposed tip and keep it from sticking to the inside of his diaper (a few tiny spots of blood on his diapers for a few days, however, is perfectly normal). Ordinarily, you'll need to keep the penis dry and the tip lubricated with petroleum jelly or antibiotic ointment. Some pediatricians recommend keeping the penis wrapped in gauze until it's healed to protect it from urine, which is very irritating. Others say not to bother with the gauze.

Burping 101

When babies drink, especially from bottles, they almost always swallow some air. And because they do most of their drinking on their side, all that air tends to get trapped in their stomach. Sometimes babies burp on their own, but most of the time they need a little help.

You should burp your baby at the middle and the end of every feeding, more often if necessary. There are three basic ways to bring up a belch. Pick the one that works best for you or alternate them.

- Hold the baby facing you, upright, her body against your chest, head above your shoulder. Pat or rub her back gently.
- Lay the baby face down across your knees, head carefully supported. Pat or rub her back gently.
- Hold the baby on your knee in a sitting position, leaning forward slightly. Pat or rub her back gently.

Whichever option(s) you choose, remember this: keep the baby's head higher than her butt, always support the head, and gentle patting or rubbing is just as effective as—and less dangerous than—thumping hard (it's also just as likely to produce one of those loud, satisfying belches). Since burps sometimes bring some liquid with them, be sure to protect yourself and your clothing before you start.

Finally, keep in mind that there's a difference between spitting up and vomiting. Spitting up is essentially a wet burp that dribbles out of the baby's mouth. Vomiting involves a lot more fluid. Spitting up is nothing to worry about, but if your baby vomits or there's blood in the spit-up, call your pediatrician.

The exception to this is if your baby received a plastibell (a plastic ring that goes between the foreskin and the head of the penis). In this case you'll want to stay away from any kind of ointment or dressings until the plastibell drops off (usually 5–10 days after it was put on). If you have any questions or worries, the person who performed the circumcision or the hospital nursing staff should be able to give you more specific and detailed care instructions.

THE UNCIRCUMCISED PENIS

Even if you elect not to circumcise your son, you'll still have to spend some time taking care of his penis. The standard way to clean an uncircumcised penis is to retract the foreskin and gently wash the head of the penis with mild soap and water.

Parents, In-Laws, Siblings, and Other "Helpers"

One of the most common questions you'll hear from people is whether they can help out in any way. Some people are serious, others are just being polite. You can tell one group from the other by keeping a list of chores that need to be done and asking them to take their pick.

Be particularly careful about accepting offers of help from people—especially parents (yours or hers)—who arrive on your doorstep with suitcases and open-ended travel arrangements. New grandparents may have more traditional attitudes toward parenting and may not be supportive of your involvement with your child. They may also have very different ideas about how babies should be fed, dressed, carried, played with, and so on. It's important, then, to be very clear that although you appreciate the help and advice, you and your partner are the baby's parents, and what the two of you say ultimately goes.

Much the same applies to just about anyone else who offers to move in with you for a few days, weeks, or months to "help out," especially people who have their own kids. With all your other responsibilities, the last thing you want to do is play host to a bunch of relatives. If someone does stay with you to help out after the birth, great—my sister-in-law spent a week with us after the birth of my youngest and ended up filling our freezer with months' worth of incredible food. But it's important that everyone understands that you and your partner are going to spend most of your free time sleeping, not socializing.

However, 85 percent of boys under six months have a foreskin that doesn't retract, according to the American Academy of Pediatrics. If this is the case with your son, don't force it. Check with your pediatrician immediately and follow his or her hygiene instructions carefully. Fortunately, as boys get older, their foreskins retract on their own; by age one, 50 percent retract, and by age three, 80–90 percent.

Knowing When to Get Help

If you have older kids, you already know that most of the stuff first-time parents panic about turns out to be perfectly normal. But if you're a first-time parent, you're going to worry about everything, no matter what anyone tells you. Your pediatrician will probably give you a list of what's normal and what's not for the first few weeks of life. But here are some things that warrant a call:

- If your baby seems unusually floppy and/or nonresponsive.
- If your baby cries for a very long time or sounds strange—whooping, gasping, high-pitched crying—or is completely inconsolable.
- Infection at the circumcision or umbilical cord site. Swelling, red streaks on the penis or near the cord, continued bleeding, or pus-like discharge could indicate a problem.
- Excessive sleep. It can be a little hard to determine this in the early days, but generally speaking, your baby should wake up every 2–3 hours and be ravenous.
- Yellow skin. This could be jaundice, which is very common but requires medical attention to keep it from becoming dangerous.
- Not enough pee and poop. If, after the third or fourth day of life, your baby isn't producing two to three poopy diapers and five wet ones every 24 hours, she could be dehydrated. Other signs include dark-colored or strong-smelling urine, a sunken soft spot on the baby's head, dry mouth and tongue, sunken eyes, and listlessness.

Getting to Know You

1 MONTH

WHAT'S GOING ON WITH THE BABY

Physically

- Most of your baby's physical movements are still reflexive, but the leg and arm thrashing should be fairly symmetrical. Sometime this month, while flailing his arms around, your baby will accidentally stick his hand into his mouth. After getting over the initial shock, he'll realize that sucking—even when there's no milk involved—is downright fun. By the end of the month, he'll probably be able to get his hand in his mouth—on purpose—fairly regularly, and if he had any hair to start with, he'll have worn away a nice bald spot on the back of his head.
- Lying on his tummy, he's now able to lift his head just enough to turn it so his nose won't be smashed into the mattress. Lying on his back, he should be able to lift his head up 45 degrees and hold it there for a few seconds.
- If you put him in a sitting position, he'll try to keep his head in line with his back, but he won't be able to hold it steady for more than a second or two without support.
- He wants to eat every 2–4 hours, but waste production is way down: 2–4 bowel movements and 6–8 wet diapers per day.
- Although his 3-D vision hasn't fully developed, his eyesight is improving, and he can now see and focus on objects a foot away or more.

Intellectually

- Your baby is alert for 30–60 minutes every 10–12 hours or so. He's already beginning to express an interest in finding out what's going on in his world. He'll stare at a new object for much longer than a familiar one, and his favorite things to look at are high-contrast black-and-white patterns and faces. By the end of this month, he'll probably follow an object moving slowly by in front of him.

- According to psychiatrist Peter Wolff, an object exists for a baby only as "something to suck, or something to see, or something to grasp, but not as something to grasp and to see at the same time."

Verbally

- As his vocal chords mature, your baby will expand his collection of animal sounds to include some small, throaty, and incredibly cute cooing noises.
- He is already beginning to differentiate between language and the other kinds of noise he hears throughout the day. He may respond to voices—especially your partner's and yours—by turning toward them. And he really enjoys being spoken to.
- Still, his main form of using his vocal chords will be to cry—something he'll do for as much as three hours a day.

Emotionally/Socially

- Don't expect many hints from your baby about what he's thinking—most of the time his expression is pretty blank. However, he loves being held and rocked, and may stare intently at you (actually, he's looking at the outside edges of your face) for 15–20 seconds or so before being distracted by an insect flying by or a light being turned on or off.
- Not quite ready for the cocktail circuit, your baby is probably sleeping 16–20 hours a day. In fact, he may use sleep as a kind of self-defense mechanism, shutting down his systems when he gets overstimulated.
- He's starting to form an emotional attachment to and feelings of trust for the people who care for him.
- He may cry as a way of demanding more attention or in protest at being overloaded with attention.

WHAT'S GOING ON WITH YOUR PARTNER

Physically

- Reduction in lochia (the normal, bloody vaginal discharge that happens after birth). Color will change from red to pink to brown to clear.
- Reduced pain around the C-section incision or episiotomy.
- Breasts may become engorged with milk. This may make them feel (and actually be) enormous.

GETTING TO KNOW YOU

- Lots of sweating and frequent urination as her body continues to eliminate excess fluids any way it can. Fortunately, her bladder control is improving, and any incontinence will probably be gone within another few weeks. A few hundred daily Kegels (tightening of the muscles used to hold back urination) will help the process along.
- Some continued hair loss.
- Stretch marks, if she had them at all, will start fading, as will the darker pigmentation around her nipples and that odd dark line that starts at her belly button and goes south.

Emotionally

- Continued irritability and moodiness. Some of this is hormonal, some is brought on by sleep deprivation and/or pain.
- She may experience all sorts of conflicting emotions. Some are the same as the ones you may have been feeling (like joy, possible disappointment about the way the birth went, and worries about what kind of a mother she's going to be). Others will be her very own (such as emptiness or sadness that the pregnancy is over, guilt if she doesn't love the baby as much as she thought she would or thought she was supposed to).
- She may feel confused, absent minded, forgetful, and generally like she's losing her mind.
- Depression or the blues (see pages 59, 62–63 for more)

WHAT YOU'RE GOING THROUGH

Bonding with the Baby

In one of the earliest studies of father-infant interaction, my colleague Ross Parke made a discovery that shocked a lot of traditionalists: fathers were just as caring, interested, and involved with their infants as mothers were, and they held, touched, kissed, rocked, and cooed at their new babies with at least the same frequency as mothers did. The sooner and more frequently dads have a chance to spend time with their babies, the more quickly the bonding process will start. Generally speaking, men who attend their babies' birth bond slightly faster than those who don't. Same goes for men who cut the baby's umbilical cord vs. those who don't. But if you weren't able to be there for the birth, don't worry—being there doesn't guarantee attachment, and not being there doesn't automatically interfere with it.

51

Attachment and Bonding Are Not the Same Thing

While there's no question that bonding with your baby is an important goal, it's essentially a one-way street: you establish a relationship with the infant and don't get much back. But attachment is more of a two-way street: you and the baby establish a relationship with each other.

This relationship isn't even close to being equal, the way it is between adults. It is, however, balanced in some very interesting and delicate ways. Basically, it works like this: as you learn to read your baby's signals and satisfy his needs in an appropriate way, he learns to view you as a reliable and responsive person—someone he can count on in times of trouble. And he'll find some way (babies always do) to get you the message that you're needed and wanted.

Meanwhile, babies who have two-way "chats" with their parents come to prefer them to any of the other adults around who might be able to satisfy a need or two. Over time, this kind of preference (based on feelings of security and the parents' reliability) develops into self-confidence and becomes the foundation for all of the growing baby's future relationships.

But What If I Don't Bond Right Away?

If you haven't established an instant bond with your baby, there's absolutely nothing wrong with you. In fact, it turns out that 25–40 percent of new parents—mothers and fathers—say that their first response to the baby is "indifference." Putting it in slightly stronger terms, researcher Katharyn May says, "This bonding business is nonsense. We've sold parents a bill of goods. They believe that if they don't have skin-to-skin contact within the first fifteen minutes, they won't bond. Science just doesn't show that."

This really makes more sense to me than the love-at-first-sight kind of bonding you hear so much about. And anyway, there's no evidence whatsoever that your relationship with or feelings for your child will be any less loving than if you'd fallen head over heels in love in the first second. So, just take your time. Don't pressure yourself, and don't think for a second that you've failed as a father.

If your baby is very sick, the situation may be a little different. Some dads whose babies were born very prematurely or are in intensive care, deliberately (though subconsciously) try to keep some psychological distance between themselves and the babies. They feel that they have to be strong for their partner and that not bonding with the baby will somehow protect them from the pain they'll experience if something bad happens. It won't. In fact, establishing a close physical and psychological bond with your baby can actually improve his chances for survival. So jump in. The sooner you hold your baby, the sooner those feelings of love work their way to the surface.

My Baby Doesn't Love Me

For about the first six to eight weeks of life, your baby probably won't give you much feedback about how you're doing as a father: you'll tell your best jokes, make your funniest faces, but he won't smile, laugh, or react to you in any noticeable way. In fact, just about all he will do is cry. This can easily make you feel unloved and, surprisingly often, a need to "get even" with the baby by deliberately withholding your own love from him.

As the grown-up, it's your job to nip this destructive cycle in the bud before it gets out of hand. So if you find yourself feeling unloved or unappreciated by your newborn, here are a few things you can do:

- Change your perspective. Although your baby can express preferences for sounds, tastes, or patterns, he's not yet capable of expressing love. However, the fact that he often stops crying when you pick him up and that he easily falls asleep on your chest are signs that he feels close to you and trusts you—critical steps on the way to the love you want him to feel. Allow yourself the pleasure of stroking his incredibly soft skin, of admiring his tiny fingers, and of filling your lungs with his clean, new-baby smell. If that doesn't hook you, nothing will.
- Pay attention. Your baby's needs and wants are fairly limited at this stage—feed me, change me, hold me, put me to bed—and he has a different way of letting you know which one he wants. If you pay close attention, you'll soon be able to figure out what he's "telling" you. Getting to know your baby in this way will make you feel less anxious and more confident as a parent, which will make the baby more comfortable with you, which in turn will make your mutual attachment more secure.
- Read. Another important way to get to know your baby is to carefully read the "What's Going On with the Baby" sections of this book. Knowing what your baby is capable of—and what he isn't—at various stages can go a long way toward helping you understand his behavior and establish reasonable expectations.
- Get closer. There's a lot of evidence that parent-child bonding comes as a result of physical closeness. So if you'd like to speed up the process, carry the baby every chance you get, bring him with you whenever you can, and take care of as many of his basic needs as possible.

Bonding and Attachment for Non-Biologically Related Dads

Plenty of adoptive parents—particularly those who adopted because of infertility—feel a little insecure or inadequate. They often believe that the process of bonding and forming an attachment with a baby comes more naturally to birth parents than to them, and that since they weren't with the baby from the beginning, they'll never be as close to their child as a biological parent would. That's just plain wrong.

Similarly, many men who became fathers through donor sperm (sometimes called donor insemination, or DI, dads) feel inadequate or less than completely masculine, and worry that the lack of a biological connection will make it impossible for them to bond with their baby or that the baby will never see them as the "real" father. They may also feel some resentment of their partner because she has that coveted biological connection.

Studies of adoptive parents have shown that a majority feel some kind of love for their children right from the very first contact; it doesn't matter whether it's when they went to pick up the baby, when they first looked at a picture that had arrived months before, or right at the birth, if they're lucky enough to be there. At the same time, "most infants, if adopted before the age of nine months will take to their new parents as if they were born to them, developing an attachment to them as they would have done to their birth parents," according to adoption psychotherapists Judith Schaffer and Christina Lindstrom.

The prognosis is even better for DI dads. To start with, you and your partner aren't biologically related (hopefully), and that hasn't kept you from loving

The Incredible Shrinking Baby

In their first week or so of life, most babies lose some weight—often as much as 10 percent of their birth weight. This can be pretty scary. After all, babies are generally supposed to get bigger over time, not smaller. This disappearing act is perfectly normal (in the first few days the baby isn't eating much), and your baby will probably regain his birth weight by the time he's two weeks old. After that, the rate of growth—for the next few months, at least—is phenomenal: about an ounce a day and an inch per month. Doesn't sound like much, but if he continued at this rate, by his eighteenth birthday he'd be nearly twenty feet tall and weigh in at about 420 pounds.

During every visit to the pediatrician your baby will be weighed, his overall length and head circumference will be measured, and the results will be given each other. And anyway, think about how involved you were during the pregnancy. You're the guy who went to the OB visits, who saw the baby squirming around in the ultrasound, who helped your partner keep her hair out of the toilet when she was vomiting, who ran out for ice cream and pickles at 2:30 in the morning, who picked out names, was there for the labor and delivery, and cut the cord. In my book, anyone who goes through all of that is a real father—biologically related or not.

There are things, of course, that can interfere with attachment in these situations, the most common being the feelings of inadequacy discussed above, which can become a self-fulfilling prophecy. With adoption, there's also the age and physical health of the child. If you're adopting a complete newborn, it's going to be a little easier to establish a bond. But a lot of adoptions aren't finalized until the babies are a few months older. Realistically, this makes the bonding process a little tougher for all concerned, as babies and parents take a little time to get used to each other. It's by no means an impossible task.

And remember, in all but the rarest cases, the desire for attachment to a child can overcome even the most formidable obstacles. (If you aren't consumed with paternal feelings right away, start by taking a look at the "But What If I Don't Bond Right Away?" section on pages 52–53.) So if you're an adoptive or DI dad and you're worried for any reason about your abilities as a parent, there is support out there. You'll find a lot of great resources in the Resources appendix.

not only in inches (or centimeters) but in percentile. (If your baby is in the 75th percentile for weight, he's heavier than 75 percent of babies the same age.) Newer growth charts also include your child's BMI (body mass index), which is a ratio of weight to height and has been very successful in predicting obesity.

Try not to get too caught up in these numbers. As with most things, bigger isn't necessarily better, plus it's normal for different parts of a baby's body to grow at different rates. My two older daughters, for example, were built like nails—90th percentile for both height and head size, but 40th percentile for weight. The youngest was more of a pyramid: 50th percentile head, 90th in length and weight.

Keep in mind that these height and weight charts, which are created by the National Center for Health Statistics (and included as an appendix in this book), are guidelines, and can't possibly account for every situation. For the first few months, for example, breastfed babies tend to bulk up a little more quickly than their formula-fed agemates. But after that, formula-fed babies tend to be a bit heavier. Unless your child is in an extreme part of the range (5th percentile and lower or 95th percentile and higher), what's important is that he grow steadily over time, not that he's achieved some kind of milestone.

YOU AND YOUR BABY

The most important thing you can do for your baby is to make him feel loved and cared for. And the best way to do this is to continue to do the activities listed on pages 28–29, only more so.

Reading and Language

At this age, you can read just about anything to your baby—even *War and Peace* or those *New Yorker* profiles you're so behind on. The goal at this stage isn't to actually teach him anything; it's simply to get him used to the sounds and rhythms of language and to have him start associating reading with calm, quiet, and security. So try to read to your baby every day and set up a regular time and place. And as with most baby-related things, he'll let you know whether he's interested or not, so don't force him to sit through the end of a chapter. If he lasts over five minutes, that's a lot.

If you feel like taking a break from reading, try a little singing instead. Infants love their dad's deeper voice.

If you and your partner are fluent in different languages, and you want your baby to grow up speaking both, this is the time to start compartmentalizing them. What I mean is that you should establish some clear boundaries—English only with Daddy, Russian with Mommy, French with the babysitter—and stick with them. We'll talk more about this throughout the book.

Toys and Games

Giving your baby a rattle, stuffed animal, or anything else that needs to be grasped is a total waste of time at this stage. He simply isn't interested in toys right now. That doesn't mean, however, that he doesn't want to play. In fact, if you pay close attention, he'll actually "tell" you when he's ready for some fun and games. It'll probably happen during the active alert stage (see pages 26–27): your baby will catch and hold your eye and make some kind of non-crying noise—possibly a coo or a squeal.

At this point, it's important that you maintain eye contact with the baby and respond by mimicking the sound he made and adding some excited sounds and

"You have the right to remain silent..."

facial expressions of your own. Researchers have found that this type of "conversation" increases infants' brain activity and promotes growth. Oh, and it's fun too.

It's also very important that you learn to recognize the clues your baby gives you when he wants to quit. He'll start by turning his head or body away, and if you ignore the message, he'll escalate to squirming, minor fussiness, and eventually, crying or screaming.

Visual Stimulation

Since your baby still isn't capable of grabbing or holding on to much of anything, he's doing most of his learning with his eyes. Here are a few ways to stimulate your baby visually:

- Fasten an unbreakable mirror securely to the inside of the baby's crib.
- Make sure the baby has a lot of different things to look at. For the first few months, infants are particularly responsive to high contrast. Black-and-white toys and patterns are popular, but anything with high contrast will be a big hit.
- Have your baby show you what he prefers. Hold up different patterns 12–18 inches from his face for a few seconds. Which ones does he stare at intently? Which ones does he turn away from?
- Play some visual tracking games. With the baby on his back, hold a small object 12–18 inches from his nose. Move the object slowly to one side. Does he follow the object with his eyes? Does he move his head? Do the same thing for the other side.

Whatever you're doing, pay attention to the baby's mood and don't play any longer than 5 minutes unless he really wants to. Your baby is not a trained seal, and these activities are games, not college entrance exams.

Mobiles

Mobiles are among the most popular furnishings in almost any baby's room. And this is the perfect time to put some up: one over the bed and perhaps another, smaller one over the changing table. When considering mobiles, keep these ideas in mind:

- Get the kind of mobiles that allow you to change the figures. As your baby gets older, his taste will become more sophisticated and you'll need to keep up. My wife and I found that mobile characters were quite expensive; we could have bought a year's worth of clothes for the baby with what it would have cost us to buy five or six sets of mobile characters. The solution? Unleash the artist inside you and make your own.
- When buying or making mobile characters, keep in mind that the baby will be looking at them from underneath. Quite a number of manufacturers produce mobiles that are gorgeous when viewed from the parents' perspective, but from the baby's perspective they're essentially blank.
- Your baby is still interested in simple lines: stripes, large squares, and the outlines of things. Intricate patterns or complicated designs aren't appropriate yet.
- Keep the mobile 6–18 inches above the baby's face but slightly to the side; babies don't like to look straight up for long.

Exploring Your Baby's Reflexes

"The newborn is faced with two fundamental and simultaneous challenges during the first weeks of life," writes child psychiatrist Stanley I. Greenspan. "The first is self-regulation—the ability to feel calm and relaxed, not overwhelmed by his new environment. The second is to become interested in the world about him."

Unfortunately, babies can't do much to accomplish either of these goals on their own. That's your job. And you'll do it by caring for and responding to your baby, and by providing him with a stimulating environment. But because your baby can't be expected to sit around waiting for you, he came fully equipped with a wide range of reflexes (see pages 60–61) to get him started. Yes, all that wild, seemingly random arm and leg flailing really has a purpose.

Your baby's reflexes are normal, involuntary actions. Some happen by themselves, others are triggered by outside events or stimuli. Because they come and go in a fairly predictable pattern, your pediatrician will track their presence and strength as a way to assess your baby's growth and development (reflexes that are asymmetrical, don't appear at all, disappear too quickly, or hang around longer than they're supposed to may indicate a problem, and could lead to developmental delays).

In addition to these reflexes, your baby also came with some self-protection features. For example, if he sees an object coming straight at him, he'll take defensive action—leaning back hard, turning away, closing his eyes, bringing his arms up in front of his face, and possibly trying to wriggle out of the way. Incredibly, if the object isn't on a collision course, he'll ignore it. If you want to try this, strap your baby into his car seat and, from a few feet away, move a ball or other fairly large object straight at his head and again past him.

Similarly, if you cover your baby's face (be very, very careful when doing this), he'll open and close his mouth, twist his head, and flail his little arms in an attempt to keep from suffocating.

Turning your baby into a science project by exploring his reflexes can teach you a lot about infant behavior, plus it's a fun way for you to get to know your baby better by connecting with him physically. The best time to do your experimenting is during his active alert stage (see pages 26–27). Three warnings: limit playing with the reflexes that frighten your baby, be extra careful with his head, and respect his desire to quit.

FAMILY MATTERS: YOU AND YOUR PARTNER

Dealing with Postpartum Blues and Depression

Somewhere between 50 and 80 percent of new mothers experience periods of mild sadness, weepiness, stress, moodiness, sleep deprivation, loss of appetite, inability to make decisions, anger, or anxiety after the baby is born. These "baby blues," which many believe are caused by hormonal shifts in a new mother's body, can last for hours or days, but in most cases they disappear within a few weeks. One researcher, Edward Hagen, claims that postpartum blues has little, if anything, to do with hormones. Instead, he says, it's connected to low levels of social support—especially from the father. And it could be the new mother's way of "negotiating" for more involvement. Either way, if you notice that your partner is experiencing any of these symptoms, there's not much you can do except be supportive. Encourage her to get out of the house for a while and see to it that she's eating healthily.

For about 10–20 percent of new moms, postpartum blues can develop into postpartum depression, which is far more serious. Symptoms include:

- Baby blues that don't go away after two weeks, or feelings of depression or anger that surface a month or two after the birth.

Fun with Reflexes

👍 (thumb up) = okay to play with

👎 (thumb down) = *not* okay to play with—may frighten the baby or cause injury

IF YOU . . .	THE BABY WILL . . .
👎 Tap the bridge of your baby's nose (gently, please), turn on a bright light, or clap your hands close to his head	Close his eyes tightly
👎 Make a sudden, loud noise or give the baby the sensation of falling	Fling legs and arms out and back, throw head back, open eyes wide, and cry, then bring arms back to the body and clench fingers
👍 Straighten the baby's arms and legs	Flex arms and legs
👍 Pull baby up to a sitting position (be sure to support the head while doing this)	Snap eyes open, lift shoulders, try (usually unsuccessfully) to lift head
👍 Stand baby up (while holding him under the arms) on a solid surface and lean him a little bit forward	Lift one leg, then the other, as if marching
👍 Put baby on tummy on flat surface; never do this on a beanbag or other soft surface—baby can suffocate	Squirm around as if he were crawling
👎 Support baby's chest in the water (but never let go—your baby can't really swim)	Hold his breath and move his arms and legs as if swimming
👍 Stroke back of hand or top of foot; gently poke the side of the palm or sole of the foot	Withdraw hand or foot and arch it
👍 Stroke or put an object on the baby's palm	Tightly grasp with enough strength to allow you to pull him to sitting position (be sure to support head)
👍 Stroke the sole of the foot from heel to toe	Raise the big toe, spread the small ones, and flex the foot as if grasping
👍 Stroke cheek or lips	Turn head toward the side being stroked, open mouth, and start sucking
👍 Place baby on his back and gently turn his head to one side	Straighten arm on the side he is looking, bend arm and leg on other side
👍 Place baby on his tummy and gently stroke one side of the spine	Hips and torso will bend toward the side you're touching

WHAT IT'S CALLED AND WHY IT'S THERE	HOW LONG UNTIL IT'S GONE
Glabella (nasopalpebral) reflex. Protects baby's eyes from being injured by an object or a harsh light	2–4 months
Moro or startle reflex; a fairly primitive way for the newborn to call for help	3 or 4 months
Probably the body's attempt to resist being held down	3 months
Doll's Eye or China Doll reflex; an attempt to get self upright and to support his oversized head	1–2 months
Walking reflex; baby can protect himself by kicking away potentially dangerous things—has absolutely nothing to do with real walking	About 2 months
Crawling reflex; a way for baby to get away from danger	2–4 months
Swimming reflex; possibly a way for baby to escape sharks or other underwater dangers	6 months
Protection against pain	2–4 months
Palmar reflex; encourages baby to start understanding the shape, texture, and weight of whatever he's grasping	2–4 months
Babinski reflex; a throwback to our monkey days	The end of the first year
Rooting reflex; helps baby get ready to eat	3–4 months
Tonic Neck (Fencing) reflex; encourages baby to use each side of body and to notice own hands	1–3 months
Galant reflex; helps baby wriggle his way through the birth canal	3–4 months

- Feelings of sadness, doubt, guilt, helplessness, or hopelessness that begin to disrupt your partner's normal functioning.
- Inability to sleep when tired, or sleeping most of the time, even when the baby is awake.
- Marked changes in appetite.
- Extreme concern and worry about the baby—or lack of interest in the baby and/or other members of the family.
- Worries that she'll harm the baby or herself, or threats of doing either one.

Sadly, a lot of moms who have postpartum depression don't get the assistance they need—often because they feel too embarrassed to admit to anyone else what they're feeling. Helping your partner cope with her depression is important for both her and your baby. Depressed new moms are often emotionally withdrawn around their newborns and have trouble taking care of them. Those babies—because they're such great imitators—mimic their mother's behavior and become less engaged with the people around them. They also cry and fuss more and are more frightened in new situations.

If your partner is suffering from postpartum depression, your help is critical. Engaged, involved dads act as "buffers," shielding their baby from the negative effects of his mother's condition. Here are some important things you can do to help your partner through this difficult time:

- Remind her that the depression is not her fault, that you love her and the baby loves her, that she's doing a great job, and that the two of you will get through this together.
- Spend more time with the baby and make a special effort to be as upbeat, smiling, expressive, and engaging as possible.
- Do as much of the housework as you can so she won't have to worry about not being able to get everything done herself.
- Encourage her to take breaks—regularly and frequently.
- Take over enough of the nighttime baby duties so your wife can get at least five hours of uninterrupted sleep. This means that you'll probably do a feeding or two, which is a great way to get in some extra dad-baby bonding.
- Help her snack on protein instead of carbohydrates throughout the day. This will help keep her blood sugar levels as even as possible, which will help smooth out her moods. If she doesn't have much of an appetite, make her a protein-rich shake.
- If you see that she's feeling anxious or obsessive, keep her as far away as possible from caffeine and make sure she drinks a lot of water (dehydration has been linked to anxiety).

- Turn off the TV news, and don't let her read the news section of the newspaper.
- Find a support group for her that's specifically geared for people with postpartum depression. She'll probably feel safer sharing what's going on in your house and in her head with others who are going through the same thing.
- Get regular breaks to relieve your own stress. Yes, she's relying on you to help her, but if you're falling apart yourself, you're not going to do her or anyone else any good.

One or two out of every thousand new mothers will develop postpartum psychosis. The symptoms usually start right after the birth and are usually immediately recognizable by anyone. They include wild mood swings, hallucinations, being out of touch with reality, doing something to harm herself or the baby, and making crazy or delirious statements. Postpartum psychosis is treatable—often with powerful antipsychotic drugs—but women who have it need help, and they need it fast. So if you see that your partner has any of these symptoms, put down this book and call her doctor immediately. Fortunately, despite the extensive media coverage of mothers who drown five of their children, the majority of women with postpartum psychosis don't hurt their babies or anyone else.

Even Guys Get the Blues—and Worse

Although baby blues or depression are almost always associated with women, the fact is that many men also get the blues after their babies are born. In some cases, men's blues are hormonally based like their partner's. Canadian researcher Anne Storey found that new fathers' testosterone levels often drop by as much as a third right after the birth of their children. Since testosterone is involved in energy and mood, lower levels could explain why some men feel a little down. It's also quite likely that the feelings of sadness, the mood swings, and the anxiety you may be experiencing are the result of facing the stress, the responsibilities, the bills, and the reality of your changing life.

Here's how author S. Adams Sullivan put it: "The hearty congratulations at work last a few days, but then your status as a celebrity wears off and you begin to notice that you're coming home every night to a demanding baby and a distraught wife.... You look at your wife and ... the healthy, radiant glow that made her beautiful while she was pregnant has disappeared, and you're tempted to agree with her when she gripes about her looks ... you're getting maybe four and a half hours of sleep, total, and that's broken up into hour-and-a-half naps, so that you're nodding off every day at work and falling behind."

In most cases, your baby blues—like your partner's—will be gone after a few weeks. But recent research is finding that between 10 and 25 percent of new dads develop actual postpartum depression. Unfortunately, men don't express their depression the same way women do; we tend to get more angry and anxious than sad. As a result, if you're feeling depressed, people (including yourself) might not recognize the symptoms and you won't get the help you need.

According to researcher Sherri Melrose, "left untreated, paternal postpartum depression limits men's capacity to provide emotional support to their partners and children." Like moms, dads with postpartum depression are more likely to spank their children and less likely to play with or read, tell stories, or sing to their infants. Their children (especially boys) are more likely to have emotional and behavior problems and more difficulty relating to their peers at age three and a half. And researcher James Paulson found that infants of depressed dads (but not of depressed moms) have smaller vocabularies at age two than those with non-depressed dads.

Breastfeeding Problems

As natural as breastfeeding is, a large percentage of women have some kind of difficulty, ranging from stress and frustration to pain and infection. Researchers at the University of Utah recently discovered that a specific gene called xanthine oxidoreductase (XOR) may actually put some women at risk of developing breastfeeding problems. Most of the time, though, the difficulties are the result of not having been given proper instruction on how to breastfeed. But whether it's genetic or operator error, the fact remains that women who have problems breastfeeding are far more likely to give it up than those who don't.

Because breastfeeding is so important to both your baby and your partner, it's important that you learn about the potential problems and ways of dealing with them. Here are the possibilities:

- Leaky breasts. It's exactly what it sounds like. Some women's breasts never leak; others' do during every feeding or every time they hear their baby cry. It's most common in the morning when the breasts are at their fullest. Breast leaking peaks during the first few weeks and tapers off over the next few months.
- Sore nipples. Breastfeeding usually takes some getting used to—for the mom and the baby—and a little discomfort is normal. Sore nipples aren't the result of frequent nursing; rather, they're usually caused when the baby doesn't latch on to the breast properly. Untreated, the nipples can go from simply being sore to cracking and bleeding, which can make the entire experience miserable for your partner.
- Engorged breasts. Within a week after giving birth, your partner's milk will "come in," and her breasts may become painfully full, swollen, enormous, or hard. She may also develop a low fever. Oddly, this is actually a good thing,

because it means that she's producing milk. Although engorgement is most common during the first few days of breastfeeding, it can happen any time. Painful engorgement can, for example, wake up your partner in the middle of the night. The easy solution to the problem is to empty the breast, either by having the baby do it or by pumping. Unfortunately, it's sometimes hard for babies to latch on to an engorged breast.

- Clogged ducts. This happens when milk flow within the breast is interrupted and backs up. It can cause uncomfortable lumps inside the breast and hardness, redness, and heat on the skin above the blocked duct. Clogged ducts can be caused by wearing tight bras or from not fully emptying the breast at each feeding. They usually clear up by themselves within a day or two.
- Mastitis. Mastitis is a bacterial infection. It can feel a lot like a clogged duct but is more painful and is often accompanied by fever and/or other flu-like symptoms. It can be caused by not completely emptying the breast, but the number-one reason is lowered resistance to illness, which is the result of exhaustion, stress, and poor diet. Mastitis can develop anytime but is most common during the first month of breastfeeding. Diagnosed early, it's easy to treat, usually with antibiotics. Untreated, though, it can become an abscess, which has to be drained surgically.

If your partner experiences these or any other problems breastfeeding, she's going to need as much support from you as possible. In addition to the suggestions on pages 42–43, here's how you can help:
- Make sure she's comfortable. A lot of women love breastfeeding pillows, which keep the baby high enough so they don't have to lean over, and free up their arms. Two very good ones are Boppie and My Brest Friend (I have no idea why they spell it that way, unless they're World War I fans).
- Encourage her to nurse the baby frequently. She should also change the baby's position every feeding and have the baby empty the breast.
- Suggest that she cover the breasts with warm, wet compresses for a few minutes before every feeding. If the breasts are engorged, she should try to express some milk before letting the baby latch on. After feedings, try cool compresses. Some women swear that putting cabbage leaves on their breasts after feeding works wonders. Hey, it's worth a try.
- Buy Lansinoh cream. It helps soothe sore, cracked, and bloody nipples and doesn't contain any ingredients that could be harmful to the baby.
- Help the baby latch on. The baby should have a great big mouthful of breast, including as much of the areola (the dark part around the nipple) as will fit. Sucking on just the tip of the nipple will hurt.

- To unclog ducts during feedings, massage the area of the clog gently and toward the nipple.
- Call her doctor if she has a fever of 100°F or more. She should check with her doctor if she has pain or other symptoms that persist for more than twenty-four hours. She may need antibiotics.
- Encourage her to continue. The pain can be intense, and she may be tempted to quit, but in many cases, nursing through the problem can help resolve it, whereas stopping can make things worse.
- Call in the pros. If none of these steps help your partner's pain or discomfort within a few days, she should talk to the pediatrician to get a referral to a lactation consultant. Or, she can contact the La Leche League (www.lalecheleague. org) or the International Lactation Consultant Association (www.ilca.org).

YOU AND YOUR BABY

Crying

Since the moment your baby was born, he's been trying to communicate with you. That's the good news. The bad news is that he settled on crying as the way to do it. It will take you a while to teach him that there are more effective, and less annoying, ways of getting your attention. In the meantime, though, if he's like most babies, he's a real chatterbox: 80–90 percent of all infants have crying spells that last from twenty minutes to an hour every day. Of course, not all of your baby's tears mean that he is sad, uncomfortable, hungry, or dissatisfied with something you've done. Nevertheless, holding an inconsolably crying baby can bring out a range of emotions, even in the most seasoned parent, running from pity and frustration to fury and inadequacy.

Fathers are likely to experience these feelings—especially inadequacy—more acutely than mothers. As with so many mother/father differences, the culprit is socialization: most men come into fatherhood feeling less than completely confident in their own parenting abilities, and a baby's cries are too easily seen as confirmation that Daddy is doing a less-than-adequate job.

As difficult as crying can be to deal with, you obviously don't want your baby to be completely silent (in fact, if your baby doesn't cry at least several times a day, you need to have a talk with your pediatrician). Fortunately, there are a few things you can do to make your baby's crying a less unpleasant experience for both of you:

- When (not if) your child starts to cry, resist the urge to hand him to your partner. She knows nothing more about crying babies than you do (or will soon enough). Since each of you instinctively has a different way of interacting with the baby, your hanging in there through a crying spell will double the chances that you'll find new ways to soothe the baby.

- Learn to speak your baby's language. By now, you can almost always tell your baby's cry from any other baby's, and you can probably recognize his "I'm tired," "Feed me now," and "Change my diaper" cries. And while the language he speaks isn't as sexy or as vocabulary-rich as French, your baby has added a few more "phrases" to his repertoire, including "I'm as uncomfortable as hell," "I'm bored out of my mind," and "I'm crying because I'm mad and I'm not going to stop no matter what you do." Responding promptly when your baby cries will help you learn to recognize which cry is which. You'll then be able to tailor your response and keep your baby happy.
- Carry your baby more. The more you hold him (even when he's not crying), the less likely he is to cry. In one study, researchers found that a two-hour increase in carrying time per day resulted in a 42 percent decrease in crying time.
- Get to know your baby's routine. Keeping a diary of when your baby cries, how long the crying spells last, and what (if anything) works to slow him down can really help. Some babies like to thrash around and cry a little (or a lot) before going to sleep; others don't.
- If your partner is breastfeeding, watch what she eats. This is especially important if the baby suddenly and inexplicably deviates from his normal crying routine. Broccoli, cauliflower, Brussels sprouts, and milk, when consumed by nursing mothers, may result in gastrically distressed (and weepy) babies.

After you've tried soothing, feeding, changing the diaper, checking for uncomfortable clothing, and rocking, the baby may still continue to howl. Sometimes there's really nothing you can do about it (see the next section, "Coping with Crying"), but sometimes all it takes is a new approach. Here are a few alternatives you might want to try:

- Hold the baby differently. Not all babies like to be held facing you; some want to face out so they can see the world. One of the most successful ways I've learned to soothe a crying baby—and I've tried this on many kids besides my own—is the Magic Baby Hold. Quite simply, have the baby "sit" facing you in the palm of your hand—thumb in front, the other fingers on the baby's bottom. Then have the baby lie face down on your forearm, with his head resting on the inside of your elbow. Use your other hand to stroke or pat his back.
- Distraction. Offer a toy, a story, a song. If that works, be prepared to repeat it over and over and over. And don't be surprised if whatever stops the crying today seems to make it worse tomorrow. Babies are just like that.

- Make some noise. Singing is good, or try one of those machines that make thunder, rain, ocean, and jungle sounds that many babies find soothing. Running a vacuum cleaner or tuning a portable radio to static has worked for some new parents.
- Give the baby something to suck on. Just take a guess why they call them "pacifiers." If you don't approve of pacifiers, you can either help the baby suck on his own fingers or loan out one of yours (for more on pacifiers, see pages 198–99).
- Give the baby a bath. Some babies find warm water soothing. Others freak out when they get wet. If you do decide to try bathing a crying infant, don't do it alone. Holding on to a calm soapy baby can be a challenge. Keeping a grip on a squirming, screaming, soapy baby takes a team of highly trained specialists.
- Wrap him up. Swaddle him in a lightweight blanket, snuggle with him skin-to-skin in your arms, and/or put him into a front pack (no matter how strong you think you are, carrying a baby around—even a newborn—is rough on the arms and back).
- Get moving. Take the baby for a walk—sometimes a change of scenery is all it takes. If that doesn't work, try rocking the baby in your arms, putting him into a baby swing, taking him for a ride in the car, or putting him on top of a running washing machine or dryer—but do not walk away, even for a second. You might also try a car-ride simulator (a device that, when attached to the baby's crib, vibrates and makes sounds like a car).

Your Baby on Drugs?

During the entire time that your partner is breastfeeding, there's a risk that almost any drug she takes—whether it's for pain or for some kind of chronic or acute medical condition—could get passed into her milk and affect the baby. Most of the time the risk is very small, but sometimes it's not. Unfortunately, a lot of doctors aren't familiar with the potential risks medications pose to lactating mothers and nursing infants. As a result, they may either prescribe something that's potentially dangerous or suggest that the woman stop breastfeeding. There is an easier solution.

LactMed is a free, online, searchable database (run by the U.S. National Library of Medicine. It's a comprehensive listing of prescription and nonprescription drugs, herbal remedies, other chemicals, and even illegal drugs, which are evaluated for safety to both mother and baby during breastfeeding. They even suggest safer alternatives where available. You can access it at toxnet.nlm.nih.gov/newtoxnet/lactmed.htm. You'll find a few more options in the Resources appendix.

- Call the doc. Your pediatrician may prescribe medication that can help in certain situations. If your partner is breastfeeding, the doc may also suggest that she drink herbal tea (chamomile, licorice, and a few others—but talk to the doctor before she starts), or that she eliminate some common allergens (wheat, nuts, milk, eggs) from her diet. If you're using formula, the doc may suggest switching to a more hypo-allergenic brand.

Coping with Crying

Starting at about two weeks of age, some 10–20 percent of healthy, well-fed babies develop colic—a word that strikes fear in the hearts of parents everywhere. The official definition is "crying more than three hours a day, more than three days a week, for more than three months. But for the rest of us, colic is crying that goes on and on and on and just won't stop. Although many colicky babies limit their crying to certain times of the day, some cry all day or all night or get progressively fussier as the day goes on. The duration and intensity of crying spells peaks at about six weeks, and usually disappears entirely within three months.

As hard as crying is on your baby, it's going to take a toll on you and your partner too. Here are some things that may help you cope:

- Go to the drugstore. Some parents have been able to relieve (partially or completely) their colicky infants with an over-the-counter gas remedy for adults. But before you give any medication to your child, talk to your doctor about whether she thinks taking this medication would help.
- Tag-team crying duty. There's no reason why both of you should have to suffer together through what the psychiatrist Martin Greenberg calls "the tyranny of crying." Spelling each other in twenty-minute or half-hour shifts will do you both a world of good. Getting a little exercise during your "time off" will also calm your nerves before your next shift starts.
- If you're bottle-feeding the baby, try changing his formula. Some pediatricians suspect that colic may be linked to a milk intolerance and suggest switching to a non-cow's-milk formula.
- Hold the baby facing you. Put his head over your shoulder with your shoulder pressing on his stomach.
- Hold the baby a little less. I know this completely contradicts my suggestion a few paragraphs ago to hold the baby more, but some doctors believe that babies may cry because their nervous systems aren't mature enough to handle the stimulation that comes with being held and stroked and talked to. But don't do this unless your physician advises you to.
- Put a hot water bottle on your knees. Place the baby face down across it to warm his tummy, and stroke his back.

"See what Daddy has for you if you stop crying?"

- Baby massage (see pages 85–88).
- Try swaddling. Being enveloped in a blanket may make the baby feel more comfortable.
- Let the baby "cry it out." If you've tried everything you can think of and the crying has gone on for more than twenty minutes, put the baby in his crib and give yourself a break. If the baby doesn't stop screaming after five minutes, pick him up and try to soothe him again some other way for ten more minutes. Repeat as necessary. Note: The "crying it out" approach should be used only after you've tried everything else. Generally speaking, you should respond promptly and lovingly to your baby's cries. Several studies show that babies who are responded to in this way develop into more confident youngsters.
- Get some help. Dealing with a crying child for even a few minutes can provoke incredible rage and frustration. And if the screams go on for hours, it can become truly difficult to maintain your sanity, let alone control your temper. If you find yourself concerned that you might lash out (other than verbally) at your child, call someone: your partner, pediatrician, parents, babysitter, friends, neighbors, clergy person, or even a parental-stress hotline. If your baby is a real crier, keep these numbers handy and see the section on anger (pages 270–73).
- Don't take it personally. Your baby isn't deliberately trying to antagonize you. It's all too easy to let your frustration at this temporary situation wear away at your confidence in your abilities as a parent, and it could even permanently interfere with your relationship with your child.

Helping Older Kids Adjust to Their New Sibling

Handling your older children's reactions to their new baby brother or sister requires an extra touch of gentleness and sensitivity. Kids often start out wildly excited at their new status as big brother or big sister, but most will have some adjustment problems later on—as soon as they realize that the new kid is going to be sticking around for a while.

Some react with anger and jealousy. They may cry, have tantrums, and even try to hit the baby. They need to know immediately and in no uncertain terms that you understand how they feel and that it's okay to be mad and talk about how mad they are. It's even okay to draw hateful pictures or beat up a doll. But it's absolutely not okay to do anything to hurt the baby.

Others may react by regressing. My oldest daughter, for example, was completely potty trained before her sister was born, but began wetting her bed again a few weeks after we brought the baby home. Some kids start talking baby talk again, suck their thumbs, need more bedtime stories and cuddling, or make demands for attention that you may not be able to satisfy.

Here are some ways you can help your older children cope with the big changes in their world:

- Get them involved from the very start. My oldest daughter stayed at my parents' house while my wife was in labor with our second daughter. But as soon as the new baby was born, we called and gave her the chance to break the news to everyone else that she was a big sister. We also had her come to the hospital right away (even though it was past her bedtime), where she got to hold her new sister "by herself."

  If your older child comes to the hospital, keep the visit short. It won't take long for the initial excitement to wear off. And be sure to let him spend some time visiting with Mom too. He may have been worried about her, and seeing her in a hospital bed, possibly with IV tubes hanging out of her arms, can be a scary sight.

- Don't push too hard. Letting the older sibling help diaper, bathe, feed, push the stroller, and clothe the new baby is a great idea if it helps bring him into the process by making him feel that the baby is "his." But don't force the older child to get too involved. It can make him feel as though you want him around only to wait on the more important new baby, which can make him resent the little interloper even more.

- Prepare them for reality. The first lesson is that infants aren't a whole lot of fun to have around for a little while. All they do is poop and cry and eat. They can't even play any games. It might be helpful to show your big kids their own baby pictures and talk to them about how they were when they were young and how you cared for them. Also, before going out as a family, warn your older child that everyone's going to be oohing and aahing over the baby, and he may feel a little left out.

- Model good behavior. Show your older kids the right ways to hold and behave with a new baby. Practicing with a doll is a great, risk-free way to get the hang of it—particularly the all-important head-supporting part. If you're bottle-feeding, show the older kids the right way to hold a bottle and how to recognize when the baby's had enough. Never, ever leave the baby unattended with an older sibling (unless you've got a teenager), and make sure the older child is always sitting down when holding the baby.

- Be patient. If your older child is angry or jealous, encourage him to talk about his feelings. If he's having trouble articulating them, you might offer a few suggestions ("Are you mad that that the baby is getting more attention than you are?") or have him draw pictures of how he feels. If your child is regressing, resist the urge to demand that he "grow up." Kids who adopt baby behavior are usually doing so because they figure that being helpless is a good way to get people to pay attention. So instead of snapping, point out some of the big-kid things they get to do that babies don't, such as using a fork and knife, riding a trike, putting on their own shoes, washing their own faces, going down a slide by themselves . . .

- Spend some extra time with them. Your older child really needs to know that you still love him just as much as before. So make sure you get some private time together reading, going for walks, drawing, talking, seeing movies, doing things that are "for big kids only" (babies can't eat ice cream—ha!), or just hanging out. And make sure the big kid gets to spend some private time with Mom too.

- Teach them about safety rules. Your older children are probably going to want to hold and carry their new sibling. If you're going to allow it, they have to understand the proper way to hold a baby (supporting the head at all times), and they must go along with your rules about the whens and wheres. Children under about twelve shouldn't be allowed to carry a baby up or down stairs. And children under nine or ten should do all their baby holding sitting down.

Safety First

It may seem strange to talk about safety at a time when your baby is practically immobile and can't possibly get into any serious trouble. But even at this age babies can do the most surprising things. Here are a few precautions you should take now to start making your home a little safer:

- Avoid beanbags. Most beanbag chairs and baby rests have been taken off the market, but there are still plenty of them in garages all over the country. There is more than a coincidental link between beanbags and suffocation deaths.

- Never leave the baby's car seat—with the baby in it, of course—balanced on anything. A flailing arm or leg, even a sneeze, might move the car seat enough for it to tip over.
- Put together a good first aid kit. You'll find a list of items on page 204.
- Take an infant CPR class. Instruction is usually available fairly inexpensively at your local Red Cross or YMCA.
- Take a quick look at the safety measures described in later chapters (pages 199–205, for example). Start putting together the materials you'll need and get into the habit of doing such things as pointing pot handles toward the rear of the stove.

First Smiles

WHAT'S GOING ON WITH THE BABY

Physically

- By the end of this month, many of your baby's innate reflexes will have disappeared. Sad but true. Nevertheless, she still holds her arms and legs away from her body, and there's plenty of twitching to go around.
- Lying on her tummy, she can now easily hold her head up at a 45-degree angle. And when she's sitting (a position she probably prefers by now—even though she can't get there or stay there by herself), she's a lot better at keeping her head straight.
- Your baby is now beginning to reach for objects. Grasping and unfolding her hands, which were once purely reflex actions, are slowly becoming voluntary. If she manages to grab something, she may be able to hold on to it for a few seconds before dropping it.
- The neurons in your baby's brain that govern vision are going through a major growth spurt. As a result, her vision is improving, and she's paying a lot more attention to what's going on in her world. And because you're such an interesting sight, she'll follow you with her eyes everywhere you go.

Intellectually

- As her brain develops, your baby will appreciate more complex patterns. Instead of the simple, relatively motionless outline of your face, she now prefers your eyes and mouth, which are constantly changing shape. Toward the end of this month she may begin to stare intently at very small items.

- If you touch her cheek now, she probably won't start sucking—an indication that she can now tell the difference between your finger and a milk-bearing nipple.
- She is also now able to accommodate herself to various situations. If you're holding her upright against your shoulder, she'll hold herself differently than if you're resting her on your knees.
- She gets excited when she sees familiar objects, but she has no sense of "object permanence" (which means that as far as the baby is concerned, anything she can't see simply doesn't exist). At the same time, though, she's developing a primitive understanding of cause and effect: when she cries, you take care of one of her needs.

Verbally

- Leaving behind the grunting and squeaking, your baby is expanding her vocabulary to include some delightful cooing (a combination of a squeal and a gurgle), as well as some impressive oohs, ohhs, and ahhs.
- Crying, however, is still one of her favorite ways of communicating and is in no way a comment on your parenting abilities.

Emotionally/Socially

- And now, the moment you've been waiting for: your baby is finally able to smile at you (sorry, but until now those things you thought were smiles were probably just gas), which she'll often do in response to something that pleases her.
- As she becomes more and more interested in learning about her world (a process that hopefully won't stop for the rest of her life), your baby will really enjoy regular changes of scenery.
- Her range of emotions is still fairly small, limited mostly to excitement and distress. But she's giving you a lot of hints about her future personality.
- She's awake about ten hours a day. Although she's stimulated more by touch than by social interaction, she'll stay awake longer if there are people around to amuse her.

WHAT YOU'RE GOING THROUGH

Thinking about Sex

Most OB/GYNs advise their patients to refrain from intercourse for at least six weeks after giving birth. But before you mark that date on your calendar, remember that the six-week rule is only a guideline. Resuming intercourse ultimately depends on the condition of your partner's cervix and vagina, and, more impor-tant, on how you're both feeling. Many couples begin having sex again in as little as three or four weeks, but it's not at all uncommon for couples to take six months or longer to fully reestablish their prepregnancy sex life.

Many factors—both physical and psychological—influence when and how a couple decides to resume their sex life. Here are a few:

- One or both of you may be too exhausted, too stressed, or just unable to fit it into your schedule. And one or both of you might worry about being inter-rupted by a crying baby, which has a tendency to limit spontaneity.
- When you had sex with your partner before, she was the woman you loved. Now she's also a mother—a thought that may remind you of your own mother and can be a big turnoff. At the same time, in your new capacity as parent, you may remind your partner a little too much of her own father. She may also find it tough to reconcile her roles as lover and mother, and may see herself as unsexual.
- Your partner may not have fully recovered from her episiotomy or C-section.
- Your partner may be embarrassed if milk leaks from her breasts when she's aroused. A lot of men find leaking breasts erotic. But if you don't—and she senses your feelings—she may worry that you don't find her desirable anymore.
- A lot of women find it difficult to think of their vagina as a sexual organ after seeing a baby come out of it. And some men have trouble coping with the idea that their partner's breasts and vagina can be functional as well as fun. And images of a vaginal birth or having the woman you love sliced open for a C-section can be hard to get out of your mind.
- You may resent your baby's unlimited access to your partner's breasts and feel that your partner is focusing more on the baby than on you. And she may be.
- Your (or your partner's) motivation to have sex may have changed since your baby was born. If, for example, you or she were motivated to have sex because you really wanted to be a parent, sex after having a baby may feel a little anti-climactic, so to speak. Been there, done that.
- Now that you have concrete proof (the baby) of your virility, you may feel more intimate with your partner than ever before.

When You and Your Partner Are out of Sync

Just as you and your partner can't always agree on what movie you want to see or what you want to have for dinner, you can't expect that you'll both feel sex-ually aroused at the same time. She might want to make love at a time when you're simply too tired to move. Or you might want to have sex when she's feeling "touched out," having spent an entire day with a baby crawling all over her, suck-ing her breasts.

Nonsexual and Almost Nonsexual Affection

Most adults have a limited repertoire of ways to please each other. But there are plenty of ways to be sensual short of intercourse. Hand holding, back rubs, hair stroking while watching TV, and even gentle, nonsexual kissing are good for those times when one of you isn't in the mood. If you're not in the mood but want to give—or receive—some nonsexual affection, tell your partner up front that there are no strings attached. Researchers have found that men and women who don't want sex are frequently afraid that the kiss or hug they need from, or want to give to, their partners will be misinterpreted as a sexual overture.

The months right after the birth of a baby are a particularly vulnerable time for your sex life. If you had great sex before or even during the pregnancy, don't take it for granted that everything will be as it was—you'll still have to work on it. And if your prebaby sex life wasn't that great, don't count on it getting better anytime soon. Either way, here are a few suggestions that might help smooth over some of the rough spots you'll invariably encounter:

- Figure out what, exactly, is motivating you to want to have sex. That may sound ridiculous—you want to have sex because it feels good, right? Well, sort of. "Sex can be an expression of monogamy, intimacy, love, or even an affirmation of one's sexual identity ('I'm a man and this is what men do')," says Linda Perlin Alperstein, an associate professor at the University of California, San Francisco. And for some people (this is pretty rare, though) sex is solely a way to reproduce.
- Talk. Most of us—men and women—feel embarrassed to tell our partner exactly what we like and don't like. But doing so is absolutely essential—not only to getting your sex life back on track but to the overall health of your relationship.
- Negotiate. If you really want to have sex, and she doesn't, ask her—without putting a lot of pressure on her—what, if anything, she'd be willing to do. Would she, for example, be willing to masturbate you? Would she hold you in her arms or let you touch her breasts while you stimulate yourself? In sexuality expert Sari van Anders's research, 58 percent of partners of new moms received oral sex. It goes without saying (or at least it should) that you should be prepared to reciprocate. The object here is not to convince her to have sex; the two of you should be working toward creating an environment in which you both feel safe expressing your desires and in which each of you can turn the other down without fear of causing offense or hurting feelings.

The First Time . . . Again

When you do finally get around to making love, you should expect the first few times to be a period of tentative rediscovery for both of you. Her body has changed, and she may respond differently than she used to. Some studies have shown that after giving birth, women experience a slightly decreased interest in vaginal stimulation and an increased interest in clitoral and breast stimulation. Also, women who experienced multiple orgasms before giving birth are less likely to do so, or will do so less frequently, now.

She may also be worried that having sex will hurt, and you may be afraid of the same thing or that those extra pounds she hasn't lost yet will interfere with her pleasure (or yours). Go slowly, take your cues from her, and give yourselves plenty of time to get used to each other again.

Sex researchers William Fisher and Janice Gray found that nursing mothers generally resume their sexual lives sooner than women who don't breastfeed. This is a little odd, considering that nursing mothers produce lower levels of ovarian hormones, which are responsible for producing vaginal lubrication. As a result, if your partner is nursing, her vagina may be much drier than before, making intercourse painful. Obviously, this doesn't mean she isn't aroused by you; it's simply a common post-birth condition. In situations like these, a little K-Y Jelly, Astroglide, or other over-the-counter lubricant will go a long way.

And while you're out buying lubricant, pick up a few boxes of condoms too. Despite what you may have heard about women not being able to get pregnant during the time that they're breastfeeding, nursing is not an effective means of contraception. Your partner's periods will probably start up again between three and eight months after the birth. But since ovulation happens about two weeks before the period starts, she may not know that she's fertile again until it's too late. So unless the two of you really want two kids less than a year apart, get in the habit of using some kind of protection every time you have sex. Barrier methods (condoms or diaphragm) are probably best right now. But have your partner check with her OB to see whether any of the oral contraceptives are safe during breastfeeding.

Finally, be flexible—and patient. In the first six weeks after childbirth, only 34 percent of couples have vaginal intercourse. Meanwhile, about 74 percent of partners of new moms masturbate, according to Sari van Anders, an intimacy and sexuality researcher at the University of Michigan.

- Be completely honest. If you and your partner agree that you'll hold each other like spoons and kiss but that you won't touch each other's genitals, don't go over the line. Doing so will only make her tense and distrustful.
- Change your attitude. A lot of men have the idea that every erection has to result in an ejaculation. But is having an orgasm the only way to experience pleasure? Not a chance. Sometimes just getting aroused—and leaving it right there—can be fun.
- Start dating again. No, not someone else—your partner. Having a good sex life can certainly contribute to the happiness of your relationship, but even the wildest, most amazing sex doesn't guarantee anything. So make sure to set aside some time every day—even if it's only fifteen minutes—to talk about life, work, movies you've seen, books you've read, politics, whatever. But don't talk about anything to do with your baby.
- Ask for—and give your partner—some nonsexual affection (see page 77).

Not Ready to Be a Father

One of the most consistent findings by researchers is that new fathers almost always feel unprepared for their new role. Personally, I would have been surprised if it were otherwise. When most of our fathers were raising us, a "good father" was synonymous with "good provider." He supported his family financially, mowed the lawn, washed the car, and maintained discipline in the home. No one seemed to care whether he ever spent much time with his children; in fact, he was discouraged from doing so, and told to leave the kids to his wife, the "good mother."

Yesterday's "good father" has now retroactively become an emotionally distant, uncaring villain. And today's "good father," besides still being a breadwinner, is expected to be a real presence—physically and emotionally—in his kids' lives. This, in a nutshell, is exactly what most new fathers want. Most of us have no intention of being wait-till-your-father-comes-home dads and want to be more involved with our children than our own fathers were. The problem is that we just haven't had the training. The solution? Quit complaining and jump right in. The "maternal instinct" that women are supposedly born with is actually acquired on the job. And that's exactly where you're going to develop your "paternal instinct." If you need a little extra guidance, think about starting a dad blog and connecting with other new and more experienced dads (see pages 192–94 for more).

Confusion

If there's one thing that set my first few months of fatherhood apart from the next few years, it was the confusing and often conflicting emotions I felt:

"You're not real experienced at this father business, are you?"

- On the one hand, I had a sense of incredible virility, power, and pride at having created a new life. On the other, I often felt helpless when I couldn't understand—let alone satisfy—the baby's needs.
- Most of the time I felt the most powerful kind of love for my tiny child. But sometimes I also felt ambivalent. And once in a while I felt a powerful anger— one that seemed to come out of nowhere—toward the very same baby.
- Most of the time I felt particularly close to my wife—especially when we would admire our children together. But every so often I'd get suspicious that she loved them more than she did me.

Being confused leads a lot of guys to feel that there's something wrong with them. You'd be amazed at the number of questions I get via email or in person, at workshops I do with fathers, that start with the same seven words: "Am I the only one who feels ...?"

Before you go off and check yourself into a mental hospital, there are a few things you should know. First, being confused isn't abnormal at all. If you want proof, all you have to do is start asking a few of the other new dads you know whether they're feeling some of the same things you are. You'll probably find that (a) they have the same feelings you do, and (b) they also think they're abnormal. That begs the question: if almost everyone thinks he's abnormal, then isn't being abnormal the norm? If that doesn't reassure you at least a little, maybe this will: this state of confusion—and the accompanying suspicions about your sanity— usually disappear by the end of the third month.

Fears—Lots of Them

The combination of feeling unprepared and confused at the same time can be rather frightening, and the first few months of fatherhood are riddled with fears. Here are some of the most common:

- Fear of not being able to live up to your own expectations.
- Fear of not being able to protect your children from physical harm as they grow and develop.
- Fear of not being able to deal with the most basic parenting responsibilities: feeding, clothing, earning enough money, dealing with the baby's illnesses.
- Fear of not being able to shield your child from some of the more abstract horrors of modern life: poverty, war, disease, the destruction of the environment . . .
- Fear of simply not being "ready" to assume the role of father.
- Fear of picking up the baby because you think you might hurt her.
- Fear of your anger at the baby.
- Fear of not being able—or willing—to love the baby enough.
- Fear of not being in control (see pages 82–83).
- Fear of repeating the mistakes made by your own father (see pages 105–8).
- Fear that if you discuss your fears with your partner, she'll misinterpret them and think you don't love her or the baby.
- For dads in the military, fear that if you deploy when your baby is young, she won't know who you are when you come back or will cry when you try to hold her.

Some fears—such as fear of poverty and war, or of not being ready—you just can't do anything about. But others you can. For example, fear of not being able to handle the little things can be overcome by practice; fear of hurting the baby can also be overcome by spending more time carrying, stroking, picking up, and holding her—babies are not nearly as fragile as they look; fears about staying in touch with your baby during a military deployment (or any extended absence) can be alleviated somewhat by reading my book *The Military Father: A Hands-on Guide for Deployed Dads*; and the fear of discussing things with your partner can be cured (to a certain extent) by taking a deep breath and telling her what you feel. She's going through many of the same things you are and will be relieved to find that she's not alone. Guaranteed.

Whatever your worries, you need to start by admitting to yourself that they exist and remembering that all new fathers are afraid sometimes. In his book *Fatherjournal*, David Steinberg eloquently describes coming to terms with himself and his fears. "I was going to be the perfect father: loving, caring, nurturing, soft. . . . I was going to do it right. . . . Tonight I see how scared I am. There is so much to do for this little creature who screams and wriggles and needs and doesn't know what he needs and relies on me to figure it out. . . . I need to accept my fear, my reluctance, my instinct to flee. I have to start from where I am instead of where the model new-age father would be." Does that sound familiar?

Hey! Who's in Charge Around Here Anyway?

It's hard to admit, but like it or not, your baby's running your life. She cries, you pick her up. She's hungry, you feed her. She fills her diaper, you change it. She wants to play, you play. She needs a nap, you drive around the block twelve times until she falls asleep. She wakes up in the middle of the night, you're up too. The ancient rabbis of the Talmud described it pretty well. The first stage of life, they said, "commences in the first year of human existence, when the infant lies like a king on a soft couch, with numerous attendants about him, all ready to serve him, and eager to testify their love and attachment by kisses and embraces." It's all happening on your baby's schedule, not yours.

Being out of control is hard for anyone, but it's especially discombobulating for men, who are supposed to know everything and be in control all the time. Before my oldest daughter was born, I was incredibly anal about time; I always showed up wherever I was supposed to be exactly when I was supposed to, and I demanded the same from others. But, as you now know, going on a simple trip to the store with baby in tow takes as much planning as an expedition to Mount Everest. And getting anywhere on time is just about impossible.

You may be a great salesman or negotiator or a cult leader, but your ability to turn adults to your way of thinking won't work with a baby. Babies are, almost by definition, irrational and not at all interested in your timetables. In no time at all your baby will figure out what you're most rigid and impatient about, and she'll begin pushing your buttons. That leisurely walk in the park you planned might have to be cut short when the baby panics and won't stop crying after a friendly dog licks her hand. Or you might end up having to stay a few extra hours at a friend's house so as not to wake the baby if she's sleeping or, if she's awake, not to upset her nap schedule by having her fall asleep in the car on the way home. And just when you think you've figured out her routines and the surefire tricks to comfort her or get her to sleep, she revamps everything.

So you've got a very Zen choice to make: you can either learn to accept change and bend, or you can break. It took a while, but I eventually learned that trying to be a father and Mr. Prompt at the same time just wasn't going to work. Most of the men I've interviewed have said basically the same thing: since becoming dads, they'd learned to be a lot more flexible and tolerant—not only of themselves

Don't Panic

Taken together, the feelings of unpreparedness, the fears, and the confusion so many new fathers experience can be overwhelming. Unfortunately, some men respond to this turmoil by running away—emotionally, physically, or both—from their kids and their partners. If you're feeling unable to deal with your anxieties and your feelings, do not run. Find yourself a more experienced father about your age and ask him to help you sort things out (see pages 192–94 for information on fathers' groups). If you can't find another dad, talk to your partner. And if none of those alternatives work, find a good therapist, preferably one with experience dealing with men's concerns. Most important, remember that all this is absolutely normal and that you're not the only one going through it. There is help out there; you just have to find it.

and their limitations but of other people's as well. It's all a part of becoming a grown-up.

YOU AND YOUR BABY

Awakening the Senses

Your baby was born equipped with the same five basic senses you were. And although they'll probably develop just fine without any outside intervention, gently encouraging them along by exposing your baby to a broad range of stimulation can be a lot of fun for both of you. As we've already discussed, pay attention to your baby's cues and don't drag any of these activities out for more than a few minutes. If she's interested, she'll let you know by paying attention. If she's not, she'll let you know that too, by crying or fussing or turning away.

TASTE

By putting drops of various foods on babies' tongues, researchers have proven that babies have definite likes and dislikes. And one of their biggest likes is sweet stuff. In one fascinating study, newborns who drank a sugary solution before a painful medical procedure (usually a heel prick to take a few drops of blood) cried less than those who didn't. You're not going to try this, of course. At this age, your baby has no business eating anything but breast milk or formula. Save the experiments with real taste sensations for when you start introducing solid foods (see pages 162–67). In the meantime, give the baby lots of different objects to put in her mouth. But be extremely careful that none of them has removable pieces or sharp edges, or is small enough to be a choking hazard. (Anything that can fit through the tube in a standard roll of toilet paper is too small.)

SMELL

Smell and taste are very closely related. In another study of babies' reactions to painful heel pricks, babies were soothed by the smell of breast milk—as long as it was their mother's. The foods that pregnant women eat make their way into the amniotic fluid. And babies whose mothers ate strong-flavored foods like anise turn toward the smell when it's nearby. But babies who'd never drunk anise-laced amniotic fluid are revolted by the smell.

To help develop your baby's sense of smell, offer her a wide variety of things to sniff:
- If you're cooking, let her smell the spices and other ingredients.
- If you're out for a walk, let her smell the flowers.
- Try some experiments to see whether she prefers sweet smells to sour ones.
- Be careful, though. Make sure she doesn't get any of these things in her mouth, and don't experiment with extremely strong smells. Also, stay far, far away from ammonia, bleach, gasoline, paint thinner, pool or garden chemicals, and any other toxic materials you may have around the house.

VISION

Your baby's eyes are still getting used to being outside the womb, and she focuses best on objects that are 8–12 inches from her, so be sure to hold toys and other objects within that range.
- Play tracking games, moving objects slowly back and forth in front of her eyes. She may even begin to anticipate what you'll do next. You can also help boost her hand-eye coordination by holding an object within arm's reach and letting her try to grab it.
- Emphasize high-contrast (black-and-white or bright) colors. Regularly change the patterns and keep track of which ones she prefers. Over the course of the next few months she'll advance from simple shapes and patterns to more complex ones.
- Show her mirrors, pictures, and photographs.
- Regularly change the baby's position in her crib so that she has different things to look at. This is also a great time to hang a mobile.
- Take the baby out for a walk and let her see what's going on in the world.

TOUCH

- Expose the baby to as many textures as possible: the satin edges of her blanket; the plastic (or cloth) on her diaper; the family dog; a window; your computer keyboard; warm things and cool things; smooth ones and rough ones. The produce section of your local grocery store is a great place for experimenting. Have her feel the difference between a kiwi or a peach and a coconut or a pineapple. Let her feel each object for as long as she's interested. It's a good idea to carefully wash the baby's hands after you do this, especially if you had her touch the family pet or anything else that could cause problems if she were to put her hands in her mouth or rub them in her eyes.
- Don't limit yourself to the baby's hands; you can gently rub objects on her cheeks, arms, or legs. (From a very young age, all of my kids loved me to rub the bottoms of their feet on my two-day beard growth.) Again, use common sense here. Be gentle and don't leave any objects with the baby.

HEARING

- Expose the baby to as wide a variety of sounds as possible: the radio; any musical instruments you have around the house; construction sites (if they're not too loud). Does your baby seem to prefer one kind of noise—or music—to another? If you do opt for music, don't feel limited to Mozart. Instead, let her listen to as many different styles as you can stand. Simple melodies and moderate tempi are best at this stage—very fast music may overstimulate her. And be sure to keep the volume down; babies' hearing is very sensitive and easily damaged by excessively loud noise.
- For fun, take a small bell, hold it behind the baby, and ring it gently. Does she try to turn around? Now move the bell to one side. Did she notice the change?
- Don't forget about your own voice. Make sounds, changing the pitch of your voice; sing; and even have leisurely chats (okay, monologues) with the baby.
- Play imitation games. Make a noise (a Bronx cheer is always a good place to start) and see whether the baby responds. It may take a few minutes or even a few days to get a reply. Once you do, try the same noise a few more times and then switch roles, having the baby initiate the "conversation" so you can imitate her.
- Don't overlook one of the most important sounds of all: silence. Babies need plenty of downtime, so don't leave the stereo or your iPod running all the time.

Baby Massage

Many parents in other countries massage their babies every day, but in the United States the idea is still pretty new. And in the eyes of some, it's about time. According to researcher Tiffany Field and other experts, massage may:

No Baby Talk, Please

There's some evidence that shows that babies prefer their mother's voice to anyone else's. But if you talked to your baby before she was born, she will definitely recognize yours too. Whenever you talk to your baby, pay close attention to your voice. Your natural, conversational voice is best because it exposes the baby to English as it is actually spoken. For some reason I've never been able to understand, many people can't bring themselves to speak naturally to a baby. Instead, they smile the biggest fake smile they can and say things like "Cootchie-cootchie widduw baby-poo, can I pinchy-winchy your cheeky-weeky?" Some babies respond well to that kind of speech, but is that really the way you want your baby to learn how to speak? What your baby will respond to most—whether it's mom or dad—are eye contact, a sincere smile, and an enthusiastic-but-normal voice that's directed at her. Need I say more?

- Help you and your baby bond.
- Help your baby feel safe and secure.
- Reduce stressful responses to painful procedures like vaccines (at least for the baby).
- Reduce pain associated with teething and constipation.
- Reduce colic.
- Help reduce sleep problems.
- Lower your stress levels while raising your self-esteem and self-confidence as a parent.

As fantastic as that all sounds, keep a lid on your expectations. While massage *may* provide some or all of the above advantages for some people, it may not be as successful for you. However, it's still a wonderful way of interacting with and getting to know your baby.

Sounds like it's at least worth a try, doesn't it? Let's start with a few general guidelines first:

- Schedule it. The best time is when both you and the baby are relaxed and calm and when you can have 10–20 minutes without interruption (although if you only have 5 minutes, do it anyway). Right after the baby's bath or right before putting her to bed are good, but you can do it anytime you want, as long as it's not right when you expect the baby to start fussing. Try to do at least a few minutes of massage every day (or split the duties with your partner).

- Find a warm room with a clean, flat surface you can put the baby on.
- Cover the surface with something soft and absorbent, since your baby will be naked.
- Sing or talk to your baby while you're doing the massage.
- Use firm but gentle pressure. Newborns don't like too light a touch—it seems like tickling and annoys them. At the same time, you're not doing deep-tissue, shiatsu, or Rolfing, so there's no need for any gouging, banging, or thumping.
- Pay attention to your baby's cues. If she seems unhappy, bored, or upset, stop.

There are all sorts of techniques out there for doing baby massage. Here's my favorite:

1. Pour a little bit of baby lotion or baby-appropriate oil (meaning natural, unscented, and edible) into one palm, then rub your hands together to warm the oil.
2. With the baby on her back, start with her arms and legs, rolling each one between both of your hands the way you used to do when you made snakes out of clay when you were a kid.

Hey, What Happened to My Baby's Head?

Your baby's skull is made up of several bones that will remain somewhat flexible until she's two. For that reason, babies who lie on their backs for too long (particularly preemies) may develop a flat spot on the skull. In most cases, this kind of "positional molding" isn't anything to worry about. But if you don't deal with it relatively early, it can cause the ears and eyes to be out of alignment, or lead to even more severe facial deformities.

If your baby's head looks asymmetrical or you think she's got a flat spot, the best thing to do is to frequently switch her sleeping positions. Every time you put her down for a nap or for the night, put her in a different position in her crib (head toward one side, then the other). That way, even if your baby likes one particular view from the crib, she'll have to turn her head from side to side to see it.

If you don't notice any improvement within a week, take the baby in to see her doctor. In very rare cases, a flattened head could be an indicator of a more serious condition that can be corrected only through surgery or by wearing a corrective headband or helmet.

3. Roll each of the toes between your thumb and forefinger in kind of a This-Little-Piggy fashion.

4. Put one palm on your baby's tummy, your little finger close to her rib cage. Pressing firmly, move the hand downward. As soon as that hand reaches the pubic bone, repeat with the other hand. The complete motion is kind of like digging in the sand with your hands.

5. Alternatively (or in addition), place both palms on the baby's tummy, index fingers touching. Pressing firmly, move both hands out, as if parting the Red Sea.

6. Turn the baby over onto her tummy.

7. Starting with the back of the head, move your hands slowly, in one smooth stroke, all the way down to her heels.

8. Now do it again, except this time, use two or three fingers on each hand and make circles as you move from head to heels. Don't forget to massage the butt.

9. Using both of your thumbs, gently press on the bottom of each of the baby's feet, stroking from heel to toe.

The Importance of Squirming Around

Your two-month-old isn't really mobile yet. While on her back, she can raise her head to about 45 degrees, but rolling over is still a few months away. Nevertheless, your baby's muscles need a little exercise. Here are a few ways to help her get a workout:

• Stop swaddling (if you haven't already). Your baby needs to practice using her arms and hands, something she won't be able to do if she's all bundled up in a blanket.

• Encourage tummy time. Although your baby should always sleep on her back, make sure she spends plenty of time in other positions while she's awake. This will encourage her to use different muscles. Babies who don't get much tummy time don't learn to roll over as quickly as those who do (although does a month or two difference really matter? How many adults do you know who can't roll over from front to back or vice versa?) Spending time on her tummy gives your baby a little upper-body workout, strengthening her arms and neck muscles and encouraging her to use them more.

Introducing the Doctor

If you went to all your partner's prenatal doctor appointments, the schedule of visits to your baby's pediatrician will seem quite leisurely—assuming your baby is healthy, you'll have only eight the entire first year (usually called well-baby checkups). Whether or not you got into the doctor-visit habit before the baby was born, make every effort to go to as many well-baby visits (and not-so-well-baby visits) as you can. Doing so is good for everyone; here's why:

- Your baby will know that she can turn to you for help and that you'll be there to comfort her when she needs it.
- Your doctor will be able to get some of your family history to apply to the baby. And since most of what pediatricians know about their young patients comes from what the parents tell them, your input doubles the amount of information the doctor can use to make a diagnosis.
- You'll be more in touch with your child and more involved in her life.

Most doctor visits will be pretty much the same: the nurse will try to convince the baby to lie flat enough to be measured and to keep still on a scale long enough to get weighed. Then the doctor will poke the baby's stomach, measure her head, and ask you a series of questions about the baby's health. He or she may also ask you to immobilize the baby to facilitate a quick ear exam.

Between visits, keep a running list of questions and concerns that you and your partner want to discuss, and don't be shy about going through every item. No one expects you to know everything. At this point, most new parents are worried about whether their baby is developing normally. Rest assured, even though well-baby visits may not seem all that thorough, your pediatrician is focusing on exactly that question.

Break out the Needles

The big event at most doctor visits for the first several years are the immunizations, so if you're squeamish about needles, you'd better get over it. We'll discuss some specific medical questions in later chapters. But for now, here's a fairly typical schedule of well-baby checkups and the immunizations your baby will receive at each visit:

But What Does "Normal" Mean?

At the very beginning of each chapter in this book, I discuss the developmental milestones that your baby will *probably* achieve by the end of that month. Keep in mind that these milestones are only guidelines and that not all babies of the same age are in the same place at the same time. This is especially true if your baby was born prematurely.

To get a better handle on what's "normal" for a preemie, you'll need to use her adjusted age (that's her actual age minus the number of months she was born early). For example, a four-month-old baby who was born two months early would have an adjusted age of only two months and will be evaluated against two-month-old standards. Premature babies usually catch up to their agemates by the time they're two or three. But the more premature the baby, the longer it takes to pull even.

At this point, red flags that might concern your baby's doctor include:

- Not being able to hold her head up for at least a few seconds, holding her hands in fists most of the time, or generally poor muscle tone.
- Asymmetrical movement. Does your baby seem to be using one leg or arm a lot more than the other? Most babies don't develop a true "handedness" until about age two. Some interesting research links asymmetrical movement with development of autism later in life.
- Absence of or extended persistence of various reflexes (see the chart on pages 60–61).

Immunizations

There has been a lot of controversy lately about immunizations (Are the vaccines themselves dangerous? Are the risks worth the rewards?), and a small but growing number of people are electing not to have their children inoculated. On pages 92–95 you'll find a chart listing the vaccines, the possible side effects, and what might happen to someone who's not inoculated. If you're thinking of skipping the vaccinations, keep these points in mind:

- If your partner was immunized, your baby will piggyback on mom's antibodies and be protected from the same diseases she is. However, that immunity disappears before the baby's first birthday—unless she gets her own immunizations.
- Almost all public schools, and many private ones, require proof of vaccination before admitting a child.
- Not vaccinating your kids is a viable option only if everyone else's kids are vaccinated, thus reducing the chance that your child will be exposed to health risks. This is known as "herd immunity": if enough people are immune, they'll protect the rest of the "herd." Imagine what would happen if everyone decided not to vaccinate.
- Today's vaccinations protect babies against more than a dozen diseases. Twenty-five years ago, they covered only four.
- Many vaccines work by introducing an *antigen* into the body. Antigens are

A Few Important Health and Safety Issues

Getting your home completely childproofed is a process that never ends. We'll talk extensively about it on pages 199–205, but there are a few things you should really take care of now.

- Turn your water heater down to 120 degrees. You may decide to take a shower or bath with your baby, and water hotter than that could cause permanent injury and scarring.
- Check out your baby's sleeping area. Whether she's in a bassinet, cradle, or crib, all of the following should apply:
  - The mattress should fit into the frame snugly enough that it's hard to get your hand into the gap.
  - If the crib is painted, make sure the paint is not toxic. Your baby's going to be chewing on it in a few months, and the last thing you want to worry about is poisonous paint chips.
  - The bars or slats on the crib should be no farther apart than 2⅜ inches.

incredibly tiny amounts of the actual disease they're supposed to protect against; they ready the body's immune system to attack similar (but much larger) invasions later on. Some people believe that too many antigens can overwhelm a baby's immature immune system. But thanks to a number of medical developments, babies are getting exposed to fewer antigens today than they were when you were immunized. In 1980, for example, the pertussis vaccine alone had 3,000 antigens. Today, it contains about 5. And there are fewer than 130 antigens total contained in the eleven standard vaccines.
- Some very high-profile celebrities have jumped on the antivaccine bandwagon and blame vaccines for autism and a variety of other problems. The research they cite has been completely debunked, so before you take their advice, carefully consider their medical qualifications.
- There are risks involved with any vaccine, but the rewards far outweigh the risks. In fact, most serious side effects are so rare (1 in 1 million) that it's impossible to be sure that the vaccine itself caused the effect. You quite literally have a better chance of being hit by lightning. According to the National Weather Service, in any given year, the odds are about 1 in 960,000; over your lifetime, the odds go to 1 in about 12,000.
- Vaccine refusal has been directly linked with deadly outbreaks of previously controlled diseases in many communities.

VACCINE	RISKS 👎 / REWARDS 👍
Diphtheria, Tetanus, and Pertussis (DTaP) or **Diphtheria, Tetanus (DT)**: same as above, minus pertussis part for babies who have: • history of seizures • suspected or known neurological disease • reactions to previous shot	👍 almost all children protected after 3 doses plus booster 👎 you'll need to observe baby carefully for 72 hours after shot 👎 some fussiness, drowsiness, soreness, or a lump at injection site 👎 mild fever for 24 hours after the shot is common 👎 seizures or uncontrollable crying are extremely rare (so much so that it's not entirely clear whether the vaccine caused the reaction or not) *Note:* Most of the risks are associated with the pertussis component. The only risk associated with the diphtheria and tetanus parts is local (injection site) swelling and slight fever
Hepatitis B—a noninfectious vaccine produced from cultures	👍 almost all children protected after 3 doses 👎 7–25 percent get soreness at the injection site, fussiness, headache, or fever over 99.9 degrees 👎 severe allergic reaction 1 in 1.1 million
Rotavirus (RV)	👍 keeps the virus from spreading to others in the community 👎 Side effects can include exactly what it's supposed to protect against: diarrhea and vomiting, along with fever 👎 could cause reaction if child has a latex allergy (one of the applicators is latex)
Haemophilus influenza type B (HiB)	👍 90–100 percent protection rate after the full series of shots 👎 soreness and/or lump at the injection site 👎 fever (rarely above 101 degrees) for 12–24 hours after shot

WHAT IT PREVENTS	RISKS IF BABY GETS THE DISEASE
Diphtheria, a severe respiratory illness; rare in the U.S.	• extremely contagious • attacks the throat and nose, interferes with breathing, and causes paralysis • damages heart, kidneys, nerves • up to 20 percent death rate (5–10 percent for those over age 5)
Tetanus (lockjaw), caused by dirt getting in cuts	• causes painful muscle contractions • without treatment, over 25 percent of babies die
Pertussis (whooping cough): prior to the invention of this vaccine, pertussis caused as many deaths as all other contagious diseases combined	• causes coughing so severe that the baby can't eat or breathe • can cause brain damage, pneumonia, and seizures • can cause death (1–2 percent) • most severe in young babies
Hepatitis B	• contagious liver disease • complications include cirrhosis, chronic active hepatitis, and liver cancer • rare in children, but an infected mom may pass it on to the baby via breast milk
Rotavirus	• a common virus that can cause severe vomiting and diarrhea in infants that can lead to dehydration and may require hospitalization • before the vaccine, 80 percent of children in the U.S. had symptoms, 1 in 7 required medical attention; 1 in 70 was hospitalized
Haemophilus Influenza type B, bacterial infection of children under 5	• before the vaccine, HiB caused 12,000 cases of meningitis and 8,000 cases of deep-seated infections (bones, joint, heart, lungs, blood, and throat) each year • may lead to blindness, mental retardation, or paralysis • 5 percent mortality rate

VACCINE	RISKS 👎 / REWARDS 👍
Measles	👍 virtually wiped out in the U.S.
	👍 over 95 percent protected after one dose
	👎 10–20 percent have mild fever or rash that appears 6–10 days after the shot
	👎 1 in 1,000,000 may develop a brain disorder
Mumps	👍 99 percent protected after one dose
	👎 rare fever, rashes, and swelling of glands after vaccination
Rubella	👍 over 95 percent protected after one dose
	👍 getting it now protects future fetuses of girl babies
	👍 children of pregnant women can be vaccinated without risk to mother
	👎 1 percent of young children will have temporary leg, arm, or joint pain
MMR—measles, mumps, and rubella vaccine	👍 protection is as good as when vaccines are given separately
	👍 side effects are the same as when given separately
Varicella (Sometimes given along with MMR as MMRV)	👍 extremely effective in preventing the disease
	👎 1 in 5 may get soreness or swelling
	👎 1 in 10 may get fever
	👎 seizures (1 per 1,000 vaccinations) and pneumonia are very rare
Inactivated Polio Vaccine (IPV); an injection has replaced the riskier **Oral Polio Vaccine (OPV)**, which you probably got (drops, usually in a sugar cube)	👍 very effective; no new cases of polio in the U.S. for over 35 years
	👍 95 percent receiving all 3 doses are protected
	👎 may cause mild fever and redness at the injection site
	👎 1 in 4 million chance of paralysis
Pneumococcal Conjugate Vaccine (PCV13)	👍 90 percent effective
	👍 the best way to protect against pneumococcal bacteria, which is very resistant to antibiotics
	👎 minor side effects include pain, swelling, fever, drowsiness

WHAT IT PREVENTS	RISKS IF BABY GETS THE DISEASE
Measles	• a highly contagious childhood disease • high fever (103–105 degrees), cough, and rash for up to 10 days • may cause pneumonia or ear infection, seizures, brain damage (1 percent of kids), and can be deadly
Mumps	• a contagious viral infection, causes fever, headache, swollen cheeks, and swollen glands • serious symptoms include meningitis, brain damage, and deafness
Rubella (German measles)	• Generally a mild illness that lasts only about three days • symptoms are mild, often missed (mild fever, swollen lymph nodes) • if a pregnant woman gets it, it can cause miscarriage or birth defects in fetus (deafness, eye and heart problems, mental retardation)
Measles, Mumps, Rubella	See above
Varicella (Chicken Pox)	• mild in adults, but can be serious for babies • may cause rash, itching, fever, tiredness • can cause skin infection, scarring, and pneumonia • rarely fatal (about six deaths per 100,000 infants) • may get shingles years later as an adult
Polio	• contagious • symptoms often minor, but can cause permanent paralysis of arms and legs • can interfere with breathing or damage the brain • 2–5 percent death rate
Protects against the 13 most dangerous strains of pneumo-coccal disease (there are more than 90)	• causes meningitis, pneumonia, and blood infections • symptoms include fever, chills, shaking, weakness, fatigue, and nausea • 5–7 percent death rate

AGE AT TIME OF VISIT	VACCINATION(S) GIVEN
Birth–2 weeks (before hospital discharge)	Hepatitis B, 1st dose (can be delayed for two months if the mother tests negative for the antigen)
2 months	Hepatitis B (2nd dose), 1st dose of RV, IPV, PCV, DTaP, HiB
4 months	2nd dose of RV, IPV, PCV, DTaP, HiB, Hepatitis B (if not already given)
6 months	3rd dose of RV, IPV, PCV, DTaP, HiB, Hepatitis B, optional flu shot
12 months	PCV (4th dose), MMR, Varicella, Hepatitis A (1st of 2 doses), TB

- No pillows, blankets, stuffed animals, or anything else that could possibly be a smothering hazard. It you're worried that your baby will get cold, put her in a warm sleep suit. If you're using crib bumpers or you've hung toys across the crib for the baby to swat at, make sure they're attached very, very securely.

Is Your Baby Working the Graveyard Shift?

By the end of this month, your baby's sleep and nap schedule should start to get a little more regular and predictable. Unfortunately, there's a pretty good chance that her schedule is going to be exactly the opposite of what you'd hoped it would be: she'll sleep more during the day and be up at night. If you think about it, this makes perfect sense. While she was pregnant, your partner was probably awake during the day, and all of her movements rocked the baby to sleep. At night, though, when your partner slowed down, the baby woke. That's exactly why most pregnant women say that within a few minutes after lying down, the baby would start kicking up a storm.

Eventually, your baby will get her timetables straightened out and start living in your time zone. If you don't feel like waiting, there are a few things you can do that might help speed up the process:

- Help the baby get lots of naps during the day. At this age she shouldn't be up for any more than an hour or two at a stretch. Although you might think that depriving her of daytime naps would exhaust her and make her sleep through the night, it doesn't work that way. Overtired babies actually wake up more than well-rested ones.

- Set a regular bedtime—somewhere around 7 P.M. is good, just try to time it so it coincides with the baby's natural nap time.
- Establish a bedtime routine. Something like nursing, reading, massage, a song, and into bed. Do the same things in the same order every night. Babies love routines and once they figure out the pattern, they'll get drowsier and drowsier the closer they get to the "into bed" part.
- Keep the house darker than during the day. But do not buy blackout shades. You need a baby who can fall asleep with some lights on. Otherwise, you'll all be miserable.
- Keep the house quieter than during the day. Yes, take off your boots and don't slam doors, but don't insist that everyone tiptoe around in their socks. You need a baby who can fall asleep with some noise. Again, otherwise, you'll all be miserable.
- No playing around. When the baby wakes up at night, feed her, change her—without turning on the lights—and put her back to bed. No games, no songs, no stories. You want her to start making associations between dark and sleep.
- Adjust the time between feedings. Pediatricians Lewis Jassey and Jonathan Jassey turned this discovery into a very successful sleep-training method, which they write about in their book, *The Newborn Sleep Book*. To sum up the Jassey Way, you want to get your baby to the point where she's feeding only five times per day, the ideal schedule being 8 A.M., noon, 4 P.M., 8 P.M., and midnight. If your baby is feeding more often than that, gradually extend the time between feedings by 15 minutes per day until you're able to cut out the excess meals. That may result in some extra crying, but if you keep the baby entertained, she may not even notice. And don't worry: your baby will still get the same amount of food every day; it'll just be in slightly larger quantities each time. The Jasseys also suggest that if your baby is going longer than four hours between daytime feedings, you should gently wake her to gradually get her on the right schedule. This is one of the very, very few times that you'll ever want to wake a sleeping baby.

YOU AND YOUR PARTNER

No One Ever Told Me It Was Going to Be Like This . . .

During the first few days of parenthood, you and your partner may experience a kind of honeymoon period where you marvel at the little baby you made and feel closer to each other than ever before. Life seems as though it just couldn't get any better.

But as the days turn into weeks and months, the charm wears off and reality sets in. You're both getting used to a new schedule and new responsibilities. And instead of focusing on each other, as you used to do before you had kids, your world—and most of your conversations—now revolves around the baby. You barely get any uninterrupted adult time together, and neither of you is getting your needs met. Throw in a little sleep deprivation and a few disagreements on parenting style, and you've got a perfect recipe for conflict.

As hard as all this is on you, it's probably even tougher on your partner, especially if you're back at work. Staying at home with a newborn is a thankless task, and your partner really needs to know that you appreciate what she's doing. Here's how you can get the point across:

- Start off by coming right out and saying so. Tell her she's a great mom, that you love her, that you're proud of her, and that you're amazed at how big the baby's getting on a diet of nothing more than the milk she's producing.
- Buy her flowers. Or text her, bring little gifts for her and the baby, and call a few times a day to see how she's doing.
- Take her out on dates. That could mean anything from ordering in pizza to actually leaving the baby with a sitter for a few hours while the two of you go for a walk. In many cities, there are movie theaters that set aside a few shows a week for new parents. The places are packed with moms, dads, and howling babies. But they crank up the volume (and in some theaters, actually bring food right to your seat), and it's a great way to escape.
- Encourage her to socialize. As someone who's been a stay-at-home dad, I can tell you that spending all day alone with a baby can drive you nuts, no matter how much you love her. New moms' groups are everywhere, and they're a great way for women to hang out, talk about their problems, and compare labor and delivery stories ("I was in labor for 14 hours and the pain was so awful I had to have an epidural." "Oh, yeah? Well I was in labor for 27 hours and I had the baby naturally." It gets worse from there.). These groups also give new moms an opportunity to have a real conversation with someone who doesn't need a breast in her mouth to be happy.
- Help her get some time to herself. Take the baby, even if it's only for a half hour, and let your partner take a break. Don't be surprised if all she wants to do is shower and take a nap.

Library Books, Okay. But Can Fathers Be Renewed?

Well, according to sociologists, the answer is yes. A "renewed father" is a man who had children from a previous relationship, gets into a new one years later, and becomes a new dad all over again. (Actually, sociologists call these dads

Breastfeeding and Older Kids

Despite how wonderful breastfeeding is for the new baby, your older kids may see it as little more than an attempt to displace them from the center of the universe. And seeing Mom holding and cuddling and nursing often brings up all sorts of feelings—anger and jealousy being at the top of the list (see pages 71–72 for more on coping with this). Some new big brothers and sisters will want to be held the same way the baby is being held. Some will even want to nurse. If the older sibling is young enough, your partner may actually want to give in to the request. If so, it should only be on a very temporary basis. (Giving a tea-spoonful or two of breast milk might be a better solution—most older kids won't like the watery consistency or the sweet taste.) Older children need to know that your partner's milk is for the baby and that big kids get to have—and do—lots of other things that newborns don't.

"recycled fathers," but that's such a horrible phrase that I changed it to "renewed" instead.) There are a lot of differences between renewed fathers and their first-edition brothers. First, the renewed dads tend to be more financially secure and less concerned with career advancement. They also have more interest in—and more time to spend with—their young children. Overall, the older the father, the more relaxed, caring, flexible, and supportive he is, according to my colleague Ross Parke. Parke has found that men and women age differently. Women get more task and goal oriented as they get older, while men get more nurturing.

On the downside, renewed fathers don't usually spend as much time rolling around on the floor with their kids as younger dads who haven't turned themselves in for the deposit yet. But their intellectual level is still high enough to more than make up for the difference, says Parke.

In intact families, women whose husbands are involved fathers are generally happier and more fulfilled. But if you're a renewed dad, your new partner may have a very different experience. She may have been very supportive of your relationships with your older kids. In fact, seeing how you were with your kids might have been one of the things that attracted her to you in the first place. But now that she and you have a child, she may resent the time that you spend with your other kids, fearing that you won't be as attentive to your new family.

Being a renewed dad can bring up other potentially sticky problems as well. A lot of new dads I've interviewed complain that new moms act as though they know a lot more about parenting than dads do. They jump in to soothe the crying baby, change the diapers, and give very specific instructions for everything else, from bottle-feeding and getting the baby to sleep to dressing and bathing. The fact that mom and dad came into parenthood with equal amounts of experience doesn't seem to matter. What these dads resent most of all is not being allowed to learn the way their partners did, by making mistakes.

But if you're a renewed dad, there's an excellent chance that you really do know a lot more about parenting than your partner does. After all, you've been through it all before, and you probably still remember what babies need and how to give it to them. You're more relaxed around the baby and not nearly as worried as your partner about every little thing.

Here's where the problem comes in. Being a brand-new mom is sometimes tough because our society gives women the message that if they aren't fantastic, loving, caring, nurturing mothers right from the start, they've failed. So imagine how she feels when Mr. Experienced Dad comes along, reversing the traditional roles, and already knows better than she does how to soothe and feed and carry and dress the baby.

From my own experience, I can tell you that what you need to do if you're in this situation is back off. Bite your tongue and let your partner make her own mistakes. It's how you learned what you know, and it's what you'd want her to do for you if the situation were reversed.

Let the Games Begin

3 MONTHS

WHAT'S GOING ON WITH THE BABY

Physically

- As more and more of his reflexes disappear, your baby's body is changing. He can now keep his hands open (instead of in tiny fists), and when you put him down on his tummy, he extends his legs instead of automatically rolling up into a little ball like a pill bug. But he can't yet tell one side of his body from the other, and he moves both legs or both arms together. By the end of this month, though, he'll realize that the two sides can be controlled independently.
- He can roll from his back to his side, and when he's on his tummy, he can lift his head and lean on his elbows. Sometimes he may arch his back and raise his head and legs off the floor and rock like a little seesaw.
- When you pull him from a reclining position, he'll try to stand up, pressing his feet against whatever he was lying on. If you hold him upright, he may be able to "stand."
- His head is bobbing around a lot less, although it still needs support, and if you can get him into a sitting position, he can probably sit fairly well for a few seconds before keeling over.
- Your baby reaches for things with both hands and is getting much better at grasping things (although he still misses a lot). This is a development that some experts believe is a new reflex, designed to develop your baby's hand-eye coordination. "Everything that the child grasps is brought to the eyes and everything he sees evokes an effort to grasp," says child psychologist Peter Wolff.

Intellectually

- Moving objects are a source of nearly endless fascination. Your baby will follow with his eyes and head an object moving slowly from one side of his head to the other. If you drop something, he'll stare at your empty hand, wondering where the object went—but not knowing anything at all about gravity, he won't follow the object as it falls.
- One day your baby will catch sight of his own hand on its way into his mouth. Until this very moment, he had no idea that the thing he's been sucking on for the past few months actually belongs to him. Better still, he now realizes that objects (or at least his hand) can exist for at least two reasons at the same time: to look at and to suck on.
- As a result of this startling, and incredibly important, revelation, your baby will spend as much as fifteen minutes at a stretch intently staring at his squiggling fingers and then shoving them into his mouth. He'll repeat the process over and over and over.
- The baby is now able to tell the difference between various objects; he prefers circular shapes to stripes and complex patterns to simple ones.
- He is also able to make associations between certain objects and qualities linked to them. For example, he may associate your partner with food and you with play, and will react differently to each of you.

Verbally

- Although most of your baby's vocalizing is crying, he's making some delightful, soothing, ooohs, aaaahs, and other single-syllable sounds.
- He's now beginning to use his vocalizing for a purpose—if you listen carefully, you should be able to tell the difference between his "Feed me now!" "Put me down, I want to take a nap," and "Change my diaper" cries.
- He's now also attentively listening to all the sounds around him and distinguishes speech from any other sound.

Emotionally/Socially

- At this point your baby's schedule of eating, sleeping, diaper filling, and being alert is getting fairly regular.
- When it comes to people, he has strong likes and dislikes, crying or calming down depending on who holds him. He'll also smile or laugh at familiar people, and stare at strangers.
- He's very perceptive about your moods and will react to them. If you're tired and anxious, he'll be harder to calm and soothe, but if you're calm and happy, it'll be easier.

- He'll stare, absorbed in his surroundings, for several minutes at a time. He wants to interact with people and may stop what he's doing (which is usually sucking something) and listen if you talk to him.

WHAT YOU'RE GOING THROUGH

Worry, Worry, Worry

A lot of new dads find themselves obsessed with worry about the health of their infant. In most cases, these worries are completely irrational. However, every year about 150,000 babies in the United States alone are born with some kind of birth defect (there are more than 1,000 known defects; some are harmless, others are life threatening), and about 5,000 of those babies don't live past the first year. But the thing that worries dads most is SIDS (sudden infant death syndrome), which is the sudden, unexpected death of an otherwise healthy baby. Striking one out of every 2,000 babies (about 2,000 per year), SIDS is the most common cause of death of children between one week and one year old. Although government and private agencies spend millions of dollars each year in the fight against SIDS, scientists have been unable to figure out what, exactly, causes it. And there's no medical test to determine which babies are at the greatest risk. That said, here's what we do know:

- SIDS is most likely to strike infants one to four months old.
- Ninety percent of deaths happen by six months, but SIDS still strikes children up to one year old.
- It is more likely to occur to boys than girls, to preterm babies, to multiple-birth babies, to babies from low-income homes or homes in which a parent or caretaker smokes, and to babies born to women who smoked or drank alcohol while pregnant. African American and American Indian/Alaska Native babies are much more likely to die of SIDS than white babies. Bottle-fed babies are also somewhat more likely to die of SIDS, but not because of the bottle-feeding itself. Bottle-fed babies are more likely to have been born prematurely or have mothers who smoke, which are more accurate risk factors.
- SIDS is not caused by colds, other minor illnesses, vomiting, choking, or by any immunizations (in fact, immunizations may actually reduce SIDS risk). It's also not contagious and not the same as suffocation.
- There's even a theory that SIDS may be caused by babies' dreams. Australian researcher George Christos has suggested that babies may stop breathing when they dream they're back in the womb, getting all the oxygen they need from their blood, and don't have to breathe on their own.

Although two-thirds of all SIDS babies have no risk factors, there are still a few things you and your partner can do to minimize the risk:

- Make sure your baby sleeps on his back—even when napping. When my two older daughters were born in 1990 and '93, the then-current wisdom was that babies should sleep on their tummies because of the risk of choking if the baby spit up. But in 1994, the American Academy of Pediatrics debunked the spit-up theory and started recommending that parents put babies to sleep on their backs. The number of cases of SIDS immediately dropped by 50 percent. If your baby has been sleeping on his stomach, it's not too late to change (sure, he's been doing it all his life, but still, it's only been three months). About 30 percent of babies who die of SIDS were sleeping on their tummy. Side sleeping is *not* a safe alternative—it's too easy for the baby to fall over and land belly down.
- Don't smoke, and don't let anyone else smoke near the baby.
- Don't overdress the baby. (See the section on dressing, pages 120–22).
- Have your baby sleep on a firm mattress: no pillows, fluffy blankets, cushiony sofas, waterbeds, thick rugs, or beanbags. Make sure the mattress fits snugly into the crib so that the baby can't slip between the mattress and the crib frame. And take out of the crib all the plush animals, extra blankets, and other things that might accidentally cover the baby. Use a blanket sleeper or sleep sack (basically a sleeping bag with arms) instead of a blanket.
- Don't cosleep (share a bed) with your baby. The problem isn't the bed itself, but the increased risk of the baby being suffocated by the adults' pillows and blankets. We'll talk about how to cosleep safely on pages 145–48.
- Breastfeed.
- Once breastfeeding is well established, try to get your baby to take a pacifier every time you put him down to sleep. If the pacifier falls out, don't worry about putting it back. And if your baby really doesn't want the pacifier, don't force the issue.
- Don't panic. Although SIDS is a horrible, devastating experience for any parent, remember that 1,999 out of 2,000 babies don't die of it.

Coping with the Death of a Child

Losing a child is every parent's worst nightmare, something no one who hasn't experienced it can possibly imagine. It can bring up grief, anger, denial, and even feelings of guilt at not having been there enough or inadequacy at not having been able to prevent the death.

As in most areas of parenting, men and women cope with and adapt to the loss of a child differently. Women have two basic needs: one is to focus on the surviving children, if any; the other is support systems. Men do what men usually do: they try to ignore their feelings and dive headlong into their jobs. It's as if they try to make up for having failed (only in their eyes) to protect their child from harm by succeeding as a breadwinner. Unfortunately, that isn't an effective way of coping with grief—in either the short or the long term. "Grief will change you," writes Amy Hillyard Jensen, author of *Healing Grief.* "But you have some control over whether the changes are for better or worse."

The process of coping with a child's death starts in the hospital with the health-care professionals. Fathers (and mothers) too often feel "sad, hurt, or angry when providers [are] nonchalant and indifferent and when they [perceive] providers to be uncaring and disrespectful toward their baby," says Joanne Cacciatore, an expert in trauma and bereavement. They want to see their newborn treated "with respect and without fear," and they're deeply grateful when providers treat the mom and dad like parents and help them do things to create memories, such as doing hand- and footprints, cutting a lock of hair, and taking photos of them holding the baby. Now I Lay Me Down to Sleep (www.nowilaymedowntosleep. org/) can put you in touch with a volunteer photographer. The work they do is beautiful.

Besides being devastating to the parents, losing a child to SIDS or some unexpected medical condition can also destroy the marriage itself. But it doesn't have to. Researcher Kim Wendee Schildhaus identified a number of factors shared by couples who adapted to their loss and stayed together.

- They accept different ways of grieving and allow each other space in the relationship without making judgments. Men and women must accept each other's individual style (see "Grief: Not for Women Only" on pages 106–7).
- They believe in and utilize family support networks, asking for help when needed, accepting it when offered.
- They have other children to focus on.
- They concentrate on work, job, career.
- They agree that the death of the child was the most tragic loss imaginable, and that the thought of losing the spouse too is unbearable.
- They develop new friendship networks that include other parents who've lost children.
- They get therapy.
- They keep the memory of the deceased child alive.
- They communicate with each other.

Examining Your Relationship with Your Father

As you continue to grow and develop as a father, you may find yourself spending a lot of time thinking about your own father. Was he the kind of dad you'd like to

Grief: Not for Women Only

For better or worse, men and women are socially and culturally conditioned to behave in certain ways in certain situations. Men are brought up to be tough, strong, competent, knowledgeable, and in control of our emotions. Weakness—especially tears—is discouraged. Anger and frustration are okay, but sadness and pain are not. This kind of socialization is very effective in a lot of ways. But when we face some kind of emotional upheaval, such as the loss of a child, too many of us have no idea how to react. Instead of acknowledging our grief and dealing with it, we ignore it. Instead of getting help, we pull away from the people closest to us. The results can be physically, emotionally, and psychologically dangerous—to ourselves and to those who love us.

One of the biggest obstacles grieving dads face is that what they're going through emotionally tends to be ignored by everyone around them. Most of the questions they get are about how the mom is doing. Rarely does anyone ask how he's doing. The assumption is that he's there solely as a support person for his partner and that he'll put his own needs aside to be there for her. He's also expected to stoically handle all of the practical things (planning a funeral or memorial, notifying family and friends). He gets the message that expressing his own emotions somehow detracts from the more important job of being strong for his partner.

With little or no support, and believing that no one understands, men withdraw and suppress their emotions even more. Grieving becomes even harder than it already was, according to researchers Joann O'Leary and Clare Thorwick. Here are some effective ways to cope:

- Talk to your family—especially your partner. "Grief is the stone that bears one down, but two bear it lightly," said Wilhelm Hauff, a nineteenth-century

use as a role model, or was he exactly the kind of father you don't want to be? Was he supportive and nurturing, or was he absent or abusive? One way or another, the relationship you had with your father when you were young sets the tone for your relationship with your own children.

Depending on your perspective, this is either good news or bad news. If you're satisfied with your relationship with your dad, and you'd like to be the kind of father he was, you don't have much to worry about. "A cohesive boyhood home atmosphere in which the father and mother worked together," writes researcher John Snarey, "predicts that the boy who grew up in it will provide more care for his own children's social-emotional development in adolescence."

author. Let people know you're doing as much as you can and let them know how they can help you.

- Have quality "alone" time. You need time to sort through all the questions running through your brain. Think about keeping a journal or starting a blog, such as A Blog for Fathers When a Baby Dies, by Tim Nelson (fathersgrieviнginfantloss.blogspot.com/) or Grieving Dads: To the Brink and Back, by Kelly Farley (grievingdads.com/).
- Decrease your social activities. Many men seek out new hobbies or other activities to distract them, but these only take away from the grieving you really need to do.
- Cry. It's just about the hardest thing to do for most of us, but don't try to keep down that lump in your throat or swallow your tears. Crying releases some tension and can actually make you feel better.
- Get angry. Anger is a natural part of the grieving process, and holding it back or ignoring it won't make it disappear. There's nothing wrong with being angry; it's what you do with the feeling that counts, so find a way to express your anger that won't hurt others. Exercise is perhaps the best outlet for it.
- Find a support system. For many men, asking for help is even tougher than crying. But research has shown that what men find most helpful is a caring listener, someone patient, someone, perhaps, who is going through (or has recently gone through) the same experience. Local hospitals are an excellent source of referrals to support groups. So is the SIDS Alliance, which has counselors available twenty-four hours a day. You can reach them at (800) 221-SIDS (7437). The SIDS Alliance (www.firstcandle.org) and GriefNet (griefnet.org/) have great resources.

But if your relationship with your father wasn't everything it should have been, you may be afraid that you're somehow destined to repeat your father's mistakes. And you may have started to act accordingly. If your father was abusive, for example, you may worry that you will be too, and you may emotionally and/or physically pull back from your baby as a way of protecting him.

If you find yourself doing—or not doing—things with your baby out of fear, you can relax. At least a little. Dr. Snarey found that new fathers seem to take the good from their fathers and throw away the bad. In fact, many new fathers are able to turn to their advantage the example of a less-than-perfect relationship with their fathers. Here are some common scenarios:

- Men whose fathers were distant or non-nurturing often provide high levels of care for their children's social-emotional and intellectual-academic development in adolescence.
- Men whose fathers provided inconsistent or inadequate supervision tend to provide high levels of care for their children's physical-athletic development in childhood.
- Men whose fathers used or threatened to use physical punishment that instilled fear in them as boys generally provide high levels of care for their own children's physical-athletic development in childhood.

Taking On More Responsibility

Whenever I ask men to tell me how their lives have changed since they became fathers, some variation on the phrase "I'm more responsible" almost always comes up in the first sentence or two. Of course, that phrase doesn't mean the same thing to everyone. Here are a few of the most common definitions I've heard:

- Being more involved at home. That could mean doing more housework, sharing the child care with your partner, planning and cooking more meals, doing more laundry, and so on.
- Getting real. One new father, a man who had been out of work for four years, said that becoming more responsible meant looking more realistically at his employment situation. "I just have to lower my sights," he said. "I can't hold out for the exact position I want."

Issues for Adoptive Fathers and DI Dads

Fathers and their non-biologically related children—whether they're adopted or conceived using donor sperm—develop in very much the same ways as biologically related fathers and kids. Many experience feelings of inadequacy at not having been able to produce their own children, although by the time the child enters preschool, most have gotten past that and shelved their fantasies of having a biological child. Instead, they're "coming to see themselves as they really are, the eminently entitled and very 'real' psychological parents," writes expert Gordon Finley.

This might seem pretty simple, but it's usually not. For many parents, adoption or conceiving using donor sperm is a second choice, a decision reached only after years of unsuccessfully trying to conceive on their own, and after years of disappointments and intrusive, expensive medical procedures. Infertility can make you question your self-image, undermine your sense of masculinity (How can I be a man if I can't even get my partner pregnant?), force you to confront your shattered dreams, and take a terrible toll on your relationships—with your wife and, perhaps more important, with your child. If you're having trouble accepting that you won't be having biologically related children, I urge you to talk to some other people about what you're feeling. Your partner certainly has a right to know—and she might be feeling a lot of similar things. In addition, the agency you're working with will probably have a list of support resources for adoptive fathers. Give them a try.

- Looking at things from other people's perspectives. A lot of guys admit that they were somewhat selfish and self-centered before having kids, according to Rob Palkovitz, a researcher who did an exhaustive study of how fatherhood changes new dads. This isn't necessarily a negative thing; it's simply an acknowledgment that having people depend on you and putting their needs before your own isn't something that comes naturally to most people before they become parents. What's especially interesting is that, according to Palkovitz, getting married didn't trigger this same realization.
- Honing your skills as a role model. Almost everything you do will influence your child. He'll be imitating your mannerisms in a few months, and the moment he learns to talk, he'll start repeating back all those swear words you thought he wouldn't understand. That's bad enough, but how are you going to feel when he pretends to smoke a cigarette or drink a beer or copy any of your bad habits?

"A DWI would put a hardship on the family," said one new father who quit having a few drinks before driving home from the golf course. And of course you've never fudged on your taxes, but some guys who did before they had kids don't anymore. Rob Palkovitz found that a lot of dads gave up destructive or risky behavior, criminal activity, and even drug abuse. I got better at obeying the speed limits (or trying to) and stopped accelerating at yellow traffic lights. For you, it might mean anything from giving up bungee jumping or alligator wrestling to reducing the aggressiveness of your investments.

• Living the healthy life. Many also change their attitude about their health. Most men don't go to the doctor (for themselves, anyway) unless a woman in their life forces them. But having kids often motivates us more than we or anyone else can. All of a sudden, being around for our kids seems a lot more important. We may start exercising more regularly, eating better, and even cutting down on the amount of junk food that makes its way home from the grocery store.

• Thinking about religion or spirituality. About 80 percent of the men in Rob Palkovitz's study and a similar majority of the dads I interviewed said that they'd made some kind of shift in their basic values or life priorities. Also, since teaching right from wrong is such a stereotypical dad thing, it's not surprising that a lot of new dads spend some time thinking about how they're going to handle those tough questions when they start cropping up. In some cases this means increasing church or synagogue attendance and/or planning to send their kids to religious school. About half of Palkovitz's sample didn't make any changes at all. Religion was already central in their lives, or they'd had such bad experiences as kids or young adults that they were turned off for good. Younger fathers in particular were less likely to take any big steps either way. Their religious and spiritual views tend not to be as fully developed, and they're not as sure as more mature dads what they're embracing or rebelling against.

YOU AND YOUR PARTNER

Heigh-Ho, Heigh-Ho, It's Back to Work She Goes

With more and more women in the workforce, there's a lot of pressure on new moms to go back to work. That explains why a third of them are on the job again only six weeks after giving birth, and two-thirds are working after twelve weeks.

While some of these women are glad to be back at work, a large percentage are anything but glad. In fact, a lot of them are just plain miserable, worried that they've failed as mothers and wishing they'd win the lottery so they could quit their jobs. This can be a very tough time for your partner, and she's going to need your help and support to get through it. Here's what you can do:

- Be flexible. When it comes to coming up with an acceptable work/family balance, your partner may not be operating completely rationally. Let me give you an example of what I mean. Before my youngest was born, my wife and I discussed having her stay home full-time for five months, work part-time for four months, and then transition back to full-time. All that changed when the baby was born. Suddenly she didn't want to go back to work at all. But in the interest of being able to make our mortgage payment (California real estate is outrageously expensive), she decided to do a full year part-time before going to full-time. Everything changed again after her first week back at the office, when she decided that she wanted to stay part-time until the baby entered preschool.

Obviously, you and your partner have to keep talking about this stuff. And you have to find a reasonable (and fiscally responsible) way of making sure that everyone's needs are met, or that they're at least taken into consideration. That means listening to each other carefully and respectfully and acknowledging the pressures that each of you faces.

- Get your child-care situation in order. Fear that the baby won't be adequately cared for is what many new mothers find most unsettling about going back to work.
- Take the pressure off her. In most families, regardless of how enlightened and egalitarian they want to be, working mothers still do most of the work at home. Because so much of women's identity is tied up in motherhood, your partner may try to do more than she can really handle—just to show herself and anyone else she thinks might be paying attention. Don't let her. Instead, anticipate what has to be done and take care of it in advance. Simple things like making sure the table is set and dinner is ready when she comes home are great and will do wonders for her mood. If you get home later than she does, make a habit of doing something nice for her on a regular basis. Massages, a few hours alone with you, and/or maybe just catching up on all those shows you haven't had the time to watch will really help. And make sure that you remind her frequently what a great mom she is even though she has to be away.
- Let her spend more time with the baby. If you and your partner are both working, you're both going to miss your baby, and you're both going to want to spend time with him from the moment you walk in the door. Be a nice guy and let your partner have first dibs. This is especially important if she's still nursing; her breasts may be ready to explode by the time she gets home, and she may need to have the baby Hoover her out.

Breastfeeding and the Working Mom

As we've talked about earlier, in a perfect world your partner would breastfeed exclusively for six months and then, over the next six months, gradually phase out the breast milk while phasing in "real" food. Unfortunately, most of us don't live in a perfect world. The reality is that on average, just 41 percent of new moms breastfeed exclusively for three months and only 19 percent make it as long as six months, according to the CDC's 2014 *Breastfeeding Report Card*. But since *some* breastfeeding is better than none, there is some good news: 79 percent of newborns in the U.S. start out breastfeeding. At six months, 49 percent are getting some breast milk, and at twelve months, 27 percent are.

Overall, researcher Erika Odom and her colleagues found that 60 percent of new moms stopped breastfeeding their baby sooner than they would have liked. One of the main reasons for this is that when women go back to work (which most do within twelve weeks after giving birth), breastfeeding becomes a real challenge. Brian Roe and his colleagues at Ohio State found that over half of moms who returned to full-time work before twelve weeks stopped nursing. But of those who stayed out of the office longer than twelve weeks, only 35 percent had stopped breastfeeding.

It doesn't have to be that way. If you really wanted to, you or your child-care provider could bring the baby to your partner's office for feedings. But that's a fairly rare—and quite impractical—scenario. The truth is that when we talk about all the great benefits of breastfeeding and how long it should go on, the breasts themselves are really just the delivery device. What's really important is the milk.

So a more viable option than spending half your life ferrying your baby to the mommy milk bar is for your partner to express milk from her breasts, which someone else can feed the baby while your partner is at work. There are two basic ways to do this: manually or with a pump. The manual option is kind of like milking a cow by hand and is one of the many reasons I'm glad I'm a man. Pumps tend to be either battery operated or electric and can handle one or both breasts. As you might guess, they can be expensive, but they're a lot faster and a lot more convenient. Plus, if your partner is planning to pump for more than a few weeks, buying a pump will probably be cheaper than renting one.

Using an electric pump can be uncomfortable and will take a lot of getting used to. (If you're wondering why, go ahead and give it a try. I was curious myself, and one morning when I was alone in the house, I lifted up my shirt, turned on the pump, and positioned the suction devices on my chest. The shock of having both nipples nearly sucked off my chest was matched only by my embarrassment when I looked up and saw my wife standing there. For weeks afterward she'd break in to giggles every time she looked at me.)

If your partner isn't 100 percent sure about pumping, I suggest that you rent a pump for a month or so before you buy. Your pediatrician should be able to give you some suggestions on the best places to rent (although Babies Я Us and many other retailers will have rentals as well). One important note on pumps: if a friend or relative offers to let you have or borrow her breast pump, respectfully decline. Unlike with rental pumps, there's no way to properly clean the machine's internal mechanism, and there's a slight risk of infection.

A few more pumping/work-related things to keep in mind:

- Introduce your baby to a bottle now if you haven't done so already. If you wait too long, you may miss your window of opportunity. Some babies may get used to the feel of a silicone nipple pretty quickly, but others, like my middle daughter, may absolutely refuse. If your baby balks at taking a bottle of perfectly good breast milk, start the feeding when he's just a little hungry instead of ravenous. A very hungry baby won't be in the mood to participate in your little experiment and will demand the real thing.

- Get some practice. If at all possible, *you* should do the bottle-feeding. Your baby associates your partner's smell with feeding, and if she tries to give him a bottle, he may refuse, preferring what she's got in her blouse to what she's got in her hand.

- Help her arrange things at work. As of 2010, there's a federal law called "Break Time for Nursing Mothers" that requires certain employers to accommodate certain (usually hourly) employees by providing a private place to pump and "reasonable time" to do it. And even if your partner isn't covered by the federal law, she may be covered by a similar state law. The easiest way to see whether your partner is covered by any of these laws is to check with the United States Breastfeeding Committee (www.usbreastfeeding.org/).

- Learn how to store and retrieve expressed milk. Here are the basic requirements:
  - Breast milk can be stored at room temperature for four to five hours.
  - It can be refrigerated for no longer than a week.
  - If your partner is freezing the milk, do so within forty-eight hours of pumping. Also, make sure she gets bags that are specially designed to store milk—regular or freezer Ziplocs just won't do. The ones at Walgreen's or Target are usually about half the price of the ones that the pump manufacturers sell. Make sure you have a permanent marker so you can record the date the milk was pumped on the bag itself.
  - Milk can stay in the freezer section of your fridge for up to two weeks. If the freezer has a separate door, you're good for three–six months. If you have a stand-alone freezer, you may be able to go as long as six–twelve months. Put the bag of milk toward the back of the freezer, where it will be coldest. The reason for the storage-time differences is that freezers inside refrigerators

get opened a lot, which can slightly warm the milk. Separate-door freezers are generally colder and get opened less, and stand-alone freezers don't get opened all that often.

- To thaw, either put the bag of frozen milk in the refrigerator overnight or, if you need it sooner, put it into a container of warm water. Never warm milk in the microwave—besides possibly interfering with the health benefits of the milk, microwaves often heat unevenly, meaning that while some of the milk feels fine to your touch, other parts could be hot enough to hurt your baby.
- After thawing, milk can stay in the refrigerator for up to twenty-four hours, but don't refreeze it.
- Before giving milk to the baby, swirl it around to mix the cream back in with the rest of the milk.

A Work/Family Solution You Might Not Have Thought Of

On pages 178–88 we'll discuss a number of the child-care options you and your partner will have to sift through sometime soon. But what if you'd both really prefer to have your child raised in the arms of a loving relative? Most families that make the decision to have a parent stay home automatically assume that it has to be Mom. Sometimes, though, that just doesn't work. Your partner might have a more stable career than you, make more money, or simply have no interest in staying home. Well, all is not lost. If you and your partner truly want to have your children raised by a parent, it may be up to you.

Now before you throw this book down and run screaming out of the room, take a minute to consider the idea. Actually, take longer than that—take at least as much time considering this option as you would any other. You may discover that it's not as crazy as it sounds. Brad Harrington and his colleagues at Boston College's Center for Work & Family found that more than half of new fathers would "seriously consider" being a full-time, at-home dad. Let's start with some of the benefits:

- You won't have to agonize over picking the right babysitter or nanny or day-care center.
- You'll get a wonderful opportunity to get to know your child.
- You'll be giving your child what you and your partner agree is the best possible upbringing.
- You'll be able to help your partner's career and give her some peace of mind at the same time.

Deciding to be a stay-at-home dad is a decision that will affect everyone in your family. If you're even remotely considering it, start by asking yourself the following very important questions:

- Can we afford it? Going from two incomes to one will probably require some major changes in your lifestyle. But it can be done. If you're really committed to the idea, there are all sorts of ways to cut your expenses, including buying food in bulk, eating out less often, raising your insurance deductibles, taking vacations closer to home, making presents instead of buying them, getting rid of the housekeeper, and moving to a smaller house or a place where the cost of living is lower.

- Can I take the career hit? This is a big one, since earning power and masculinity are inextricably linked in so many people's minds. ("If I'm not a good provider, I'm not a good man/father," the thinking goes.) If you can get over this one, you may still be able to keep a finger or a foot in the work world by teaching, consulting, writing, or starting a home-based business. But be realistic. If you decide to reenter the workforce later, that employment gap on your résumé could cause you some problems with potential employers, many of whom may be a lot more traditional than you.

- Can I handle it? Staying home with a child is a lot more work than you think. It can also be a bit lonely. According to researcher Robert Frank, about two-thirds of stay-at-home dads feel isolated, but only one-third of stay-at-home-moms do. You'll probably find that women—moms, nannies, babysitters—tend not to welcome men into their groups at parks or playgrounds or malls and the other places people take their kids during the day. And you'll have to get used to the funny looks and stupid comments you'll hear from people who see you with your kids in the middle of the day—and who tend to see anything related to child care as "women's work." Several stay-at-home dads I've interviewed have told me that it's actually easier to tell people that they're unemployed than to deal with the raised eyebrows and "Where's the mother?" questions.

- Can my partner handle it? If you become an at-home dad, your partner's career may thrive, and she may feel less anxious or guilty about work-family conflict, according to University of Maryland researcher Marianne Dunn. At the same time, she may feel (and actually be) judged by others who say she isn't a "good mother." She may miss your baby while she's at work, feel guilty that she's not spending enough time with him, and be a little jealous of your relationship with each other. She may also be put in the position of having to defend you from the people who say (to her, not to you), that you're lazy or not very masculine. And there's a very good chance that she won't be thrilled with how clean the house is when she gets home (men and women tend to have different standards in this area).

- Can our relationship handle it? Bucking gender stereotypes is generally easier for women than it is for men. But having the freedom to choose between pants or dresses is hardly the same as going back to work while you take care of the baby. Unless the two of you can speak openly and honestly with each other about what you're feeling, your relationship could be severely hurt.

- Where can I get help? In reality, you won't be quite as alone as it might seem. At least 2 million stay-at-home dads are doing it every day, and the number is rising all the time. At-home dads with strong social support networks (including their partner, family, and friends) tend to be happier and less likely to feel isolated than those who don't get support. If you're looking to connect with other at-home dads, the National At-Home Dad Network (athomedad.org) has a growing list of dads' groups all over the country and all sorts of other resources. Who knows? There may be one right around the corner. You'll find more resources for at-home dads in the Resources appendix of this book.

YOU AND YOUR BABY

Let the Games Begin

Playing with your baby is one of the most important things you can do for him. Researchers have found that early parent-child play can speed up the attachment process. In addition, kids who play a lot—especially with their dads—as babies are more attentive and interactive as they grow up, and end up with higher self-esteem than kids who don't get as much physical activity. But before you mount that basketball hoop, remember that at this stage of life, babies have literally just discovered themselves, and watching and experimenting with their own little bodies is quite enough to keep them occupied for a big chunk of their waking time.

You are your baby's first—and most-important—toy, and the first "game" you play with him starts with nothing more than his giving you a smile. If you respond nicely, he'll smile at you again. After repeating this a few times (it may even take a few days), your baby will learn that what he does can lead to a response from you. That seemingly simple realization is the basis for any kind of meaningful interaction your baby will have with other people.

Nuts and Bolts

Now that your baby has developed some control over his hands, this is the perfect time to introduce some rattles, or keys, or other similar toys. Early this month he'll probably tentatively reach for interesting-looking objects with both hands at the same time. By the end of the month, he may start using them independently. Regardless of how many hands he uses, just make sure that whatever you give him is soft enough that he can smack himself in the head without doing any damage—he's going to be doing that a lot. If he's not quite ready to actually grab anything, you can still have fun by simply holding a toy nearby and encouraging him to reach for it. Just don't take it personally if your gesture is completely ignored.

Make sure you set aside at least a few minutes a day to play with your baby. Don't worry about getting bored or needing any fancy equipment—you can have plenty of fun just walking around and keeping up a running commentary on everything you see. Sing some songs or do some baby weight-lifting: Lie on your back, holding the baby chest-to-chest. Then lift him straight up, saying "Up" and lower him while saying "Down." Be sure to watch out for the drool or worse, if he just ate.

A fun experiment: Tie one end of a ribbon loosely to the baby's ankle and the other to a mobile. Make the ribbon taut enough so that if the baby moves his leg, he'll also move the mobile. After a few minutes, most (but definitely not all) babies at this age will begin to see a cause-and-effect relationship developing and will begin to move the tied leg more than the other. Move the ribbon to the other leg, then to the arms, and see how well the baby adapts. A note of caution: never leave the room—even for a second—with the baby tied to the mobile.

Music

While it's way too early to start private cello lessons, it's not at all too early to start making music a part of your baby's life. Babies come prewired for music. Studies have shown that babies who listened to music while still in the womb (which they can do anytime after about twenty-four weeks) often stop crying and focus when they hear a familiar song. If you pay attention, you'll notice that he already has a rudimentary sense of rhythm. Lay him on the floor and turn on the stereo (not too loud, please). Notice how he moves his arms and legs rhythmically—not in time to the music, but definitely in response to it. He may also make some sounds, as if trying to sing along. Here are a few things to keep in mind as you're thinking about introducing your baby to music:

- Kids are surrounded by language from their first days (in fact, there's plenty of research showing that kids respond to linguistic rhythms and patterns they heard even before they were born). And since kids learn music in much the same way as they do language—by listening and absorbing—play as much music as you can. But don't go crazy. Your baby—just like you—needs some regular downtime.
- Play a wide variety of music. Major or minor keys, fast or slow tempos, and the types of instruments are not important at this stage. For some reason, babies seem to prefer simple melodies to more complex ones, so save the fusion jazz for later. Stay away from anything that's very loud or might startle the baby.

And pay attention to your baby's reactions. Do his movements change as you change the style of music?

- Select music you like too (after all, you'll be listening as well). There's plenty of music out there written specifically for babies, but that can get a little boring for you. So you may want to check out lullaby versions of your favorite songs (yep, they exist) and see whether your favorite bands have recorded some music for kids. Some babies this age may try to imitate tones they hear. This is, however, extremely rare.

- It doesn't have to be expensive. Kindermusik (www.kindermusik.com) and Music Together (www.musictogether.com) offer music-related programs all over the country for kids of all ages. Check the websites to see whether there's a franchise near you. They also sell some excellent CDs of music that babies really like. That said, you can accomplish the same thing at home with the music in your own collection. Just follow the guidelines above. Have fun. Although music has been shown to stimulate brain development in infants, don't try to raise the next Beethoven. Just enjoy yourself and make sure your baby's doing the same.

Reading: From Birth through Eight Months

Feeling a little silly about the prospect of sitting down and reading to your baby? Consider this: "When children have been read to, they enter school with larger vocabularies, longer attention spans, greater understanding of books and print, and consequently have the fewest difficulties in learning to read," writes Jim Trelease, author of *The Read Aloud Handbook*.

Still not convinced? How about this: 60 percent of prison inmates are illiterate, 85 percent of juvenile offenders have reading problems, and 44 percent of adult Americans don't read a single book in the course of a year. Clearly, reading is an important habit to develop, and it's never too early to start.

What to Read When

For the first few months of your baby's life, your reading probably won't seem to be having much effect on him. Sometimes he'll stare at the book, sometimes not. Once in a while a flailing arm might hit the book, but it's completely accidental. It doesn't really matter what you read at this stage, just as long as you do it. It's a great opportunity for you and the baby to snuggle together and for him to get to know the rhythm and feel of our language.

At about three months, your baby may start holding your finger while you read to him. While it doesn't seem like much, this tiny gesture is a clear indication that he's starting to become aware of the book as a separate object and that he likes what you're doing. Look for books with simple, uncluttered drawings as well as poetry and nursery rhymes.

At four months, your baby will sit still and listen attentively while you're reading. He may even reach out to scratch the pages of the book. Don't get too excited, though—he's a while away from being able to identify anything on the page. Nursery rhymes, finger plays (this little piggy went to market and so on), and books with pictures of other babies are big hits at this stage.

At about five months most babies are just starting to respond to your pointing. There are two ways to take advantage of this new development: first, watch your baby's eyes, then point to and talk about what he is already focusing on. Second, point to something and encourage the baby to look where you're pointing. It's now time for the seven Rs: rhythm, rhyme, repetition, repetition, repetition, repetition, and repetition.

At six months babies will respond to what you're reading by bouncing up and down or chuckling before you get to a familiar part of the story. If you've been reading regularly to your baby for a few months, you may notice that he has developed clear preferences for books and will let you know which one he wants you to read. A word of warning: at this age babies have an irresistible need to put everything into their mouths, and books are no exception. But first they'll want to scratch, tear, pat, rub, hit, and get into a serious tug-of-war with you over the book. To avoid these problems before they start, give your baby something else to put in his mouth while you're reading to him, and try to distract him with noise books (the cow says "moo," the airplane goes "whooosh"). Just in case your baby manages to outfox you, keep those family heirlooms far away, and stock your shelves with board and cloth books.

At about seven months your baby's grabbing and tearing are now slightly more purposeful, and you may notice an occasional attempt to turn pages. It will be another month or two, though, until he's actually able to do so. Plot is pretty well wasted on babies this age. But he'll like books with brightly colored pictures of familiar objects, as well as those that encourage you to make different sounds or funny voices.

READY, SET . . .

Here are a few things to keep in mind when you're getting ready to read:
- Select a regular place for reading.
- Set aside a regular time, when you will be able to devote your full attention to the baby and the book. Just before or just after a nap is usually good.
- Try to read for at least fifteen minutes each day. Be prepared: you may have to do this in several installments. Kids' attention spans average only about three

minutes at this age, but vary widely (my oldest and youngest daughters would sit in my lap for an hour at a time, but the middle one couldn't sit still for more than three seconds).

- Use lots of vocal and facial expression.
- You don't have to finish the story. Reading to your child is for him, not for you. So if he arches his back, squirms, lurches forward, or does anything to let you know he's not happy, stop immediately—you're wasting your time. If you don't, the baby will begin to associate reading with discomfort.
- Make it interactive. Take plenty of short breaks from the text to point out interesting things going on in the illustrations and to ask questions ("Where's the piggy hiding?" "What does the big bad wolf say?").
- Don't read things that are developmentally inappropriate. It's not so much the actual content as the tone of your voice. So unless you plan to act out all the parts in *War and Peace*, stick with kids' books.

...GO!

You'll find a list of appropriate titles in the Books for Babies appendix in this book. It is by no means definitive. With about five thousand new children's titles published each year, the pool of good books never stops growing. I strongly urge you to get to know your local children's librarians, who are always up to date, or to visit Children's Literature (www.childrenslit.com) or The Children's Book Review (www.thechildrensbookreview.com/) for suggestions and reviews.

Hittin' the Road

One of the great myths about babies is that you have to bundle them up like Nanook of the North every time you take them out of the house. Here's the truth: overdressed babies are at risk of getting heat stroke, which can result in abnormally high fevers and even convulsions. This risk is especially high if you're taking the baby out in a sling, backpack, or front pack, where he'll be even hotter.

Of course, underdressing can be a problem, too. The answer is to dress your baby just as you would dress yourself (except that you're probably not going to wear any of those cute little booties), plus one layer. When the weather's cold, it helps to dress the baby in various layers rather than one or two very heavy items. That way you can remove a layer or two if the baby gets overheated.

Most important, because you're the grown-up, you're going to have to pay close attention. If you underdress your baby, he'll probably let you know about it; babies usually complain loudly when they're too cold. Babies who are too hot, though, tend not to complain, preferring instead to lie there listlessly.

Sunscreen

Until he's six months old, don't use any sunscreen on your baby at all (that's why it's so important to keep infants out of the sun). They are usually filled with chemicals and frequently cause allergic reactions. However, if you're in a situation where you simply can't be in the shade or you can't completely cover your baby's skin, the American Academy of Pediatrics says that it's okay to apply small amounts of sunscreen (at least SPF 15) to the baby's face and the backs of the hands.

After six months, the risk of an allergic reaction from sunscreen is much lower, but stick with one that's got as few chemicals as possible. The Environmental Working Group has a comprehensive list of baby sunscreens at www.ewg.org/skindeep/browse/baby_sunscreen/. Ideally, use a product that contains zinc oxide or titanium dioxide. These sit on top of the skin and create a protective barrier. If you use a sunscreen, make sure it's at least SPF 15 and "broad spectrum," meaning it blocks both types of UV rays (UVA and UVB). Lube your baby up with sunscreen about half an hour before going outside, and add some more every few hours. Pay special attention to feet, hands, legs, and arms—even if they're completely covered. Socks can roll down, and sleeves and pant legs can hike up all by themselves, exposing baby's skin to the elements.

SUMMER

For the first six months, your baby should be kept far away from direct sunlight. Because babies' skin is at its thinnest and lightest during this period, even a little sun can do a lot of damage. This applies to babies of all races and skin tones.

When you go out, dress your baby in lightweight and brightly colored long-sleeved shirts and long pants (it's kind of counterintuitive, but even though whites and light pastel colors do a better job of reflecting heat, they actually let more light—and UV rays—through). From the time they were a few months old, none of my kids would let me put any kind of hat anywhere near them. But if you can get your baby to wear a cute hat with a wide brim, so much the better. And if you're brave enough to try putting sunglasses on him, get the kind that shield his eyes from UVA and UVB rays. For extra protection, consider getting a parasol or sunshade for your stroller and try to stay indoors during the hottest parts of the day (about 10:00 A.M. to 4:00 P.M.).

When you're putting together your supplies for an outdoor summertime excursion, throw in a sweater, a pair of socks, and some warm pants for the baby. Sounds a little strange, but if you step into any kind of air-conditioned building (such as a supermarket or your office building) after having been outside for a while, you're going to feel awfully cold—and so will the baby.

Oh, and by the way, if you were thinking that your baby can't get a sunburn on a cloudy or overcast day, think again. Studies have shown that 60 percent of the sun's UV rays make their way down here, regardless of clouds, fog, or anything else.

In the car, your baby will be in the back seat. Make sure that he's as far away from windows as you can get him. Consider applying a UV-blocking window tint or film to your windows. The sun's UV rays go through glass with no problem, but UV tinting or film blocks up to 99 percent.

Skin Problems

SUN

Despite all your precautions and good intentions, your baby may still end up with a minor sun-related condition:

- Sunburn. If it's minor, cover the affected area with a cool compress. If there are blisters, if the baby is running a fever, or if he's listless or nonresponsive, call your doctor immediately.
- Prickly heat (heat rash). A direct result of overdressing, prickly heat looks like tiny red blisters on a flushed area. It occurs anywhere sweat can build up: where the neck meets the shoulders, under the arms, inside elbows and knees, inside diapers. If your baby has heat rash, try to keep him as cool as possible. Lotions and creams probably won't help much, but putting a cool, damp washcloth or some cornstarch on the affected area may make your baby more comfortable.

INSECTS

The sun isn't the only potentially dangerous element that comes out in the summer. Here are some tips for preventing your baby from being consumed by bugs:

- Don't use any kind of scented powders, lotions, or even diaper wipes. Bugs love them.
- Avoid insect repellent if at all possible. A long-sleeved shirt and long pants can provide just about the same level of protection and are a lot easier on infant skin.

- Stay away from clothes with floral patterns: most bugs aren't smart enough to tell the difference between a real flower and your equally delicious flower-covered child. Light colors are far less attractive to bugs than dark colors.
- When outside, consider getting some insect netting to drape over the stroller. Inside, position a fan so it blows across the baby's crib. Mosquitoes and other insects prefer stagnant air to a breeze.

DIAPER RASH

You can prevent sunburn or insect bites, but no matter what you do or how hard you try, one of these days your baby is going to get diaper rash. In the pre-disposable-diaper era, when a baby urinated, the moisture stayed right there against his skin. Partly because of the acid in urine and partly because it's uncomfortable to stew in something wet, the baby would soon start complaining. And if he made what my oldest daughter used to call "a big dirty" (a bowel movement), he'd be even more uncomfortable and would "speak up" even sooner. This raised the chances that he'd get changed fairly quickly.

With disposables, however, almost all of the moisture is whisked away from the baby (just like they say in the commercials) and converted into some kind of non-liquid gel. Still, the digestive acids in the baby's waste, especially in his stool, continue to irritate his skin until—voilà!—diaper rash. But because the baby isn't uncomfortable enough to complain, his diapers somehow don't manage to get changed quite as often. This also explains why babies who grow up with cloth diapers are generally toilet trained about a year sooner than those in disposables.

A Little Diaper-Changing Fireworks

In 1999, English housewife Jill Furlough got a fright late one night when she saw green sparks shooting out of her sleeping baby's disposable diaper. She called the diaper manufacturers, who assured her that the sparks were the result of *triboluminescence*, an extremely rare—and perfectly harmless—buildup of energy probably caused by the friction of the baby's bottom rubbing against the inside of the diaper. (It's actually exactly the same chemical reaction that produces the sparks you see when you bite down on a Wintergreen LifeSaver in a dark room. Unlike static electricity, it doesn't generate any heat.) Since then, there have been numerous other sparking-diaper scares, but to date, there's no record of any injury to anyone.

Just about the only thing you can do to keep diaper rash to a minimum is to check your baby's diapers every few hours and change them even if they're only slightly wet. Also:

- When diaper rash develops, let your baby frolic for a few minutes sans diaper (on a towel, perhaps, just in case). The extra air circulation will help.
- Apply some diaper cream with each change, but be especially gentle: irritated skin doesn't like to be rubbed. A piece of advice: after you've applied diaper rash cream to the baby's bottom, wipe any residual cream on your fingers onto the inside of the diaper before fastening it.

Born to Be . . .

WHAT'S GOING ON WITH THE BABY

Physically

- She can now track moving objects, coordinating the activities of her eyes and head as well as an adult can.
- She's making better use of her hands, using them to finger each other, to grasp small objects (most of which immediately end up in her mouth), and generally to bring the world to her, since she still can't go to it. But she hasn't yet figured out what to do with her opposable thumb. So, for the next few months at least, she won't be using it much, making her grasping a little clumsy. She can retain objects in her hands voluntarily, although letting go is still a problem.
- By the end of this month, though, she'll have figured out that the two sides of her body are separate—a discovery she's glad to demonstrate by passing things back and forth between her hands. But she hasn't completely discovered how to separate them. When picking something up with one hand, she'll make the same grasping motion with the other.
- While on her tummy, she can lift her head 90 degrees and prop herself up on her forearms. And if you've had her spend a lot of time on her tummy, she may even be able to roll from front to back, although she won't be able to do it regularly for another month or so. She can, however, roll onto her side and may occasionally surprise herself by ending up on her back.
- She still tries to stand when you pull her up (don't let her do this for more than a second or two; her hips aren't strong enough to support the weight). And when she's sitting, her back is straight and her head hardly wobbles.

Intellectually

- Your baby now knows her hands and feet are extensions of herself. She'll spend a great deal of time every day staring at her hands and using them to explore her face, her mouth, and whatever other parts of her body she can reach.
- She's beginning the long process of understanding cause-and-effect relationships. If she accidentally kicks a toy and it squeaks, she may try to kick it again, hoping to get the same reaction. Similarly, she knows what a breast (or bottle) is for and may get excited when she sees one.
- She's begun to draw small distinctions between similar objects and can clearly tell the difference between a real face and a picture of one (although she may have trouble differentiating between a human and a monkey face). She is also starting to differentiate herself from some other objects in her world. She may, for example, find a special toy particularly soothing.
- She's learning that objects (and people) have labels and may occasionally respond to her own name.

Verbally

- She's trying as hard as she can to speak, using her tongue and changing the shape of her mouth. And, if she's got something on her mind, she may take the initiative and start a conversation with you. If she really wants to chat, she'll be very upset if you aren't focusing all your attention on her.
- If you wait a few seconds after saying something to her, she may "answer" you, making ample use of her expanding vocabulary of squeals, chuckles, chortles, giggles, and clicks.
- When she hears a sound—especially a voice—she actively searches for it with her eyes.

Emotionally/Socially

- Overall, your baby is a pretty happy kid. She smiles regularly and spontaneously, enjoys a rousing game of peek-a-boo, and anticipates pleasurable encounters by vigorously kicking her arms and legs. She may also use the full-body wiggle as a signal for "do it again" or "pick me up."
- She's so anxious to socialize that she can actually suppress other interests in order to play. If you talk to her while she's eating, for example, she'll gladly stop for a few minutes to talk.
- She now tries to extend her playtime by laughing or holding her gaze on a desired object, and she may protest loudly if you stop doing what she wants you to.
- Despite this hedonistic streak, she's still got clear preferences among playmates (including toys). Some will be able to soothe her, others won't.

- This is an extremely busy developmental time for your baby, and you may notice some interruption in her sleep patterns as she wakes up in the middle of the night to practice her new tricks.

WHAT YOU'RE GOING THROUGH

Reevaluating Your Relationship with Your Job

Remember the shift in focus and priorities we talked about last month—from self to family? Well, once that shift has begun, the very next thing most new fathers do is take a long, hard look at their jobs.

We've come a long way since the days when all that dads were expected to do (and, I believe, allowed to do) was go to work. Today, 70 percent of working dads say their role in the family is to be both the involved dad and the provider, according to a new study by the Boston College Center for Work & Family. It's no big surprise, then, that 60 percent of working dads in dual-earner couples say they experience work/family conflict, according to the Families and Work Institute. That's up from 35 percent in 1977 (over the same time, the percentage of women who say they have work/family conflict has stayed pretty much the same, at around 45 percent).

But being a provider-protector dad in the twenty-first century is a study in contradictions. For example, in the Boston College Study, 86 percent of working dads agreed or strongly agreed that "My children are the number one priority in my life." And other studies have found that at least half of working dads would pass up a promotion (and the accompanying pay increase) if it meant taking time away from their family. At the same time, 76 percent of working dads would like to "advance to a position with greater responsibility with their employers," and 58 percent have "a strong desire" to be in upper management. Perhaps most ironic of all, whereas 58 percent of working dads (versus 49 percent of men without children) say they'd like to work fewer hours, the dads put in an average of forty-seven hours per week on the job, while the non-dads log only forty-four hours per week, according to the Families and Work Institute. And whereas 42 percent of dads work fifty or more hours per week, only a third of non-dads do.

So why the disconnect between what we say and what we do? It's pretty simple: the culture of the workplace and society's expectations haven't kept up with dads' evolving priorities. A study by the Association of Executive Search Consultants found that while 80 percent of executives say that work/life balance is "critical in their decision whether to join or remain with an employer," 82 percent say that their company doesn't have a program to improve that balance. In fact, 73

percent are often required to work between 6 P.M. and 9 P.M., and 63 percent are often required to work weekends.

And then there's the "flexibility stigma." In most Western societies, being the provider is central to men's identity, in much the same way as being the nurturer is ingrained in women's identity. In other words, we equate working with masculinity and caring for children with femininity. So, when a man requests family leave, he's no longer behaving the way men are "supposed" to. As a result, the people around him start to see him as more feminine (weak and uncertain) and less masculine (competitive and ambitious), according to Rutgers University researchers Laurie Rudman and Kris Mescher.

Rudman, Mescher, and another team of researchers led by Joseph Vandello at the University of South Florida found that the penalties men pay for asking for family leave are quite heavy. They're seen as not serious about their jobs, they get lower evaluations from coworkers and managers, and they may get passed over for promotions and receive smaller raises than male coworkers who act more like "real men" and don't request time off for family reasons.

There's no question that women have been dealing with a flexibility stigma for decades and pay a steep financial price when they move from the fast track to the mommy track. Corporate America should be ashamed. But according to Scott Coltrane and his colleagues at the University of Oregon, "Men who leave the workforce for family reasons can expect to earn 26.4 percent less later in their careers than they would have had they never left the workforce. Women face a 23.3 percent financial penalty."

Despite all of this, most new dads are figuring out ways to move the work/family balance seesaw to a more neutral position. Though very few guys are taking advantage of family leave programs—even when they're paid (usually out of fear of committing career suicide), they still manage to cobble together an average of two–three weeks off from work using vacation days, sick days, and some white lies: some men interviewed for the Families and Work Institute study said that they had "told friends at work they were going to a bar when in fact they were going home to care for their children." Hey, whatever works, right?

Coming to Terms with Breastfeeding

Before their babies are born, nearly all expectant fathers feel that breastfeeding is the best way to feed a baby and that their partners should do so as long as possible. After the baby comes, new fathers still feel that breast is best, but many also feel a little ambivalent.

Most new fathers feel that breastfeeding "perpetuates the exclusive relationship the mother and infant experienced during pregnancy," writes Dr. Pamela Jordan, one of the few researchers ever to explore the effects of breastfeeding on men. Given all this, says Dr. Jordan, a new father is likely to experience:

- A diminished opportunity to develop a relationship with his child.
- A sense of inadequacy.
- A feeling that the baby has come between him and his partner.
- A feeling that nothing he does to satisfy his child can ever compete with his partner's breasts.
- A sense of relief when his partner weans the baby, giving him the opportunity to "catch up."
- A belief in what Jordan calls the "hormonal advantage theory"—the idea that women are born with certain knowledge and skills that give them an advantage in parenting, including guaranteed success with breastfeeding.

Whether or not you're experiencing these or any other less-than-completely-positive feelings, there's a good chance that your partner is having a few ambivalent feelings of her own about breastfeeding. Here are some of the things she may be feeling:

- Exhaustion. It may look easy and relaxing to you, but nursing a baby is tough work.
- Despite the images of smiling, happy nursing mothers, your partner may not be enjoying the experience. And if she isn't, she may be feeling guilty or inadequate. (Just goes to show you that fathers aren't the only ones boxed in by socialization.)

SIPRESS

- She may resent the way nursing interferes with some of the other things she'd like to do.
- She may want to run as far away from the baby as possible. If so, she's also likely to feel guilty or selfish (socialization again . . . mothers are always supposed to be happy to be with their children).
- She may not be interested in answering your questions about the process. (I had a million for my wife: How does it feel? How much comes out in each feeding? Does the milk come out from one hole or more than one?)

If your partner is breastfeeding, there's no question that you're at a bit of a disadvantage when it comes to feeding the baby—an activity most people would agree is the most important thing you can do for a baby. However, there's a big difference between "most important" and "only." Unfortunately, "when it comes to meeting the needs of an infant, for some parents the whole focus is on breastfeeding," writes Francine de Montigny, professor of nursing at the Université du Québec. "These fathers did not seem to be aware that all the things they were doing—the skin-to-skin contact and other physical contact that occurs during comforting, bathing, infant massage and other kinds of routine baby care—are also very, very important for their baby's well-being and brain development." Interestingly, de Montigny found that fathers whose babies were being fed formula—meaning that they could feed them just as much as the mothers could—were actually less involved than dads of breastfed babies.

For Women Only (you can read this, but only if you promise to show it to your partner when you're done)

"The breast-feeding mother has the control of parenting and must realize that she has the power to invite the father in or exclude him," writes Dr. Pamela Jordan. "She can play a vital role in establishing exclusive father-infant time, often while simultaneously meeting her own needs for time away and alone. Just as the father is viewed as the primary support of the mother-infant relationship, the mother is the primary support of the father-infant relationship . . . supporting the father during breast-feeding may help improve his, and consequently, the mother's, satisfaction with breast-feeding, the duration of breast-feeding, and the adaptation of both parents to parenthood." Just something to keep in mind . . .

So rather than focus on the one thing you can't do, pay a little more attention to what you can do—and are probably already doing. In addition to the baths and massages, think of all the skin-to-skin contact you're making, all the diapers you're changing, the stories you're reading, the playing you're doing, the bedtime routines you've created, the walks you're taking, all the times your baby has blissfully fallen asleep on your chest. Sounds pretty involved to me.

Worried That Your Life Will Never Be the Same Again (It Won't)

Before my first child was born, just about everybody my wife and I knew (and plenty of people we didn't know) pulled us aside and tried to warn us that our lives would change forever once we became parents. They told us about how hard it is to shift from worrying only about ourselves to being responsible for the safety and well-being of a completely helpless little person. They told us that we'd lose a lot of sleep and even more privacy. And they told us that we'd better go to a lot of movies and read a stack of books because we might not have another chance for a while. Everything everyone said was absolutely correct, but none of it really prepared us for our transition to parenthood.

What I often find most interesting about the changes I underwent when I became a father is the way my memories of my prefatherhood past have been subtly altered. It's not that I can't or don't remember life before children, it's just that that so much of my identity is tied up in being a father that my prechild life, in retrospect, seems somehow incomplete. Most of the new dads I've interviewed expressed the same kinds of feelings.

I have clear, fond memories of taking long walks on the beach by myself, sleeping in all day, and going out at midnight for a beer with friends—things I haven't done much since becoming a father. It's as though those things happened to someone else, however. I don't really miss my other life, but in a way, I wish I could have shared it with my children (not the beers, perhaps, but the walks on the beach and the sleeping in).

Rethinking What It Means to Be a Man

There are two major reasons why so many of us would prefer to drive ten miles down the wrong road rather than stop and ask for directions. First, from the time we were little boys, we've been socialized to associate knowledge with masculinity—in other words, real men know everything, so admitting to being lost is a sign of weakness (and, of course, a lack of masculinity). Second, we've also been socialized to be strong, independent, and goal-oriented, which makes asking for help a sign of weakness (and, again, a lack of masculinity). Nothing in the world can bring these two factors into play faster than the birth of a baby. Because of the near-total absence of active, involved, nurturing male role models, most new fathers can't seriously claim that they know what to do with a new baby (although never having cooked before didn't prevent my father from making all sorts of wild claims about his culinary skills; boy, was he wrong).

Getting help seems like the obvious solution to the ignorance problem, but most men don't want to seem helpless or expose their lack of knowledge by asking anyone—especially their partner. Now toss in a few more ingredients:

• The confusion and fears we've been feeling lately.
• The prevailing attitude that a man who is actively involved with his children—especially if he's the primary caretaker—is not as masculine as his less involved brothers.
• Cultural messages that tell us that we have to explore our "feminine" side or be more maternal in order to be better fathers.

It's easy to see how the whole experience of becoming a father can lead so many new fathers to wonder secretly (no one would ever openly admit to having these thoughts) whether or not they've retained their masculinity. All too often the result of this kind of thinking is that fathers leave all the child-rearing to their partners and thereby leave their kids essentially without a father.

So you have a choice. Either accept the hardest yet most rewarding challenge you'll probably ever face by becoming an actively involved father and taking on a significant share of the responsibility for raising your children, or take the easy way out and leave it all to someone else. What would a "real" man do?

YOU AND YOUR BABY

Your Baby's Temperament

Once upon a time, way back in the 1950s, a husband-and-wife team of psychiatrists, Stella Chess and Alexander Thomas, came up with a theory that children are born with a set of nine fundamental behavioral and emotional traits that they called "temperamental qualities." These qualities, which are noticeable within days (sometimes hours) after the baby is born, remain fairly consistent throughout life, combine differently for each child, and determine, to a great extent, a child's personality and whether he will be "easy" or "challenging." Chess and Thomas also found that a child's temperament has a major influence on his parents' behavior and attitudes.

Over the past few decades, Chess and Thomas's original research in temperament has been expanded, refined, and improved upon by all sorts of people. But it's still the gold standard and one thing that has remained constant is how learning to recognize and accept your baby's temperament can truly change your life by helping you to accept her (as well as yourself) for who she is. Here, then, are the nine temperament traits, adapted from Chess and Thomas and the work of Jim Cameron, head of the Preventive Ounce (preventiveoz.org), a nonprofit mental health organization for children. The chart on pages 134–36 has a lot of examples that will give you a good idea of what each of the nine traits looks like. When you're done reading it, take the quiz below.

1. Approach/Withdrawal: Your baby's usual initial reaction to unfamiliar situations, such as meeting a new person, tasting a new food, or being in a new situation.
2. Adaptability: Similar to Approach/Withdrawal, but deals with your child's longer-term reactions to changes in routines or expectations, places, and ideas.
3. Intensity: The amount of energy your baby commonly uses to express her emotions—both positive and negative.
4. Mood: Her general mood—happy or fussy—over the course of a typical day.
5. Activity level: The amount of energy she puts into everything she does.
6. Regularity: The day-to-day predictability of your baby's eating, sleeping, and filling diapers.
7. Sensitivity: Your baby's sensitivity to pain, noise, temperature change, lights, odors, flavors, textures, and emotions. Note: it's quite possible for her to be highly sensitive to one sensation (bright lights, for example) but not at all sensitive to another (noise).
8. Distractibility: How easy it is to change the focus of your baby's attention.
9. Persistence: Similar to Distractibility, but goes beyond the initial reaction and concerns the length of time your baby will spend trying to overcome obstacles or distractions.

The Nine Temperament Traits of Babies

APPROACHING BABIES
- separate easily from parents
- are excited to meet and interact with new people
- love to try new foods
- seem perfectly at home in new situations

WITHDRAWING BABIES
- are usually shy, cling to their parents in new situations or around strangers
- have difficulty separating from parents
- need time to warm up to new experiences
- may be extremely picky eaters and spit out unfamiliar food

FAST-ADAPTING BABIES
- fall asleep easily and without fussing, no matter where they are
- don't mind changes in routines
- can be fed easily by different people
- don't mind being handled by different people or passed around
- smile back quickly when talked to
- seem perfectly delighted to be wherever they are

SLOW-ADAPTING BABIES
- may refuse to fall asleep in a strange place (or even a moderately familiar one like Grandma and Grandpa's)—only their own cribs will do
- take a long time to get back to sleep after being awakened
- don't like being picked up and held by strangers
- take a long time to warm up to new situations, and once upset, may take a long time to calm down

LOW-INTENSITY BABIES
- display their emotions, but are often hard to read
- have subdued moods
- seem fairly nonchalant

HIGH-INTENSITY BABIES
- react strongly (positively or negatively) to strangers, loud noises, bright lights
- do everything—shrieking with delight or crying—so loudly it hurts your ears
- let you know, in no uncertain terms, when they're hungry, thirsty, or uncomfortable

POSITIVE-MOOD BABIES
- laugh and smile at just about everything
- are happy even when having their diapers changed
- enjoy being able to do new things
- seem genuinely happy to see you

NEGATIVE-MOOD BABIES
- cry when being changed
- are fussy or cranky most of the time
- whimper or cry a lot, sometimes seemingly for no reason
- complain during hair brushing

LOW-ACTIVITY BABIES
- seem content to lie still while nursing or getting changed
- will sit calmly in the car seat
- prefer less physical play (swings instead of wrestling)

PREDICTABLE BABIES
- get hungry, get tired, and move their bowels at about the same times every day
- love regular eating and bedtime schedules
- don't like to have their routines messed with

HIGH-SENSORY-THRESHOLD (OBLIVIOUS) BABIES
- love loud events (basketball games, circuses, bands . . .)
- aren't bothered by wet or dirty diapers
- are emotionally stable
- can't always differentiate between two voices
- aren't bothered by clothing labels, bright lights, scratchy fabrics, or even pain

LOW-DISTRACTIBILITY BABIES
- are quite hard to soothe once they're upset
- seem completely oblivious to interruptions (noise, familiar voices) when involved in something important (like nursing)

HIGH-ACTIVITY BABIES
- move around a lot while sleeping, frequently kicking their blankets off
- squirm and wriggle while awake, and are hard to dress, change, bathe, or feed
- often reach physical developmental milestones earlier than lower-activity kids

UNPREDICTABLE BABIES
- have absolutely no respect for your schedule
- have frequent sleep problems, get up several times during the night, and may or may not take naps during the day
- may not be hungry at mealtimes and may want to eat at different times every day
- have irregular bowel movements

LOW-SENSORY-THRESHOLD (VERY AWARE) BABIES
- are easily overstimulated
- are awakened easily by a gentle touch or lights being turned on
- may get extremely upset at loud noises
- notice tiny variations in the taste of food
- are extremely uncomfortable in wet or dirty diapers
- are very sensitive to fabrics, labels, and the fit of their clothes

HIGH-DISTRACTIBILITY BABIES
- have short attention spans
- are easily distracted while nursing
- are easily soothed when upset and quickly stop crying when picked up
- can turn from tears to laughter on a dime

The Nine Temperament Traits of Babies *continued*

HIGH-PERSISTENCE BABIES
- are able to amuse themselves for a few minutes at a time
- like to practice new motor skills (like rolling from front to back) over and over and over
- pay close attention (for more than a minute) to rattles and mobiles
- pay close attention to other children when playing
- cry when you stop playing with them

LOW-PERSISTENCE BABIES
- need constant attention—can't amuse themselves for very long in crib or playpen
- have short attention spans and are frustrated easily, even by simple tasks
- quickly lose interest in playing, even with favorite toys
- won't spend much time working on new skills (rolling over, sitting up)

Now that you know what to look for, spend a few minutes rating your baby on the following scale. And have your partner do it, too.

TRAIT	RATING		
Approach/Withdrawal	Approaching	1 2 3 4 5	Withdrawing
Adaptability	Fast	1 2 3 4 5	Slow
Intensity	Low	1 2 3 4 5	High
Mood	Positive	1 2 3 4 5	Negative
Activity Level	Low	1 2 3 4 5	High
Regularity	Predictable	1 2 3 4 5	Unpredictable
Sensitivity	Oblivious	1 2 3 4 5	Very Aware
Distractibility	Low	1 2 3 4 5	High
Persistence	High	1 2 3 4 5	Low

If you have a lot of 1s and 2s, you're one lucky guy. You've got an "easy" child (about 40 percent of parents do), and having an easy child is, well, easy. Your baby's always smiling and happy, she sleeps through the night, eats at the same time every day, and loves playing and meeting new people. When she does get upset or fussy, you can usually calm her down almost immediately. You're madly in love with your baby and you're feeling confident about your parenting skills.

However, depending on the situation, 1s and 2s might actually be "undesirable" traits. For example, a Low-Distractibility baby (who would score 1 or 2) won't be upset by noises but will be hard to soothe, while a High-Distractibility baby (who would score 4 or 5) may not be able to sit still but will be easy to soothe.

If you ended up with a lot of 4s and 5s, you most likely have a "challenging" child (only about 10 percent of parents do), and things are not nearly as rosy. She doesn't sleep through the night, has trouble eating, freaks out at the slightest noise or change in her surroundings, cries for hours at a time (and nothing you try seems to make it any better), and is generally fussy. Meanwhile, you're exhausted and depressed, angry at the baby for her "malicious" behavior, embarrassed at the way people stare at your unhappy child, guilty about your unparental feelings, and jealous of your friends and their easy babies. In short, you're not finding your parenting experience very satisfying, you're discouraged and frustrated, and you think you must be a complete failure as a father. You may even feel trapped and fantasize about running away.

As bad as it sounds, there are some things you can do to help you overcome a lot of your frustration and negative feelings:

- Recognize that challenging children are challenging because of their innate makeup. Their temperament exists at birth. It's not their fault, it's not your fault, and it's not your partner's fault. It's just the way things are.
- Stop blaming yourself, your partner, or your baby. There's probably nothing wrong with any of you. Your baby is who she is, and there's very little you can do about it. The problem is that the way you're interacting with your child simply isn't working.
- Take the quiz again, but this time rate yourself. What are the similarities between you and your baby? The differences? You can see right away where your traits and your baby's mesh nicely, and where they won't. If you're both Highly Distractible, you may never get through that book you're reading —and neither of you will care. But if you're Highly Approaching and the baby is Highly Withdrawing, you may have some real problems taking her to meet your boss for the first time.

At the very least, these steps will enable you to modify your approaches to your child's behavior and to anticipate and avoid conflicts before they occur. The result will be a far happier, more loving, and more satisfying relationship with your child. Guaranteed.

Putting Your Knowledge of Temperament to Good Use

Following are some of the most common temperament traits you're likely to encounter during your baby's first year, along with some suggestions for how to handle them.

INITIAL WITHDRAWAL/SLOW ADAPTABILITY

Just because your baby is shy, spits out new foods (which you probably won't be giving her for another few months), and refuses to play with new toys doesn't mean she'll never change. The key is to introduce things slowly and to be patient. For example, introduce new foods a few times at different meals, and give the baby a chance to "meet" a new toy from a distance before letting her touch it.

Your Withdrawing/Slow-Adapting baby will probably begin experiencing stranger anxiety (see pages 215–16) earlier—and it will last longer—than babies who are more Approaching and Fast Adapting. Tell new visitors, and even those the baby knows a little bit, to take it easy when approaching her, not try to pick her up right away, and not take it personally if she screams or cries.

Your baby will eventually get used to new things—it'll just take her a little while. One thing you can do is frequently expose her to new situations and experiences so she can get used to the idea. But be careful. Your Withdrawing/Slow-Adapting baby has a tendency to get overstimulated, so recognize those symptoms and be prepared to get her back to something more familiar if necessary.

Also, think about your baby's temperament before making any major changes in your appearance. Shaving your beard, getting a haircut, or even replacing your glasses with contact lenses can trigger a strong negative reaction. When my oldest daughter was six months old, her babysitter—whom she absolutely adored—got a haircut, and it took her more than a week to recover.

HIGH INTENSITY

Some babies just make a lot of noise, and short of leaving the room or getting earplugs (both of which are perfectly reasonable approaches), there's not much you can do about it. Just make sure you can tell the difference between a shrill, eardrum-destroying happy shriek and a shrill, eardrum-destroying unhappy one. And watch out if you're tickling your baby with your nose—her mouth is very, very close to your ears.

NEGATIVE MOOD

Not much can make you happier than going out with a smiling, happy baby. But a baby who isn't a smiler, and who whimpers and cries all the time, can be a real challenge to your self-confidence. It's hard to take pleasure in a baby with a Negative Mood, or even to feel proud of her. And it's certainly tempting to think that if the baby doesn't smile at you all the time, she doesn't love you.

If you're feeling this way, resist the urge to get angry with your baby for her whining, or to "get even" with her by withholding your love. (I know it sounds silly, but it happens.) The truth is that the lack of a smile probably doesn't mean anything at all. And the whining will subside as your baby's verbal skills improve, enabling her to get your attention in more productive ways.

HIGH ACTIVITY

Because your High-Activity baby will spend her sleeping moments doing laps in her crib, you might want to put some rubber stops underneath the crib's wheels because energetic kicking and bouncing can actually move the crib. (Believe me, it's quite a shock to walk into your baby's room first thing in the morning and find that she—and her bed—aren't where you left them.) For that reason, it's especially important that you remove anything from inside the crib (or nearby) that could possibly fall on top of the baby's head.

Never, never leave your baby unattended—even for a second—on a changing table or bed; she could very well roll off (this applies to all babies, but especially to Highly Active ones). Once, when my oldest daughter was about four months old, I was tickling her in her bassinet when the phone (located about three feet away) rang. I stepped over, said "Hello," and heard a loud thump behind me: my daughter, who had never given any indication that she knew how to pull herself up, had done exactly that, and toppled over the side of the bassinet. No harm was done, but we put that bassinet into storage and didn't take it out again until the next baby came.

Your High-Activity baby may sometimes be too busy to be held or cuddled and may squirm and cry until you put her down. It's easy to take this as a rejection, but don't. Just try to do your holding and snuggling at times when she's likely to be more receptive, such as first thing in the morning or just before bed.

UNPREDICTABILITY

Since your Unpredictable baby seems to be eating, sleeping, and filling her diaper at random, it's up to you to try to establish a regular schedule. Although she may not want to eat, try to feed her something at times that are more convenient for you. If you schedule meals at the same times every day, you may be able to help her create a modified routine.

Routines are important for bedtime too. When you go into her room at night, don't turn on the lights, don't pick her up, don't play, and get out as soon as you can. Once you stumble on a getting-the-baby-back-to-sleep routine, stick with it (although be prepared: what works with an Unpredictable baby one day may stop working a day, a week, or a month later. They are, after all, unpredictable).

If your baby's sleep irregularities are truly serious, you and your partner should divide up the night, each taking a shift while the other sleeps. If that doesn't help, talk with your pediatrician about a mild sedative—for the baby, not you.

ENFANT TERRIBLE.

MUELLER

LOW SENSORY THRESHOLD

For the first few months of a Low-Sensory-Threshold baby's life, you'll never know what's going to set her off. Sounds, smells, and sensations you might hardly notice can cause her to explode into tears: turning on the car radio, the crowd applauding at a basketball game (yes, you can take babies to basketball games), even too many toys in her crib.

One way to make your baby's life a little less jarring is to modify the amount and type of stimulation in her environment. Avoid neon colors when decorating her room, get opaque drapes to keep daytime light out during nap time, and don't play actively with her right before bedtime. When dressing your baby, stay away from tight clothes, brand-new clothes (they're often too stiff), wool, synthetic fabrics, or anything with a rough texture. Cotton blends usually offer the best combination of washability and softness. And be sure to clip off scratchy labels and tags.

HIGH DISTRACTIBILITY AND LOW PERSISTENCE

This combination of characteristics isn't usually a challenge until babies get active. Your High-Distractibility/Low-Persistence baby gets bored easily and may want constant attention from you. She may also take forever to eat, stopping every thirty seconds to follow a fly as it zips through the room or to check out a shadow on the wall. If she's being breastfed, this will probably bother your partner more than you.

This discussion of temperament should be enough for you to identify and begin to deal with your child's behavior patterns. But if you're seriously concerned about your child's temperament, check out the Resources appendix of this book.

YOU AND YOUR PARTNER

Sex

On average, couples resume having sex about seven weeks after the birth of the baby. But it may be a lot longer than that before your prebaby (and prepregnancy) sex life returns. If your partner is breastfeeding, she's also producing hormones that may mildly suppress her desire. That helps explain why a majority of women don't recover their sex drives for as long as six months after giving birth. For most couples, though, the biggest obstacles are fatigue and time.

Getting your physical relationship back to normal is going to take patience, communication, and some careful planning. Here are a few things that may give your sex life the jump start it needs:

- Go for quality over quantity. Just because you can't have sex three times a week doesn't mean you have to give up altogether. You may only be able to fit in a few rolls in the hay a month, but make them count.
- Keep it regular. When it comes to sex, it's use it or lose it. Your sex organs are muscles, and they need some regular working out to operate at peak capacity. In addition, long breaks can cause your hormone levels to change, which can reduce your desire.
- Start early and build from there. When she gets out of bed, tell your partner how good she looks; if you see her naked, compliment her body; flirt with her and let her catch you peeking down her shirt over breakfast; rub up against her as you walk past each other in the hallway; and make a few sexy phone calls to her during the day. By the time you get home, you'll be all over each other.
- Think like teens. Watch some porn together, grope each other in the back seat of the car, or have sex on the sink in the bathroom of a friend who's invited you over for dinner.
- Be good to yourselves. Both of you should you eat right, exercise at least three times a week, get plenty of sleep, and have at least five minutes alone a few times a week just to get your thoughts together.

- Reach out and touch each other. When you were younger and more awake, the need to touch your partner was sparked by desire. Now that you're a dad, things have changed and the order is reversed. Touching, holding, stroking, and kissing each other—even if you aren't really into it when you start—can actually produce the desire, which in turn will make the kissing and fondling more intense, which could lead to other things . . .

Finally, as mentioned earlier, don't forget the contraception. Condoms are best until your partner's doctor tells her that anything else is okay.

Thyroid Problems

For up to six months after birth, 5–10 percent of women experience postpartum thyroiditis, an inflammation of the thyroid, a gland that produces hormones that are involved in almost every organ and system in our body. In particular, thyroid hormones are involved in regulating your temperature, metabolism, weight, muscle strength, digestion, heart and lung function, mood, and overall mental state.

Postpartum thyroiditis causes no pain but produces a number of symptoms, including anxiety, emotional instability, muscle fatigue, lack of energy, and depression. The problem is that every one of those symptoms is also a perfectly normal part of your partner's postpartum recovery. However, by this point, she should have been over most of them, so if you're still seeing any, it's worth discussing them with your partner's doctor. Most of the time, the condition will take care of itself within a few months, but sometimes it requires some medical treatment. Diagnosing it definitively may require some tests that use radioactive isotopes, which are a big no-no if your partner is nursing because traces can be passed to the baby through the breast milk.

FAMILY MATTERS

Sleeping Tight

We all love our children, but let's face it, sometimes we want them to go to sleep—and stay that way for a while. There are all sorts of factors (many of which are beyond your control) that influence whether your child will be a "good" sleeper or a "bad" one. Fortunately, though, there are a few rules of thumb that can help tilt the odds in your favor:

- Don't become the baby's sleep transition object. Baby's last waking memory should be of her crib or something familiar in it (blankie, toy, a picture on the wall, glow-in-the-dark stars on the ceiling). That way, if she wakes up in the

Things That Go Bump in the Crib

A lot of new parents use crib bumpers (soft pads that run along the inside of the crib) in an attempt to keep their babies from running into the slats or bars and getting hurt. That's a nice idea (one that millions of people—including me—have been using for decades). But new research is showing that those bumpers could actually be more dangerous than the injuries they're trying to protect against. In one study, twenty-seven babies died (over twenty years) from factors directly attributable to bumpers: suffocation (babies may bump into the bumpers with their face and not be able to move away), entrapment (getting caught between the bumper and the mattress), or strangulation (some bumpers are tied on with strings, which can get wrapped around the baby's neck). The American Academy of Pediatrics now recommends against using bumpers of any kind, even the mesh "breathable" ones, which eliminate the suffocation risk but still could be entrapment or strangulation hazards. So, yes, while crib bumpers might keep some babies—especially High-Activity ones—from getting minor bumps and bruises, they can cause death. If you've bought crib bumpers or gotten them as a gift, return them for something else. Why take the chance?

middle of the night, she'll see the familiar object and be able to associate it with sleep. If you were the last thing she saw before dropping off, she'll want you again, even if you happen to be sleeping.

- It's perfectly natural for babies to fuss or be restless for fifteen or twenty minutes after being put down. (Please remember that fussing is one thing, screaming is another. If the baby begins to really wail, pick her up and soothe her, but try to get her back in her crib while she's still awake. It's absolutely impossible to spoil a baby by picking her up or soothing her in the first three or four months of life.)
- Keep nighttime activity to a minimum. Whether your baby is sleeping in your room or not, she needs to learn that nighttime is for sleeping, not for playing.
- Don't turn on the lights. If the baby wakes up for a middle-of-the-night breast or bottle, do it in the dark.
- Don't change diapers unless you absolutely have to (such as when you're trying to treat a particularly nasty case of diaper rash or if the baby is wearing cloth diapers; if she's wearing disposables, she'll be perfectly fine until the morning).
- Establish a routine. You'll need to make up your own, depending on what works best for you. Here's a fairly simple routine that is good for babies this age as

well as for toddlers: change diapers, do a little baby massage, get sleep suit on, read a story or two, go around the room and say "goodnight" to all the toys and animals, give a kiss goodnight, and into bed.

- When your baby is about six months old, start leaving the door to her room open. Kids that age get scared if they feel they're trapped in a small space, especially if they aren't sure you're just outside the door.
- In case of nightmares or other middle-of-the-night scares, respond promptly and be as reassuring as possible. Unless your baby is hysterical with fear, try to keep things brief and resist the urge to take her out of the crib. You can do a lot of soothing by rubbing her back or head—all from your side of the bars.
- Make sure the baby doesn't get overtired during the day. This means making sure she has plenty of naps—preferably one within 60–90 minutes after eating—and goes to bed early.
- During the day, gently wake up—and entertain—your baby if she tries to nap more than two or three hours at a stretch. The idea is to make her longest sleep of the day occur at night.

But What about Those Middle-of-the-Night Wake-Ups?

By this age, the majority of babies are sleeping through the night. But not all of them. The most common reason babies wake up in the middle of the night is that they want to eat. If your partner is breastfeeding, do everything you can to stay in bed and let her handle things. I realize that this sounds positively insensitive, but the truth is that there's really nothing you can do to help out short of bringing the baby to her. And if you do, you'll both end up sleep deprived out of your mind. Instead, ask her to handle the first nighttime feeding herself so you can get some uninterrupted sleep. While she's up, she can pump an extra bottle of milk so that you can give the baby the other nighttime feeding and let your partner get a few hours of uninterrupted sleep. Sleep deprivation is a terrible thing, and this tag-team approach will help you avoid it. You'll still be tired, but it won't be nearly as bad.

As I mentioned above, the most common reason babies wake up at night is because they're hungry. But it's not the *only* reason. Sometimes, no matter what you do, your baby is going to wake up at two or three in the morning for no other purpose than to stay awake for a few hours and check things out. So if you hear rustling and other noises coming from wherever your baby is sleeping, wait a few minutes before you go to her—she may go right back to sleep. If you do have to get up, keep your middle-of-the-night encounters as boring as possible. Until they're old enough to have sex, kids need to know that nighttime is for sleeping.

Here's something simple you can do that may reduce midnight wake-ups and could make your baby smarter: spend more time with your infant during the day.

Liat Tikotzky and her colleagues at Ben-Gurion University in Israel found that the more dads (but not moms) are involved in daytime care, the fewer times their babies wake up at night. Dads' daytime involvement also helped with *sleep consolidation*, meaning that babies do less of their sleeping during the day and more at night. Good sleep consolidation (as opposed to sleep *fragmentation*, which is the opposite) is associated with better memory, cognitive outcomes, and language ability.

Sleeping Arrangements

As hard as it may be to imagine, there's a rather basic parenting issue that regularly generates even more controversy than circumcision or the disposable-versus-cloth-diapers debate: whether or not to have your child sleep in the same bed as you and your partner.

Fortunately (or unfortunately, depending on where you stand on the issue), there's absolutely no consensus on which view is the "right" one. And just to make sure that there's no real way to decide this issue once and for all, there's very little serious scientific data supporting either position.

Our oldest daughter slept in a bassinet in our room for a month or so until we moved her into her own room. The middle one slept in bed with us for six months before being asked to leave. Personally, I kind of liked being able to snuggle up with a warm, smooth baby, but after being kicked in the head, stomach, back, face, and chest every night for six months, I was glad to go back to an adults-only sleeping arrangement. The youngest baby also started off in our bed but moved to her own room after only six weeks or so.

Here are some of the most common issues that come up in discussions of what's usually called *cosleeping* or *the family bed*:

- Independence. Proponents point to the fact that in most countries (comprising about 80 percent of the world's population), parents and children sleep in the same bed. They claim that in Western countries kids are being forced to be independent too early and that human evolution simply can't keep pace with the new demands our culture is placing on its children. They maintain that before a child can become independent, she must feel that the world is a safe place and that her needs will be met. Kids who sleep in a family bed, in this view, turn out to be more independent, more confident, and more self-assured than those who don't. Critics, however, say that what works in other countries doesn't always work here (in many emerging countries, for example, homes are so small that separate sleeping arrangements for babes just aren't possible). In America early independence is critical, and babies should therefore quickly learn to be away from their parents, especially if both work and the children have to be in daycare.

"And so the Big Bad Wolf ate Little Red Riding Hood,
Hansel and Gretel, Cinderella, and the Three Little Pigs and
that was the end of fairy tales forever. Now good night!"

- Sleep—the baby's. Despite what you might think, cosleeping children tend to sleep more lightly than children who sleep alone (blankets rustling and parents turning over in bed wake them up). But light sleeping isn't necessarily a bad thing. In fact, there seems to be a correlation between lighter sleep and a lower incidence of SIDS.
- Sleep—yours. It's perfectly normal for even the soundest-sleeping kids to wake up every three or four hours for a quick look around the room. The vast majority (about 70 percent) soothe themselves back to sleep after a minute or two. But about 30 percent will spot something they just have to play with (you or your partner, for example), and they're up for hours.
- Safety. Many parents are afraid that they'll accidentally roll over on their sleeping child if the whole family is sharing the same bed. Though this is a perfectly legitimate concern, most adults—even while asleep—have a highly developed sense of where they are. It's probably been quite a while since you fell out of bed in the middle of the night. That said, if you're drunk or stoned or otherwise inebriated, your odds of rolling over your baby go way up. Plus, your bedding is a potential smothering hazard and your blankets may overheat your baby— something that's associated with an increased risk of SIDS. That risk is exactly

why the American Academy of Pediatrics advises against cosleeping and recommends having your baby sleep in the same room with you, just not in the
same bed. Other experts disagree, saying that removing the risk factors (see
below) can make cosleeping safe.

- Sexual spontaneity. No kidding. But there are plenty of other places to make
love besides your bed.
- Breastfeeding. There's no question that it's a lot easier for a nursing mother to
reach across her bed for the baby than to get up and stagger down the hall. Some
research indicates that this may encourage mothers to breastfeed longer. Problems arise, however, when fathers feel (and they often do) displaced by the nursing baby and decide that the only place to get a good night's sleep is on the couch.

A Few Things to Consider If You're Thinking about Sharing Your Bed with Your Child

- Keep politics out of your decision making. Sleep with your child because you
and your partner want to, not because you feel you have to.
- Don't be embarrassed. You're not being soft, negligent, or overindulgent—it's a
choice made by millions of fine parents.
- Safety first. Make sure your bed is large enough to accommodate everyone.
(But no waterbeds—baby could roll between you and the mattress.) The mattress should be firm, the bed should be against the wall, and the baby should
sleep—always on her back—on the wall side, or get a guard rail if she's going

Naps and Sleep Schedules

At four months your baby has probably only recently settled into a regular
sleep routine. Every baby has her own sleeping schedule, but a typical one
for a baby this age might include an eight-to-ten-hour stretch at night plus,
if you're lucky, another four–five hours divided into two or three daytime
naps, for a total of around fourteen hours (that's the average—but the range
is from nine to sixteen hours). Over the next few months, her nighttime
sleep will get longer and the total nap time will get shorter. Keep an eye on
these naps, however; if they get too late, they may start upsetting the night-
sleeping routine. You can't expect a baby to take a nap from 4 P.M. to 6 P.M.
and then go to bed for the night at 7.

to sleep on the outside edge. No comforters, blankets, or fluffy pillows, as they may pose a risk of suffocation.

- Rethink your decision right now if you're obese, you smoke, drink, or take any medication that might make you hard to wake up, or if you're generally such a sound sleeper that you're worried you might roll on top of your baby without noticing.
- Make sure everyone's toenails are trimmed.
- Think before you start. Once your baby has been sleeping in your bed for six to eight months, it's going to be awfully hard to get her out if you change your mind.

A Few Things to Consider If You're Thinking about *Not* Sharing Your Bed with Your Child

- Don't feel guilty. You're not a bad or selfish parent for not doing it.
- There is no solid evidence that sleeping with your child will speed up the bonding/attachment process.
- It's okay to make an occasional exception, such as when a child is ill or has had a frightening experience.
- If you're making your decision because of safety issues, you may be able to compromise by setting up the baby's crib in your bedroom or by getting a "side-car"—basically a three-sided crib that attaches to the side of your bed.

Work and Family

WHAT'S GOING ON WITH THE BABY

Physically

- This month's big discovery is, yes, toes. And just as your baby spent hours wiggling and sucking his own fingers, he'll repeat the process with his lower extremities.
- He's getting a lot stronger and is now able to roll from his stomach to his back at will. He can also get himself from his tummy to his hands and knees. Once there, he may rock back and forth as if anxious for some kind of race to begin.
- When you pull him to a standing position, he'll try to help you out by leaning his head forward and bending at the waist. Once standing (which he can do quite well as long as you hold on), he may stamp his feet up and down.
- He's almost able to sit without support and can now pick up objects while sitting.
- His hands continue to get more coordinated. His aim is still a little iffy when he reaches for things, but he now plays with a toy in either hand and can turn his wrist (it's harder than it sounds) to get a better look at what he's picked up. He may even be able to hold on to his own bottle.
- There are now longer and more regular intervals between feedings and bowel movements.

Intellectually

- For the past four months, your baby was content to sit back and stare at objects or to have you put them in his hand. But no longer. In an attempt to actively engage in his world, he's energetically starting to reach for things. Watch carefully as he looks back and forth between an object and his hand—inching the hand slowly toward the object. That may not sound like much to you, but he's learning that objects exist that are separate from him.

- Handling and turning an object teaches your baby that even though something looks different from different angles, its shape remains the same.

- With these newfound skills, your baby will now get excited by seeing only a small part of a familiar object and will try to move small obstacles out of his way. He's also learning to anticipate the direction that objects move, and he may lean over to find a toy he's dropped instead of staring at his hand. But if the object is out of his sight for more than just a few seconds, it ceases to exist and he forgets about it.

- Amazingly, he can also make estimates about speed and distance. In one fascinating study, babies who heard a sound that appeared to come closer to them leaned back to get out of the way of what they thought was a threat.

Verbally

- It's finally happened: your baby is babbling. Besides the vowel sounds (*eee, aaa, ayy*) he's been making, he's added a few consonants (*bbb, ddd, mmm*) to the mix.

- He's found his voice's volume switch and will practice modulating his shrieks, coos, and yelps.

- Although he's still trying to imitate more of the voice sounds you make to him, the noises he produces sound nothing like actual language.

- He's so delighted with his newfound communication skills that he'll babble for twenty to thirty minutes at a stretch. Don't worry if you're not there to enjoy it—he's perfectly content to talk to his toys or, in a pinch, to himself.

- He may understand, and respond to, his name.

Emotionally/Socially

- He's capable of expressing a growing number of emotions: fear, anger, disgust, and satisfaction. He'll cry if you put him down and grow calm if you pick him up.

- He has—and readily expresses—strong preferences for toys and people, pushing away what he doesn't want. He also deliberately imitates faces and gestures.

- If he feels you're not paying enough attention to him, he'll try to interrupt whatever you're doing with a yelp or a cry. If he does start crying, you can usually stop his tears just by talking to him.

- He knows the difference between familiar people and strangers, and associates friends with pleasure.

- Unfortunately, he doesn't remember that his friends started off (to him, at least) as strangers. Consequently, he's a little slow to warm to new people. That can be tough on you if you're trying to show people what a fantastic baby you have, but it's a positive developmental sign. We'll talk more about stranger anxiety next month.
- He may spend some time trying to soothe himself—either by talking to himself or by clutching a favorite toy.

WHAT YOU'RE GOING THROUGH

A Crisis of Confidence: Worried about Doing Things Wrong

Just a few months ago, your baby didn't make very many demands, so satisfying them wasn't all that tough. But now his needs are far more complex, and at times you may feel that it's nearly impossible to react promptly and appropriately every time. And you'll be right.

With so much to respond to, it's perfectly normal to worry that you're not reading your baby's signals correctly and that you're doing everything wrong. These feelings, of course, are made worse by a baby who won't stop crying (a reflection of inadequate fathering skills?) or by a dissatisfied or seemingly hostile look on the baby's face (a reproach for some terrible mistake that you made?).

Perhaps the best way to overcome your worries is to spend more time with the baby. The more practice you get, the better you'll be at understanding the baby's "language" and the more confident you'll be in responding.

Also, learn to go with your gut feelings. There's almost always more than one solution to a given problem, and you'll undoubtedly settle on a good one. Even if you make a few mistakes, they aren't likely to have any long-term effects. After all, just because your partner burps the baby over her shoulder doesn't mean you can't (or shouldn't) do it with the baby sitting on your knees.

It's also important that you stand your ground. Many women have been raised to believe that if they aren't the primary caregiver, they've failed as mothers. In some cases, that leads the mother to act as a gatekeeper, not sharing in the parenting and actually limiting the dad's involvement to an amount she feels isn't a threat. If you're feeling left out, talk to your partner right away. Chances are she's not doing it deliberately. In fact, she may think she's "protecting" you—saving you the trouble of having to deal with a crying baby or a baby who needs to be changed. But the result is still the same: you don't get as much time with your baby to develop your own confidence (and competence).

Mom probably *wouldn't* buy us one, but you have to learn to make your own choices, Dad.

SIPRESS

So give her a little time, and show her—by being as much of a hands-on dad as you can be—that you're serious about wanting to be an equal participant and that you're ready and able to do the job. And gently remind her that you need her support. Studies by Brent McBride, director of the Child Development Laboratory at the University of Illinois, and others have shown that the more your partner supports and encourages you, verbally or behaviorally—and the less she criticizes the way you do things—the more involved you'll be. But it's the confidence she has in you that's most important.

Of course, if you're really sure you're making serious mistakes, ask for some help. But spending too much time analyzing things and worrying that you've done something wrong can get you into trouble. According to psychiatrist Stanley Greenspan, excessive worrying can destroy your self-confidence and lead to doing nothing at all or to adopting a hands-off attitude toward the baby. (That way, the twisted logic goes, at least you won't make any more mistakes.) This, of course, can have a decidedly negative effect on your baby's development—and on your development as a father.

Finally, before you toss in the towel, consider this: if you think you're having trouble reading your baby's signals, how can you be so sure that his crying and odd looks mean all the horrible, negative things you think they do?

Striking a Balance between Work and Family

Let me start with this: there's no such thing as work/family balance. What looks like perfect equilibrium today will be horribly out of whack a few weeks from now. As your children get older and other circumstances change, the percentage of your time you spend on each option will change.

As mentioned in the previous chapter (pages 127–29), most men place a high value on their family life and claim that they're willing to make sacrifices to spend more time with their children. But by six months after their children's birth, about 95 percent of new fathers are back working full-time. (At about the same time, only 37 percent of new moms are working full-time, and another 22 percent are working part-time.)

In the last chapter we talked a little about the seeming contradiction between what men say and what they do. But researcher Glen Palm found that the work/family trade-off isn't nearly so cut-and-dried. Many new fathers, Palm says, are "taking time off from friendships, recreation, and sleep to devote to their children, while they continue the time commitment to a full-time job." Clearly there's something keeping fathers from spending less time at the office. One explanation, of course, is financial. Since the average working woman makes less than the average working man, if one parent is going to take time off from work, many families conclude that they can better survive the loss of the woman's salary. Another important explanation is that in our society men and women have very different attitudes toward the relative value of career in their lives.

Basically, deep into the twenty-first century, we still expect men to be the primary breadwinners, to show their love for their families by providing for them financially. This is true even among Millennials (those born after 1980), who talk a lot about egalitarian relationships before they have kids, but adopt pretty traditional values and roles after they become parents. We'll talk more about this in the ninth month.

"To many people, 'working mother' means conflict," says author James Levine. "But 'working father' is a redundancy." Perhaps the most interesting explanation (and my favorite) for why we keep fathers tied to their jobs and away from their families is offered by anthropologist Margaret Mead: "No developing society that needs men to leave home and do 'their thing' for society ever allows young men in to handle or touch their newborns. There's always a taboo against it. For they know that if they did, the new fathers would become so 'hooked' they would never go out and do 'their thing' properly." I know exactly what she means.

Making Some Changes

Although you may never be able to resolve your work/family conflicts completely, there are a few ways you can maximize your time with your family, minimize your stress, and avoid trashing your career.

Depending on what your job is, there's a good chance that you don't really need to be cooped up in a cubicle from Monday through Friday, 9 A.M. to 5 P.M., with a manager peeking over your shoulder making sure you're doing your job. According

"It's your husband. The baby won't burp for him."

to the Society for Human Resource Management (SHRM), nearly 60 percent of employers offer some kind of flexible work arrangements (FWA)—and nearly half of those companies make those arrangements available to a majority of their employees. (That's great news, but it's still a long way from satisfying the 80–90 percent of working parents who say they want access to more flexible options.)

There are a variety of FWAs, which human resources experts Barbara Wleklinski and Elizabeth Jennings divide into several categories:

- Time: When and how long you'll work.
- Place: Where you'll be doing that work.
- Task: What, exactly, you'll be doing.

Let's take a look at these categories in a little more detail.

TIME-ORIENTED ARRANGEMENTS

- Flex time. You'll still work the same number of hours, but you might, for example, start at 5 A.M. and go home at 1 P.M. instead of the usual 9 to 5. The schedule you come up with will depend on what works for you, your employer, and your coworkers.
- Compressed work week. The basic idea is that you put in extra hours on certain days in exchange for a day off. Typical arrangements include four ten-hour days per week or working an extra hour every day for nine days and taking a day off every two weeks.
- Alternate work week. You still put in your forty hours, but you might work Wednesday through Sunday and take Mondays and Tuesdays off.

- Part-time work. Less than a typical forty-hour week but usually more than twenty hours/week. You'll need to find out how many hours you're required to work so you don't lose your benefits.
- Family Leave. You take off a chunk of paid or unpaid time.

PLACE-ORIENTED ARRANGEMENTS

- Work at home. You do your entire job from your home/home office. If you're considering this option, make sure you have good time-management skills and that you've got a relatively quiet space in your home that's conducive to getting work done. And if you have a tendency to obsess about your work (as I do), you'll have to train yourself to take frequent breaks. I can't tell you how many times I've realized—at ten o'clock at night—that I haven't eaten all day and that the only time I went outside was to take the newspaper in from the porch.
- Telecommuting. If you're not a construction worker or a retail salesman, you might be a prime candidate for this option. Now don't get too excited; it's not as if you and your boss will never see each other again. Most telecommuters are out of the office only a day or two a week. From your perspective, telecommuting is designed to give you more time with your family. But if you think you'll be able to save money on child care or have your baby sit on your lap while you crunch numbers, you're sorely mistaken.

  Besides the convenience aspect, one of the major advantages of telecommuting is that you don't have to shave and you can work in your underwear. There are, however, a few disadvantages. Primary among them is lack of human contact; you may hate that train ride into the city or the annoying guy in your carpool, but after a few months alone in your house, you might actually miss them. You might also miss going out to lunch with your coworkers or even just bumping into them in the halls.
- Telework center. You get together with another couple of people who live nearby and want more flexibility and you share a work area. Ideally, your employer would pay for it. The goal is to reduce commute times, traffic delays, and so on.
- Virtual office. You've got the tools you need to do your job from anywhere, whether that's home, your local coffee house, a public library, or the back seat of your car.

TASK-ORIENTED ARRANGEMENTS

- Job sharing. You and another person divide up the responsibilities of the job, usually at a pro-rated salary. You'd probably use the same office and desk. A typical job-share schedule might have you working two days one week and three days the next, while your workplace partner does the opposite. Or one of you might work the mornings and the other afternoons. Either way, be very careful to negotiate a continuation of your health benefits. Many employers drop them for less-than-full-time employees.

- Job splitting. You keep some, but not all, of the tasks in your job description, and offload the rest to someone else.

A FEW OTHER OPTIONS

There are two other FWAs to consider. One is gutsy but still pretty conservative, the other is just plain gutsy.

- Become a consultant to your current employer. This is a great way for you to get a lot of flexibility over your workday. There are also lots of tax advantages, particularly if you set up a home office (see more on this in the next section). At the very least, you'll be able to deduct auto mileage and a hefty percentage of your phone and utility bills. But be sure to check with an accountant first; the IRS uses certain "tests" to determine whether someone is an employee or a consultant. If, for example, you go into the office every day, have a secretary, and get company benefits, you're an employee. Also, remember that if you become a consultant, you'll lose your benefit package. So be sure to build the cost of that package (or the amount you'll have to pay to replace it) into the daily or hourly rate you negotiate with your soon-to-be-former employer.
- ROWE (Results-Only Work Environment). Basically you work whenever, wherever, and however you want—as long as you get the job done. This option can only work if your employer is incredibly flexible but also incredibly clear on what you're supposed to accomplish. At the same time, you have to be extremely organized and self-directed.

Making the Proposal

If you happen to work for one of the 40 percent of companies that don't offer FWAs, there's still hope. The number one reason (given by 68 percent of employers) why companies create FWA policies is "employee requests," according to SHRM. So this could be one of those ask-and-ye-shall-receive kinds of things. But before you march into your boss's office, you'll need to come up with a solid plan. And even if you're lucky enough to work for a company that offers FWA, you'll need a plan too. Here's what to do:

- Have some long talks with your partner about which arrangement works best for you and your family.
- Be as specific as possible about the days, times, and locations you're proposing to work as well as about how long you anticipate needing the revised schedule.

If You're an Employer (or a Supervisor)

FWAs are getting more popular, but most companies still look at them as a "women's issue," which means that they rarely consider that a lot of fathers might need the same benefits. The ultimate responsibility for changing this Neanderthal attitude and helping men get more involved with their families rests at the top—with you.

- Change your own schedule. Many of your male employees will be reluctant to approach you with proposed schedule changes because they're afraid of jeopardizing their career. So if you know someone has just become a father, raise the issue with him first. Chances are he'll be grateful.
- Make some changes. If you have enough employees, organize classes and support groups for new parents. Even if you don't have many employees, you can still offer free (or subsidized) on-site or near-site child care. You can also encourage your employees to take advantage of part-time, job-sharing, or flexible scheduling options. Overall, your company's policies should recognize that *all parents* (as opposed to just mothers) are responsible for their children's care and development.
- Don't worry about the cost. Companies with family-friendly policies find that the costs of implementing such programs are more than compensated for by increased morale and productivity, reduced absenteeism, and lower turnover. They're also a great recruiting tool.

- Get a group of people with similar concerns to approach your boss at the same time. That way, no one will be able to accuse you of asking for preferential treatment. Start by asking other dads with young kids as well as working mothers.
- Look at things from your employer's point of view. Unless you work for a non-profit, your company is in business to earn money. And to do that, your boss has to be sure that what needs to be done to keep the company thriving will actually get done. So give your employer all the details about how you'll be able to accomplish the various tasks you have, how often you'll be in touch, and how your boss and coworkers can reach you in case of emergency. The more secure your employer and coworkers feel, the more supportive they're likely to be.
- Experiment. If your employer is skeptical, suggest trying it out for a month or two. Come up with some concrete metrics that you'll both use to evaluate success or failure.
- Read "Sell the Benefits" on page 158. Make copies if you need to and hand them out to anyone you think could use an extra nudge in the right direction.

Sell the Benefits

Sure, offering flexible workplace arrangements is the right thing to do, but there are also as number of concrete, bottom-line-affecting benefits that your employer probably doesn't know about. Go ahead and enlighten 'em.

- FWAs boost productivity. Stanford University economist Nicholas Bloom found that employees who telecommute are 13.5 percent more productive than employees who go into the office. What accounts for the increase in productivity? Bloom says that one-third of the increase is attributable to the quieter environment at home. "Offices are incredibly distracting places," he says. The other two-thirds has to do with the longer hours people at home put in. They have no commute, they start earlier, take shorter breaks, and don't run errands at lunchtime.

- FWAs increase retention/reduce turnover. The telecommuters in Bloom's study quit their jobs at about half the rate of their peers in the office. Turnover is a huge expense. "The costs of hiring and training a new employee, and the slower productivity until the new employee gets up to speed in their new job," average about 20 percent of the worker's salary, according to economists Heather Boushey and Sarah Jane Glynn. For executives, the costs can exceed 200 percent of salary.

- FWAs improve recruitment. Companies find that offering FWAs helps attract top talent.

- FWAs improve employee morale and loyalty. When employees feel that their employer respects their need for flexibility, they're happier, don't take sick days when they're not sick, and are more committed to their employer's success.

- Loyal, happy employees are engaged employees—and engaged employees are profitable employees. Gallup recently analyzed data from 192 organizations in 49 industries—49,928 work units, including nearly 1.4 million employees—looking at the relationship between employee engagement and company performance. They found that companies in the top 25 percent in terms of employee engagement "outperformed those in the bottom 25 percent by 10 percent in customer ratings, 22 percent in profitability, and 21 percent in productivity." The top 25 percent also reported lower turnover rates, less employee absenteeism (37 percent), fewer safety incidents (48 percent), less shrinkage (28 percent), and fewer quality defects (41 percent). If that doesn't convince your employer, I can't imagine what would.

Putting It All Together

No matter how you try to keep your work life separate from your family life, there's going to be plenty of spillover between the two. This isn't necessarily a bad thing. In his four-decade-long study of fathers, John Snarey found that, "contrary to the stereotype of rigid work-family trade-off, a positive, reciprocal interaction may exist between childrearing and bread-winning."

Other researchers have come to similar conclusions. "Before they became fathers, men did not appear to be conscious that home and work life often require different personal qualities," writes research psychologist Phil Cowan. After becoming fathers, however, many men "described new abilities to juggle conflicting demands, make decisions, and communicate quickly and clearly both at home and at work. . . . Some described themselves as more aware of their personal relationships on the job, and more able to use some of their managerial skills in the solution of family problems."

YOU AND YOUR FAMILY

Caught between Two Families

Integrating your old and new families can be enormously complicated—for your kids, your new partner, and you. Many older children feel somewhat abandoned and jealous when a younger sibling comes along. But if they aren't living with you full-time, these feelings may get kicked to an even higher level when you start a new family. They may feel that your loyalty and your love (and sometimes your money) will be spent on your new baby, the one who's with you all the time, and they may resent having to share those things with anyone. They may also see how much more involved you are with their new half sibling and resent that you weren't that way with them. (This may or may not reflect reality, but your kids' feelings are just as real either way.)

Children of divorce almost always harbor a secret (or not-so-secret) hope that their parents will get back together. But your having a new family with a woman who's not their mother may make them confront their dashed hopes. At the same time, your new family may disrupt your older children's loyalties. On the one hand, they'll continue (as they should) to feel deeply loyal to their mother. On the other hand, they might feel a naturally growing allegiance to the baby and to their stepmother. But as those newer relationships deepen, the children may feel guilty that they're abandoning their mother—as if in allowing themselves to be part of a new family, they have to stop loving her. This can sometimes make them lash out at you, the baby, and/or your partner. In their minds, if it weren't for all the changes that have been forced on them, life would be great—or at least not any worse than it was before.

This is almost exactly what happened with me. My two older kids were with me half the time, and we've always had a very close relationship. That's a wonderful thing for the three of us, but it sometimes made my youngest's mother feel excluded, as though she had me only 50 percent of the time. And she naturally worried about whether I would have time (and love) enough for her and the child we had together.

As tough as your renewed fatherhood status is for your children and your partner, it's no less difficult for you. The nice, linear progression of your development as a father has been derailed. Usually, you get married, have kids, the kids grow up and get married, and they have kids of their own and make you a grandfather. But if you're a renewed dad, you'll need to be in two emotional places at the same time. You're still on your original track with your older children, but you're also starting the process all over again with your new family.

Sometimes it's easy—and fun—to be on both tracks. Having been through it before will probably make the early stages of fatherhood less stressful and more relaxing. Other times, however, you'll feel as though your two tracks are on a collision course with each other. As I discussed earlier, your new partner may interpret your laid-back attitude as a lack of interest or excitement. But the more time you spend with your new family, the more abandoned and resentful your older kids may feel, jealous of the things they never got. You might feel guilty, too, about not having been a better dad the first time around. But the more time you spend with your older children, the more your new family will feel excluded.

The good news is that you get to do something most humans wish for but never have a chance to do: go back (kind of) and do things differently. Your challenge is to figure out how to juggle the often conflicting needs of your two families in a way that works for everyone (including you), and to create a new family unit that integrates your older children, your new child, and your partner. Notice that I'm not saying to make the older kids part of your new family or to make the new family part of the old one. Either of those approaches will make one group or the other feel second best. Instead, both groups have to understand that they're part of something bigger and that your loyalties are not divided but are spread out evenly.

It's not always going to be easy, but whatever you do, *never* give in to pressure or temptation to sever ties with your older children. They need you, and you need them, even if you don't get to see each other as often as you'd like.

YOU AND YOUR BABY

Jealous, Empathetic, with a Head for Numbers?
Yep, That's Your Baby

Older siblings aren't the only children who get jealous. There's actually some indication that babies as young as five months may too. Sound crazy? Well, consider this: British researcher Riccardo Draghi-Lorenz asked twenty-four mothers of five-month-old babies to show affection to another baby or to talk with another adult while their baby watched. The results weren't pretty: over half of the babies got upset and cried when Mom cooed or tickled or cuddled with another infant. But when the mothers were schmoozing with adults, only 10 percent of the babies cried. (This bit of information probably isn't going to do much to change your behavior. But if you're in a situation where you're likely to be interacting with your baby's tiny peers, just be aware of how he might react.)

Jealousy isn't the only sophisticated emotion your baby has. You've probably already discovered that your moods and actions can affect your baby's. When you smile and sound excited, he'll try to do the same. If you're angry or sad, your baby will cry more. British researcher Elena Geangu took this concept a bit further and found that when babies hear a recording of another baby crying in pain or distress, they start crying themselves. But they don't cry when hearing recordings of an older child or a monkey crying—and yes, monkeys can and do cry when they're distressed.

Yale researcher Paul Bloom had five- and six-month-old babies watch several short puppet shows. In one, a dog is trying to open a box. He's joined by two teddy bears—one helps the dog lift the lid of the box, the other is annoying and sits on the box. In another show, babies watched a puppet cat play ball with two rabbits. When the cat rolled the ball to one of the rabbits, it rolled the ball right back. The other rabbit snatched up the ball and took off with it. After watching these puppet shows a few times, the babies were given a chance to choose a character (one of the teddy bears or one of the rabbits). About 80 percent of the time, the babies picked the "good" guys.

Now, about the math. Researcher Karen Wynn (who is married to Bloom) put five-month-old babies in front of a stage. (Doesn't it seem like babies spend an awful lot of time at the theater? Makes me a little jealous.) The researchers then—in full view of the baby—put a Mickey Mouse doll behind the curtain, followed by another Mickey a few seconds later. When the curtain opened, the babies expected to see two Mickeys. But if there was one or three, they stared at the stage longer than when there were two, and had a very surprised look on their face.

Time for Solids

When I was a baby, the current wisdom about introducing solid foods was to do it as early as possible, often as soon as five or six weeks. One of the explanations was that babies who ate solid foods supposedly slept longer than those on bottles (almost no one was being breastfed then). Today, people are more interested in the baby's health than in whether he sleeps through the night (which eating solid food doesn't affect anyway), and most pediatricians now recommend that you delay introducing solids until your baby is six months old if he's being breastfed; possibly as soon as four months if he's bottle-fed. The recommended delay may be even longer if you or your partner has a history of food allergies (for more on that, see pages 164–65).

Even if you're tempted to start solids earlier than four to six months, resist. Here's why waiting a little longer is a good idea:

- It may protect against illness. Introducing solid foods before sixteen weeks has been linked to weight problems throughout life.
- Babies who are breastfed for four months and then put on solid food have four times the risk of developing respiratory illness (such as pneumonia and asthma) and twice the risk of developing ear infections as babies who nurse for six months.
- If you, your partner, or an older child has Type 1 diabetes (sometimes called juvenile diabetes), timing is especially important. Two very recent studies found that at-risk babies who first ate cereals or other foods containing gluten before four months or after seven months had a far higher risk of developing diabetes than babies who started on solids within the traditional four-to-six-month window.
- Because younger babies' digestive systems are immature, they can't break down proteins, starches, or fats until they're at least six months old. Before then, solid foods—along with their nutrients—pass undigested through their systems.
- If the baby isn't ready, he may choke on the food.
- Feeding solids may fill up the baby and make him drink less formula or breast milk, which could deprive him of the calories and nutrients he needs.
- It can reduce the likelihood of the baby developing allergies later on.
- Breast- and bottle-feeding are a great opportunity for parents to cuddle with their babies, although it's nearly impossible for you to cuddle the baby while your partner is breastfeeding.
- With breasts, there's nothing to clean up; with bottles, only the bottle. But with solids, you have to wash spoons, dishes, high-chair trays, bibs, and perhaps even the floor and nearby walls.

If your baby was born prematurely, check with your pediatrician before introducing solids. You'll still probably start when his *adjusted* age (see pages 90–91) is six months. (If he's five months old now and was born six weeks early, his adjusted age, for food introduction purposes, is only three and a half months.

Here's how you can tell if your baby is really ready for solids:

- His weight has doubled since birth (indicating that he's getting plenty of nutrition).
- He's very underweight for his age (indicating that he's not getting enough nutrition).
- He's drinking more than a quart (32 ounces) of formula or breast milk per day.
- He chews on nipples (either your partner's or the bottle's) while sucking.
- He stares intently at you, smacks his lips, or drools when you're eating, or may try to snatch food from your plate.
- He can sit by himself or with support and has good head control.

Remember, introducing solids does not mean that breast- or bottle-feeding will end (see pages 278–82 for information on weaning). In fact, most of your baby's nutrients will still come from milk or formula for a few more months.

Getting Started

Getting your baby to eat solid foods isn't going to happen overnight. For starters, most of what he's had in his mouth thus far has come out again looking pretty much like it did when it went in. Now a full spoon is going in and an empty one is coming out. Second, he'll probably take a few days to get used to the strange new taste and texture. Then he's got to figure out how to move it from the front of his mouth to his throat, where he can swallow it (liquids kind of know where to go by themselves). Here's the way to do it:

- Offer new foods at a time when the baby isn't too tired, too fussy, or too hungry.
- Set aside a lot of time. It could take you ten or fifteen minutes to work your way through a single teaspoon of food.
- Make sure your baby is properly strapped into a high chair; you don't want to do this on your lap. Also, put a bib on the baby unless you enjoy doing laundry.
- Your baby's first food should be an iron-fortified, single-grain cereal (no, not Cheerios)—rice, oatmeal, or barley. For the first few days, add breast milk or formula—but not cow's milk—to make the cereal especially liquidy. Thicken it up as your baby gets used to it by adding a little less milk.

Allergies and Intolerances:
What They Are and How to Prevent Them

Despite the claims of about 25 percent of American parents, fewer than 5 percent of children under three are truly allergic to any foods. True allergies are abnormal responses by the immune system to ingested proteins. The most common symptoms are nasal congestion, asthma, skin rashes (eczema and hives), chronic runny nose or cough, vomiting, and severe mood swings. In contrast, symptoms such as headaches, excess gas, diarrhea, or constipation are generally caused by *intolerances*, which are usually the result of an enzyme deficiency.

While you may be tempted to say, "What's the difference? A reaction is a reaction," the distinction between an allergy and an intolerance is critical and subtle. Allergies often begin in infancy and get progressively worse with each encounter with the offending food. Intolerances don't. Fortunately, most kids—except those allergic to peanuts and fish—outgrow their allergies altogether by age five. (Only about 2 percent of children over five have true food allergies.)

The consensus among pediatricians is that the way to deal with allergies and intolerances is to prevent them before they happen. Complete prevention, of course, is impossible. But here are a few things you can do to better the odds:

• Breastfeed your baby and withhold solid foods for at least four to six months.

• Watch out for constipation. Most parents start their babies on rice cereal, and most of those babies immediately get constipated. If this happens, stop the rice and start the baby on mashed fruit until the problem resolves itself. (The best fruits for this purpose start with the letter *p* for "poop": Pears, Prunes, Peaches, Plums, and (a)Pricots. Once the baby's intestines are flowing again, reduce the fruit and add back some cereal (stay away from rice this time). Adjust the mix as needed to keep the baby regular.

• Use a plastic-coated spoon to serve. He'll probably spend some time chewing on it, and regular metal utensils are hard on gums. And be sure to have a washable toy that the baby can play with while you're feeding him. In a few years you're not going to want him to play around while he's eating. But for now, if his hands are busy with a toy, they won't be trying to grab the spoon out of your hand.

• Do *not* try to feed your baby solid foods through a bottle with an enlarged hole in the nipple. (Don't laugh—people do it all the time.) The object is to get the baby to eat with a spoon.

- If your partner has a history of true allergies, she should reduce or completely eliminate high-risk foods (see page 166) while breastfeeding.
- Introduce only one new food at a time. That way, if your baby has a reaction, you'll know right away what caused it.
- After introducing a new food, wait three to five days before introducing another.
- If your baby has any of the negative reactions mentioned above, eliminate the food right away and call your pediatrician. He will probably tell you to take the baby off the food and reintroduce it in six months. By then, your baby may have built up the necessary defenses.
- If you have *no* family history of allergies, talk to your pediatrician about when to introduce highly allergenic foods such as cow's milk, egg whites, fish, nuts, shellfish, and wheat. Conventional wisdom used to be to hold off on introducing those foods until the baby was at least a year old. According to the American Academy of Allergy, Asthma, and Immunology, however, holding off on giving your baby allergenic foods may actually *increase* his risk of developing a food allergy or eczema later. But before give your baby anything other than a breast or a bottle, ask the doc.

- Never force the baby to eat. If he turns his head away, refuses to open his mouth, or spits out whatever you've given him, it's time for a break.
- Three days after you actually manage to get some cereal down the baby's throat, add vegetables—one at a time, three to five days apart. Make sure the baby gets a good mix of yellow (carrots, squash) and green (peas, spinach, zucchini) veggies. Many people prefer to make bananas baby's first noncereal food. The problem with bananas is that they are fairly sweet, and babies may become so fond of them that they won't be interested in any other foods you may introduce later. Plus, like rice, bananas are constipating.
- After a week or so on vegetables, introduce noncitrus fruits (again, one at a time, three to five days apart). Until he's a year old, your baby can't digest raw apples, but unsweetened applesauce is okay. Hold off on the oranges for a few more months (the citric acid can cause painful diaper rash).
- No juice (see page 45 for why). However, if you have no choice, be sure to dilute it at least fifty-fifty with water.

MOST PROBLEMATIC FOODS (AND WHY)	OKAY TO INTRODUCE AT . . .	LEAST PROBLEMATIC FOODS
• Honey (may contain parasites)	8–12 months	• Rice
• Egg whites (allergen)	1 year (the rest of the egg, 7–10 months)	• Oats • Barley • Carrots
• Wheat and yeast (allergen)	6–12 months	• Squash • Apricots
• Cow's milk and other dairy products (allergen)	12 months (low fat: 2 years)	• Peaches • Pears
• Fish (mercury level in mackerel, swordfish, and tuna + choking hazard from bones)	6–12 months	• Apples • Lamb • Veal
• Pecans, walnuts, and other tree nuts (allergen)	Check with pediatrician	
• Shellfish (possible allergic reaction)	1 year (2 if there's a family history of fish allergies)	
• Peanuts and soy beans (allergen + choking risk, especially peanut butter)	Check with pediatrician	
• Beets, spinach, lettuce, radishes, and other root veggies (high in nitrates)	12 months (or go organic)	
• Citrus fruits (acidic, hard to digest)	6–12 months	
• Berries, except cranberries and blueberries (hard to digest)	6–12 months	
• Tomatoes (acidic, hard to digest)	6–12 months	
• Chocolate (caffeine + hard to digest)	12 months	
• Juice (sugar + too filling)	Never, if at all possible	
• Hot dogs, raw carrots (choking hazard)	12 months	
• Grapes (choking hazard)	12 months	
• Popcorn, hard candy, olives (choking hazard)	12 months	

- Don't add sugar or salt to any foods. Your baby doesn't need either one.
- Try not to feed the baby right out of the jar unless he's going to eat the whole thing. The bacteria in his mouth can contaminate what's left.
- When your baby is about seven months old, introduce yogurt. It's an important source of protein and can easily be mixed with other foods. Although most babies like yogurt, none of mine did, and we had to trick them into eating it by putting a blueberry (always a favorite food) at the back of the spoon.
- Breads and cereals (yes, Cheerios are okay now) are next, followed by shredded meats if you want.
- At about nine months, introduce some mushy finger foods.
- At about one year, your baby can eat almost any kind of food, but in small pieces. Some foods, such as grapes, raw carrots, nuts, and hot dogs, can still present choking hazards.
- One big warning: do not give your baby honey or corn sweeteners for at least the first year. They often contain tiny parasites that an adult's digestive system exterminates with no problem. But the baby's still-immature system won't be able to handle the chore.

I Wanna Do It Myself

When your baby is ready to feed himself, he'll let you know, usually by grabbing the spoon from your hand (babies are quicker than you'd think) or mushing around anything that's dropped onto the high-chair tray. When this happens, prepare yourself; over the course of the next few weeks, your baby will discover the joys of sticking various kinds of food in his nose and eyes, under his chin, behind his ears, and in his hair. And it won't be much longer until he learns to throw.

One way to minimize the mess is to put a large piece of plastic under the high chair; a large trash bag cut open along the side is good. But don't relax yet; your baby will soon learn to use his spoon as a catapult to launch food beyond this protective boundary. There's really nothing you can do about this, so keep the high chair far away from your carpets and avoid wearing your best clothes while the baby is eating. You might also want to consider feeding the baby while he's wearing only a diaper. He's going to need a shower after almost every meal anyway, so you might as well save yourself the trouble of having to wash his clothes too.

Making vs. Buying

Jarred food is convenient but can be expensive—especially if you're going with one of the organic brands. A cheaper but less convenient alternative is to make your own. It's easy, really. After all, the major ingredient of most baby food is cooked vegetables. You can even do it in bulk. All you have to do is boil some

Three Small Warnings

1. When you begin giving your baby solids, he's going to make an incredible array of faces: horror, disgust, fear, betrayal. Try not to take them personally—he's just reacting to the new and unknown and not criticizing your cooking.

2. Don't make a ton of food the first few times. You'll probably end up feeding the baby the same spoonful over and over again (you put some in his mouth, he spits it out; you scrape it off his cheek and put it in his mouth again . . .). This can be frustrating, but try to remember what comedian Dave Barry once said: "Babies do not take solid food through their mouths. . . . Babies absorb solid food through their chins. You can save yourself a lot of frustrating effort if you smear the food directly on your baby's chin, rather than putting it in the baby's mouth and forcing the baby to expel it on to its chin, as so many uninformed parents do." The solution: be patient and keep your camera ready at all times.

3. Be prepared for some Technicolor diaper contents. Babies are kind of like horses—whatever comes out their butts tends to look pretty much the same as what went in. I remember when my first baby was about six months old and I was feeding her mashed pumpkin (it was close to Thanksgiving and I had some left over from pie making). We did the usual I-put-it-in-her-mouth-and-she-spits-it-out routine. And I, like any loving father, dutifully scraped it up with my finger and ate it. When our "meal" was over, and I was taking my daughter out of the high chair, I noticed a glob of pumpkin on the inside of her leg. So, naturally, I scooped it up and popped it into my mouth. Unfortunately, it wasn't actually pumpkin. To this day, I'm still a little skittish around orange-colored pies . . .

vegetables, blend or mash them up, and pour them into an ice-cube tray. Whenever you need to, just pop out a cube, thaw, and serve. If you're really committed to making your own food, you may want to pick up a food mill.

Even though making your own sounds like a much healthier way to feed your baby, jarred food may be better, largely because it doesn't taste as good. Here's what I mean: jarred baby food used to be filled with preservatives, chemicals, dyes, salt, and other nasty stuff. But manufacturers have cleaned up their act, and jars are filled with an additive-free, mashed version of whatever's on the label (besides the picture of the baby). It's also usually very bland, at least to the adult palate.

When you make your own baby food, though, it's so tempting to toss in a little olive oil, a few spices, butter, and all sorts of other things to make it taste better. That's great—if *you're* planning to eat it. But what your baby needs right now (and that's what it's all about, right?) is bland. Seasonings, especially salt, aren't good for him. So save the curries and butter and sugar until he's a little older. Of course, if you plan to eat your baby's leftovers, season them up as much as you want—after he's finished.

A word of caution: microwaves heat food unevenly, leaving hot spots right next to cold ones. So if you're using a microwave, make sure you stir well and test anything you're planning to give the baby.

6 MONTHS Gaining Confidence

WHAT'S GOING ON WITH THE BABY

Physically

- By the end of this month she'll probably be able to sit by herself in "tripod position" (feet splayed, hands on the floor in between for balance). She may even be able to right herself if she tips over and pull herself to a sitting position if you grasp her hands.
- She can turn herself from back to front or front to back at will, and may even be able to propel herself short distances (usually backward at first) by creeping or wiggling. Be prepared, though: she'll be demonstrating a lot of these new moves when you're trying to change or dress her.
- She can probably get herself to her hands and knees and will spend hours rocking back and forth, picking up an arm here, a leg there—all in preparation for crawling.
- She can clap her hands and bang two objects together. And whatever isn't being banged is sure to be in her mouth.
- She can now look at one thing and reach for another and can probably pass objects back and forth between her hands.

Intellectually

- With so many new things to do and learn, your baby is now awake about twelve hours a day and spends most of that time finding out about her environment by touching, holding, tasting, and shaking things.
- Your baby recognizes her name and, if she's not too busy, may turn her head toward you if you call her.

- The idea that she is separate from other people and other objects is slowly sinking in. But she still thinks she has absolute control over all she sees or touches. As if to rub it in, she'll endlessly drop toys, dishes, and food from her high chair and revel in the way she can make you pick them up.
- Another way your baby demonstrates her complete power over the world and everything in it (especially you) is to cry for attention whether she needs any or not. Both these activities show that your baby is able to formulate plans and can anticipate the consequences of her actions.
- She's developing a solid sense of the way things should be. For example, she loves to look at drawings of faces, but if you turn the drawing upside down or mix up the features, she'll get very confused. She'll also get confused if she sees a picture of you but hears someone else's voice.

Verbally

- She's now more regularly adding consonants to vowels and creating single-syllable "words" such as *ba, ma, la, ka, pa*.
- She's getting pretty good at imitating sounds and also tries—with some success—to imitate your inflections.
- She's getting so familiar with language that she can easily tell the difference between conversational speech and any of the other noises you make. She might, for example, laugh when you start making animal noises. And she definitely prefers listening to her native language over a foreign one.
- She's also learning to like other sounds; music in particular will cause her to stop what she's doing and listen.

Emotionally/Socially

- Until this month, your baby really didn't care who fed her, changed her, played with her, or hugged her, just as long as it got done. But now, for about 50–80 percent of babies, who satisfies their needs is almost as important. You, your partner, and perhaps a few other very familiar people may now be the only ones your baby will allow near her without crying. This is the beginning of *stranger anxiety*.
- She's still very social and will smile at everyone (as long as you're nearby). She even smiles and laughs when looking at that "other" baby in the mirror.
- She'll wave her arms to let you know to pick her up, cling to you when you do, and cry if you take away a toy or stop playing with her.
- Despite all this, she's still incredibly curious in new situations, and will spend as much as ninety minutes taking in her surroundings.

- Her range of emotions is getting broader. She can, for example, express real anger if you do something she doesn't like, such as try to put her in a car seat or stroller or down for a nap.

WHAT YOU'RE GOING THROUGH

Growing Up

There's nothing quite like having a kid to make you realize that you're a grown-up. It also makes you realize that besides being a son, you're also a father. That may sound painfully obvious, but you'd be surprised at how many men have a hard time with the concept. After all, we've spent our whole lives looking at our fathers as fathers and at ourselves as sons.

Here's how a friend of mine described becoming aware that he had made the transition: "One day I slipped my arm into the sleeve of my jacket and my father's hand came out the other side." You'll know it's happened to you when you use a phrase that your father used but that you haven't heard for twenty years. Or when you suddenly find yourself doing or saying one of the dozens of things your dad did that you swore you'd never do when you became a parent. Don't be embarrassed; it happens to all of us.

Feeling Like a Father

Most men (and women) see the father's role as that of a teacher of values and skills. Besides being a little limiting, there's really nothing wrong with that attitude—except that it puts dads with infants in a tough spot. Teaching requires communicating and interacting, which is hard to do when the student is a baby who's completely helpless and essentially nonresponsive. The result is that since they can't teach, a lot of new dads don't feel particularly fatherly.

But by the time your baby is six months old, she's no longer unable to communicate. She turns her head when you call her, she gets excited when you walk into the room. And when you wrestle with her, build a tower together, or tickle her, she'll give you a smile that could melt steel—a smile that's only for you. Your baby's reactions and "praise" may not seem like much, but whether you realize it or not, they're making you feel confident that she needs you and that you're playing an important and influential role in her young life. You're finally starting to feel like a father now; and the more you and your baby interact, the more you'll feel that way.

Jealousy

"The single emotion that can be the most destructive and disruptive to your experience of fatherhood is jealousy," writes Dr. Martin Greenberg in *The Birth of a Father*.

There's certainly plenty to be jealous about, but the real question is: Whom (or what) are you jealous of? Your partner, for her close relationship with the baby and the extra time she gets to spend with her? The baby, for taking up more than her "fair share" of your partner's attention and for getting to spend more time with her breasts than you do? The babysitter, for being the recipient of the baby's daytime smiles and love—tokens of affection you'd rather were directed at you? Or maybe it's the baby's carefree life and freedom from responsibility. The answer, of course, is: all of the above.

Like most emotions, a little jealousy goes a long way. Too much can make you feel competitive toward or resentful of your partner, the babysitter, even the baby. Do you feel you need more attention or emotional support from your partner? Do you need more private time with the baby? Whatever or whomever you're jealous of, it's critical to express your feelings clearly and honestly and to encourage your partner to do the same. If for some reason you feel you can't discuss your feelings on this issue with your partner, take them up with a male friend or relative. You'll be surprised at how common jealousy is. Jealousy's "potential for destruction," writes Greenberg, "lies not in having the feelings but in burying them."

Gaining Confidence

I don't remember every day of my children's childhoods, but there's one day in particular—when my oldest daughter was about six months old—that I recall quite clearly.

It really wasn't all that different from any other day. I gave her a bottle and dressed her. When she threw up all over her clothes, I dressed her again. Five minutes later she had an explosive bowel movement that oozed all the way up to her neck, so I cleaned her up and dressed her for the third time. Over the course of the day I probably changed five more diapers and two more outfits, gave her three bottles, calmed her from crying four times, took her in and out of the car eight times as I drove all over town doing errands, put her down for two successful naps, during which I managed to do a few loads of laundry and wash the dishes. I even managed to get some writing done.

All in all, it wouldn't have been a very memorable day if it weren't for what happened at the end of it. As I sat in bed reading, I remember thinking to myself, "Damn, I'm really getting a pretty good handle on this dad stuff." The truth is that I was. And by now, you probably are too. Things that would have had you panicking a few months ago now seem completely ordinary. You've learned to understand your baby's cues, you can predict the unpredictable, and those feelings of not being able to do things right are nearly gone. You probably feel more connected and attached to your baby than ever before. The feeling is one of confidence and stability, and signals that you've entered what some sociologists and psychologists refer to as the "honeymoon period" with your baby.

The calmness and smoothness of this period can (but doesn't always) spill over into your relationship with your partner as well. It's a time when a lot of men say that things have gotten "easier," and that they feel a sense of truly being a family. I'll talk more about your relationship with your partner on pages 283–84.

YOU AND YOUR BABY

Playing Around

As your baby develops her reaching, grabbing, and shoving-things-into-her-mouth skills, she'll gradually lose interest in face-to-face play and become more focused on the objects around her (or at least the ones she can reach) and on exploring her environment.

The first, and perhaps most important, lesson your baby will learn about objects is that she can, to a certain extent, control them (unless they happen to be cats; then she's out of luck). Of course, this startling epiphany comes about as a complete accident: you put a rattle in her hand, and after swinging her arms around for a while, she'll notice that the rattle makes some noise. But over the course of several months, your baby will learn that when she stops flailing, the rattle stops rattling and that she can—just because she wants to—get it to rattle again, and again, and again.

Your baby will learn quite a bit about objects all by herself. But if you're interested, there are a number of games you can play with her that, besides being fun, will encourage object awareness and perception. That said, spending time with your little one is more important than having a list of activities. So feel free to make up your own as you go.

REACHING GAMES

To encourage your baby to reach and to expand her horizons, try holding attractive toys just out of her reach: above her head, in front of her, to the sides. See how close you have to get the toy before she makes her move. Remember, the object here is not to tease or torture the baby, it's to have fun. You can add another layer of complexity by putting the out-of-reach object on a blanket or towel. Then slowly pull the blanket and show her how it gets closer. Will she try that herself?

TOUCHING GAMES

Try this: let your baby play with a small toy without letting her see it (you could do this in the dark or with her hands in a paper bag). Then put that toy together with several other toys she's never played with. Many babies this age will pick up the familiar toy. Although this may sound fairly easy, it isn't. You're asking your baby to use two senses—touch and vision—at the same time, and to recognize by sight something she's touched but not seen. If your baby isn't ready for this one, don't worry. Just try it again in a few weeks. It's a concept that can take a while to develop.

IF . . . THEN . . . GAMES

There are thousands of things you can do to reinforce cause-and-effect thinking. Rattles, banging games, rolling a ball back and forth, and splashing in the pool are excellent. So is blowing up your cheeks and having the baby "pop" them with her hands. Baby gyms—especially the kind that make a lot of noise when smacked—are also good, but be sure to pack them up the moment your baby starts trying to use the gym to pull herself up; they're meant to be used while sitting or lying down and aren't sturdy enough to support much weight.

OBJECT PERMANENCE GAMES

When your baby is about six or seven months old, the all-important idea that objects can exist even when they're out of sight finally starts sinking in.

GOOD TOYS	BAD TOYS
• Blocks	• Anything made of foam—it's too easy to chew off pieces
• Dolls with easy-to-grasp limbs	• Anything tempting enough to swallow, having detachable parts, or small enough to fit through a toilet paper tube
• Real things: phones, computer keyboards, shoes, and so on	• Anything that could possibly pinch the baby
• Toys that make different sounds and have different textures	• Anything that runs on electricity
	• Stuffed animals and other furry things that might shed (stuffed animals that don't shed are fine)
• Musical toys	• Toys with strings, ribbons, elastic—all potential choking hazards
• Balls	• Walkers (possibly—see page 200)
• Sturdy books	

- Object permanence develops in stages. If you're interested in seeing how, try this: Show your baby a toy. Then, while she's watching, "hide" it under a pillow. If you ask her where the toy is, she'll probably push the pillow out of the way and "find" it. But if you quickly move the toy to another hiding place when she's not looking, she'll continue to look for it in the first hiding place.
- Peek-a-boo and other games that involve hiding and finding things are great for developing object permanence. Peek-a-boo in particular teaches your baby an excellent lesson: when you go away, you always come back. This doesn't sound like much, but making this connection now lets her know she can count on you to be there when she needs you and will help her better cope with separation anxiety (see page 222).

TRACKING GAMES

Hold an object in front of the baby. When you're sure she's seen it, let it drop out of your hand. At five or six months, most babies won't follow the object down. But starting at about seven months, they'll begin to anticipate where things are going to land. When your baby has more or less mastered this skill, add an additional complication: drop a few objects and let her track them down. Then hold a helium balloon in front of her and let it go. She'll look down and be rather stunned that the balloon never lands. She'll also give you a priceless look of betrayal—as though you cheated by defying the laws of physics. Let her hold the string of the balloon and experiment.

Another great game involves your baby's newly developed abilities to track moving objects even when they're out of sight part of the time. Put your baby in a high chair and sit down at a table facing her. Slowly move a toy horizontally in front of her a few times. Then put a cereal box between you and the baby and move the ball along the same trajectory but have it go behind the box for a second or two. Most six-month-olds will look ahead to the other side of the box, anticipating where the ball will emerge. If your baby's still having fun, try it again, but this time, instead of keeping the ball on the same path, make a 90-degree turn and bring the ball out from the top of the box.

You can do the same kind of thing during games of peek-a-boo. Step behind a door so the baby can't see you. Then open the door a little and poke your head out. Do that in the same place a few times and then higher or lower than where she was expecting to see you. Most babies find this endlessly amusing.

Give the Kid a Break

Don't feel that you have to entertain your baby all the time. Sure it's fun, but letting her have some time to play by herself is almost as important to her development as playing with her yourself. And don't worry; letting her play alone—as long as you're close enough to hear what she's doing and to respond quickly if she needs you—doesn't mean you're being neglectful. Quite the opposite, in fact. By giving her the opportunity to make up her own games or to practice on her own the things she does with you, you're helping her learn that she's capable of satisfying at least some of her needs by herself. You're also helping her build her sense of self-confidence by allowing her to decide for herself what she'll play with and for how long.

Again, if your baby doesn't respond to some, or any, of these activities, don't worry. Babies develop at very different rates, and what's "normal" for your baby may be advanced—or delayed—for your neighbor's. And keep in mind that you don't need to spend a lot of money on fancy toys. When my oldest daughter was about this age, one of her favorite toys was a plastic dish-scrubbing pad. And I remember taking her to FAO Schwartz in New York—zillions of fantastic toys everywhere—and thinking that she was going to want to play with everything. But all she wanted to do was play with the price tags. (She's a teenager now, and I look back at that experience as a warning—she still spends an awful lot of time looking at price tags . . .)

YOU AND YOUR PARTNER

Overcoming Tension

As I mentioned earlier, this is a time when a lot of new parents start feeling a little less strain in their relationship and a lot more like a family. Of course, this isn't true for every couple; some are still feeling a lot of tension, which can sometimes translate into lack of satisfaction with the relationship (we'll talk more about this on pages 283–84). If you're feeling this way, wake up.

As it turns out, men's satisfaction with their relationships is a major factor in determining how involved they are with their children. The more satisfying the relationship, the more involved and happy you'll be in your fathering role. But the more unhappy and volatile your relationship, the less involved you'll be, and the lower the quality of that involvement.

Oh, and in case you thought you could keep the quality of your marriage a secret from your baby, forget it. Eleven-month-olds, for example, are less likely to look to their fathers for help in novel situations (such as seeing an unfamiliar person) when their fathers are in distressed marriages.

FAMILY MATTERS

Finding Quality Child Care

Most parents instinctively feel (and there's plenty of research to back them up) that to have one or both of them care for their baby in their own home would, in a perfect world, be the best child-care option. But most couples can't afford the traditional dad-goes-to-work-while-mom-stays-at-home option or the less-traditional mom-goes-to-work-while-dad-stays-at-home scenario. So chances are that, sooner or later, you'll need to consider some form of daycare for your child. Here are some of the options and their advantages and disadvantages.

CARE IN YOUR HOME (NANNIES AND BABYSITTERS)

In-home care (your home) is probably the most convenient option for parents. You don't have to worry about daycare schedules, and your baby can stay in a familiar environment. In addition, your baby will get plenty of one-on-one attention, and because she remains at home, she'll be less exposed to germs and illness.

Leaving your child alone with a stranger can be daunting and traumatic, especially the first time. On the one hand, you might be worried about whether you really know (and can trust) the caregiver. You might also be worried—as I was—that no one will be able to love or care for your child as well as you and your partner. On the other hand, you might experience what psychologist Lawrence Kutner calls the "natural rivalry" between parents and caregivers. "As parents, we want our children to feel close (but not too close) to the other adults in their lives," he writes. "We worry that, if those attachments are too strong, they will replace us in our child's eyes." Fortunately, no one will ever be able to replace you—or your love. But there are many wonderful caregivers out there who can give your baby the next best thing.

If you do go this route, I'd strongly suggest that you have the caregiver keep a log of the basic goings-on in your baby's life: naps (when and how long), feedings (including how much), diaper changes (when, how many, contents), and overall behavior. This may sound incredibly anal, but it's actually quite helpful. It's especially important, for example, to know if the baby's gone a few days without filling a diaper, isn't napping, or is gradually losing interest in food. Having a written record of these things can help you track them over time. In the unlikely event that something is wrong, being able to tell your pediatrician what's been going on will help him diagnose the problem.

If you're an old-school kind of guy, you can keep your own log on a pad of paper—just make columns for each of the things you want to keep track of and write the time in hour increments down the side. Otherwise, there are tons of baby-tracker apps that will get the job done.

HOW TO FIND A NANNY OR BABYSITTER
The best ways to find someone to care for your baby in your home are:
- Word of mouth
- Agencies that screen candidates for experience, training, and references, and may run a basic background check
- Listing services (www.SitterCity.com and www.Care.com)

To Put Your Mind at Ease—Sort Of

Finding the perfect daycare situation for your baby is a big job, and you and your partner need to take it seriously. Of course, it isn't made any easier by the stories you hear all the time about babysitters or daycare providers who were caught beating or abusing the children they were supposed to have been caring for. It's enough to scare the hell out of anyone.

Even though those kinds of incidents are fairly rare, you're still going to want to eliminate as much of the risk as possible. Here are a few ways you can do this:

- Hire people you know and trust. If you have good friends or relatives who rave about the daycare center or nanny or babysitter they've entrusted their children to, take that into consideration. But you should still meet with the person (or check out the center) to make sure that the fit is right for your baby and your family.
- Only consider licensed facilities. Anyone working at a state-licensed facility should have gone through a background investigation. You'll need to check with your state's licensing agency to verify that the facility is licensed and to get an idea of how thorough the screening process is. See the Resources appendix for more.
- If you're hiring an individual, go through an agency. Many—but not all—

The first thing to do is to conduct thorough interviews over the phone—this will enable you to screen out the obviously unacceptable candidates (for example, the ones who are only looking for a month-long job or those who don't drive if you need a driver). Then invite the ones who make the first cut over to meet with you, your partner, and the baby in person. Make sure the baby and the prospective caregiver spend a few minutes together, and pay close attention to how they interact. Someone who approaches your baby cautiously and speaks to her reassuringly before picking her up is someone who understands and cares about your baby's feelings. And someone who strokes your baby's hair and strikes up a "conversation" is a far better choice than a person who sits rigidly with your baby on her knee.

Another good "test" for potential caregivers is to have them change your baby's diapers. Does the applicant smile or sing or try some other way to make getting changed interesting and fun for the baby, or does she seem disgusted by the whole thing? And be sure that she washes her hands when she's done.

When you've put together your list of finalists, get references—and check at least two (it's awkward, but absolutely essential). Ask each of the references why the agencies screen applicants. At a minimum they should get a driving record and criminal background check.

- Do some investigating on your own. Some states have a centralized place to do background checks—district attorney, child abuse registry, sex offender registry—and if you can't do it, you can hire companies that will do it for you; you'll need the applicant's full name, social security number, and driver's license number.
- Get a nanny cam. There are literally dozens of options. Cameras can be mounted in obvious places so the caregiver can see them or hidden inside clock radios, stuffed animals, or something else. Some are in black and white, others are in color; some make a recording that you can review later, others stream the images to your office computer, tablet, or phone.

The most important thing you can do is to trust your gut. If a daycare center or an individual gives you a funny feeling—even if it, or she, came with the most glowing recommendation—move on to the next option. The same goes for background checks and electronic surveillance. If someone won't cooperate, that should be a red flag. And if you're suspicious enough of a sitter to consider installing cameras in your home, maybe you should find someone else.

babysitter left her previous jobs, and what the best and worst things about her were. Also, make sure to ask the prospective caregiver the questions listed below.

When you make your final choice, have the person start a few days before you or your partner return to work so you can all get to know each other, and of course, so you can spy.

WHAT TO ASK

Here are a few good questions to ask prospective in-home caregivers. You may want to add a few more from the sections on other child-care options.

- How long have you been doing child care?
- What age children have you cared for?
- Do you have any special training (early childhood development, Red Cross certifications, etc.).
- Tell us a little about your own childhood.
- What would you do if . . . ? (Give several examples of things a child might do that would require different degrees of discipline.)

To Grandmother's (or Grandfather's) House We Go

If your parents, in-laws, or other relatives live in the neighborhood, they may provide you with a convenient, loving, and low-cost child-care alternative. According to the U.S. Census Bureau, 23.7 percent of children under five years old are being cared for by their grandparents while their parents are working—half of them in their grandparents' homes. Other relatives account for an additional 7.4 percent of all child-care arrangements for preschoolers.

If you're counting on your baby's grandparents for child care, be as appreciative and respectful of their time as you possibly can. Though most grandparents are usually delighted to spend time with their grandchildren—many say that it keeps them active and feeling young—they're also entitled to enjoy their retirement and spend their time the way they'd like to. However, they may be reluctant to say anything to you out of fear of offending you. So come right out and ask them directly whether you're asking too much.

Encouraging grandparents to spend time with their grandchild is great for everyone. Sara Moorman and her colleagues at Boston College followed grandparent-grandchild pairs for nearly two decades and found that those with the closest relationships were less likely to suffer from depression. Another study found that grandmothers who spend one day per week hanging with the grandkids improve their performance on tests of brain function and memory. But don't go overboard. In the same study, kids cared for by grandparents five or more days per week had "significantly lower processing speed" and "lower working memory performance."

- When would you hit or spank a child? (If the answer is anything other than "Never," find yourself another candidate.)
- How would you handle . . . ? (Name a couple of emergency situations, such as a gushing head wound or a broken arm.)
- Do you know baby CPR and first aid? (If not, you might want to consider paying for the caregiver to take a class. The Red Cross usually offers them.)
- What are your favorite things to do with kids?
- Do you have a driver's license? Insurance?
- What days/hours are you available/not available? How flexible can you be if an emergency arises while we're at work?
- Are you a native speaker of any foreign language?
- Can you/are you willing to cook or do light chores during the baby's naps?
- Will you cooperate with a background check?

OTHER IMPORTANT ISSUES TO DISCUSS

- Compensation (find out the going rate by checking with other people who have caregivers) and vacation.
- Willingness and/or ability to take care of more than one baby. Doing a "nanny share" with someone in your neighborhood can reduce the cost for both families and provide a playmate for the babies at the same time.
- How much texting and Facebook posting does the candidate do?
- Privacy issues: Do you want your baby on someone else's Instagram?
- Does she or he smoke?
- Complete responsibilities of the job: feeding, bathing, diapering, changing clothes, reading to the baby, and so on, as well as what other chores (light housekeeping, cooking) will be expected while the baby is sleeping.
- English-language skills—particularly important in case of emergency (you want someone who can accurately describe to a doctor or 911 operator what's going on).
- Immigration/green card status (more on this and other legal complications below).
- You might want to draw up a contract listing all of the caregiver's responsibilities—just so there won't be any misunderstandings.
- U.S. weights and measures. Sounds silly, but if your caregiver is going to cook for you, make sure she knows the difference between a teaspoon and a tablespoon, and between a cup and a pint. We had some very odd-tasting dishes before we figured out that our Azerbaijani nanny didn't have any idea.

LIVE-IN HELP

Hiring a live-in caregiver is like adding a new member to the family. The process for selecting one is similar to that for finding a non-live-in caregiver, so you can use most of the questions listed above for conducting interviews. After you've made your choice, try out your new relationship on a non-live-in basis for a few weeks, just to make sure everything's going to work out to everyone's satisfaction.

FAMILY DAYCARE

If you can't (or don't want to, or can't afford to) have someone care for your child in your home, the next best alternative is to have your child cared for in someone else's home. Since the caregiver is usually looking after only two or three children (including yours), your baby will get the individual attention she needs as well as the opportunity to socialize with other children. And since the caregiver lives in his or her own house, personnel changes are unlikely; this gives your baby a greater sense of stability.

Au Pairs

Au pairs are usually young women who come to the United States on year-long cultural exchange programs administered by the U.S. Department of State. Legally, au pairs are nonresident aliens and are exempt from social security, Medicare, and unemployment taxes (see page 186 for more on taxes and payroll).

What an au pair provides is up to ten hours per day or forty-five hours per week of live-in child care. If she's responsible for a child under two, she must have at least two hundred hours of documented infant-care experience. But she's not allowed to care for a child under three months old unless you, your parents, or some other responsible adult is in the home. In exchange, you pay a weekly stipend (currently about $200 and tied to the federal minimum wage) as well as airfare, the first $500 toward her education, program fees ($6,000–9,000, which usually includes health insurance), and full (private) room and board. On average, having an au pair will set you back about $18,000 for the full year.

You can hire an au pair through one of a dozen or so State Department–approved program sponsors who screen au pairs and host families and match them up. The most current list is on the State Department website, j1visa.state.gov/programs/au-pair. You could hire one through a nonapproved organization, but the au pair would be subject to immediate deportation and you to a $10,000 fine.

Having an au pair can be a wonderful opportunity for you and your baby to learn about another culture. One drawback, however, is that they can stay only a year; then it's *au revoir* to one, *bonjour* to another. In addition, it's important to remember that from the young woman's perspective, being an au pair is a cultural thing. In theory she's supposed to do a lot of child care, perhaps some light baby-related housekeeping, and take six semester hours of academic credit. But in reality she may be far more interested in going to the mall with her new American friends or hanging out with your neighbor's teenage son. And finally, understand that she's not a housekeeper, nurse, professionally trained child-care worker, or servant.

Be sure to ask potential family daycare providers what kind of backup system they have to deal with vacations and illness (the provider's). Will you suddenly find yourself without child care, or will your baby be cared for by another adult whom both you and your baby know?

GROUP DAYCARE

Many people—even those who can afford in-home child care—would rather use an out-of-home center. For one, a good daycare center is, as a rule, much better equipped than your home, or anyone else's for that matter, and will undoubtedly offer your child a wider range of stimulating activities. But remember, a toy-store-like atmosphere and a well-landscaped playground don't guarantee quality.

Many parents also prefer group daycare because it usually offers kids more opportunities to play with one another. In the long run, most parenting experts agree that being able to play with a variety of other kids helps children become better socialized and more independent. The downside, of course, is that your child won't get as much individual attention from the adult caregivers; and since your six-month-old won't really be playing with other kids for a while longer, adult-baby contact is more important. In addition, interacting with other kids usually means interacting with their germs; children in group daycare tend to get sick a lot more often than those cared for at home (whether yours or someone else's).

Where to Find Out-of-Home or In-Someone-Else's-Home Caregivers

You're most likely to find out-of-home child-care facilities through word of mouth or by seeing an ad online or in a local parenting newspaper. Perhaps the easiest (and safest) alternative is through Child Care Aware (childcareaware.org), a nationwide campaign created to help parents identify quality child care in their communities. The National Association of Family Child Care (nafcc.org) and the National Association for the Education of Young Children (naeyc.org) also have searchable databases of child-care providers—plus, they offer accreditation.

However you find out about a potential child-care facility, there's no substitute for checking it out for yourself in person. Here are some of the things the organizations mentioned above suggest you keep in mind when comparing child-care facilities:

ABOUT THE CAREGIVERS

- Do they seem to really like children? And do the kids seem to like them?
- Do they get down on each child's level to speak to the child?
- Are the children greeted warmly when they arrive?
- Are the children's needs quickly met even when things get busy?
- Are the caregivers trained in CPR, first aid, and early childhood development?
- Are they involved in continuing education programs?
- Does the program keep up with children's changing interests?
- Will the caregivers always be ready to answer your questions?

Taxes and Government Regulations

If you hire an in-home caregiver or family daycare provider, here are some of the steps you have to take to meet IRS, INS (Immigration and Naturalization Service), and Department of Labor requirements:

- Have the person you're hiring fill out I-9 (immigration status) and W-4 (withholding) forms
- Get a federal ID number (you may be able to use your social security number)
- Register with your state tax department
- Register with the U.S. Department of Labor
- Calculate payroll deductions—Social Security, Medicare, and unemployment (and, of course, deduct them)
- File quarterly reports to your state tax board and make quarterly estimated tax payments to the IRS
- Get a worker's compensation policy and compute the premium (usually a percentage of payroll rather than a flat fee for the year)
- Prepare W-2 and other reporting forms
- Demonstrate compliance with INS guidelines

If the prospect of doing all this doesn't make you want to quit your job to stay home with the baby, nothing will. Fortunately, there are some alternatives. In the Resources appendix I've listed several companies that, for a fee, will take care of all these matters and any other pesky details that may arise.

There is one piece of good news on the tax front (there's a phrase you won't hear very often). Through your employer, you may be eligible to contribute pretax dollars to a "flexible spending account" (sometimes called a "cafeteria plan") that you can use to pay for child care. And, depending on your income and other things that only your accountant knows for sure, you may be able to take advantage of the Child and Dependent Care Credit, which could offset some of your child-care expenses.

- Will they tell you what your child is doing every day?
- Are parents' ideas welcomed? Are there ways for you to get involved if you want to?
- Are there enough caregivers for the number of kids? Each state has different standards, ranging from 1:3 up to 1:6. Having taken care of two infants at the same time, I can tell you that while 1:3 is pretty tough, 1:6 is absolute insanity.

The National Resource Center for Health and Safety in Child Care (nrckids.org) has a great website that lists the latest standards in each state.

ABOUT THE FACILITY

- Is it licensed? Ask to see the certificate.
- Is the atmosphere bright and pleasant?
- Is there a fenced-in outdoor play area with a variety of safe equipment?
- Can the caregivers see the entire playground at all times?
- Are there different areas for resting, quiet play, and active play?
- What precautions are taken to ensure that kids can be picked up only by the person you select? Do strangers have access to the center?
- Are there adequate safety measures to keep children away from windows, fences, and kitchen appliances and utensils (knives, ovens, stoves, household chemicals, and so forth)?

ABOUT THE PROGRAM

- Is there a daily balance of playtime, story time, and nap time?
- Are the activities right for each age group?
- Are there enough toys and learning materials for the number of children?
- Are the toys clean, safe, and within reach of the children?

ABOUT OTHER THINGS

- Do you agree with the discipline practices?
- Do you hear the sounds of happy children?
- Are surprise visits by parents encouraged?
- Will your child be happy there?

Try to visit each facility more than once, and after you've made your final decision, make a few unannounced visits—just to see what goes on when there aren't any parents around.

A FEW THINGS TO GET SUSPICIOUS ABOUT

- Parents are not allowed to drop in unannounced. You need to call before visiting or coming to pick up your child.
- Parents dropping off kids are not allowed into the caregiving areas.
- Your child is unhappy after several weeks.
- There seem to be new and unfamiliar caregivers almost every day.
- You stop by and the kids are watching TV.
- You don't get any serious response when you voice your concerns.

Finding a good child-care provider is a lengthy, agonizing process, and it's important not to give up until you're completely satisfied. Unfortunately, most parents get frustrated with the choices and end up settling for something less than optimal. The result? Most infants get mediocre care. A recent study by the Work and Families Institute found that only 8 percent of child-care facilities were considered "good quality," and 40 percent were rated "less than minimal." Worst of all, 10–20 percent of children "get care so poor that it risks damaging their development." So be careful.

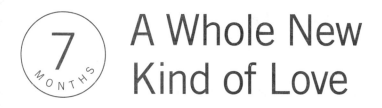

A Whole New Kind of Love

WHAT'S GOING ON WITH THE BABY

Physically

- He's getting so good at sitting that he doesn't need his hands for balancing anymore. Instead, he can—and will—use them to reach for things.
- He can get himself to a sitting position from his stomach.
- He's starting to crawl, but don't be surprised if he goes backward at least some of the time or, instead of crawling, scoots around on his bottom, using one arm to pull, the other to push.
- If you hold him upright, supported under the arms, he can bear some weight on his feet and will stamp and bounce up and down.
- He now uses his opposable thumb almost like you do, and is able to pick up what he wants confidently and quickly. He still prefers objects he can bang together and, of course, put into his mouth.
- He's got some teeth, and if your partner is still breastfeeding, you're going to be hearing a lot about them.

Intellectually

- As his brain develops, so does his ability to make associations. He recognizes the sound of your approaching footsteps and starts getting excited even before you come into his room.
- If confronted with blocks of different sizes, he will pick each one up, manipulate them a bit, then line them up to compare them to one another.
- He's so thrilled with his newfound ability to pick up and hold objects that he just can't get enough. He spends a lot of time examining objects upside down

and from other angles. And if he's holding a block in one hand, he'll reach for a second one and eye a third—all at the same time.

- The idea that objects may exist even when he can't see them is just beginning to take shape. If he drops something, he no longer thinks it's gone forever. Instead, he'll grope around for it or stare intently at the place it disappeared, hoping to bring it back. But if it doesn't show up within five to ten seconds, he'll forget about it.

Verbally

- A few months ago, your baby was capable (with practice) of producing any sound that a human can produce. But since he spends all his time trying to make the sounds you make, he's forgetting how to make the ones you don't (like rolled Rs or the clicks of the African bush people).
- In English, though, your baby's babbling is shifting from single-syllable to multi-syllable (*babababa*, *mamamama*, *dadadada* . . .). He's able to modulate the tone, volume, and speed of his sounds and actively tries to converse with you, vocalizing after you stop speaking and waiting for you to respond to him.
- Your baby's passive language skills are also improving. He now turns when he hears his own name and understands several other words.

Emotionally/Socially

- Although he's fascinated with objects, your baby really prefers social interactions and one-on-one activities, such as chasing and fetching.
- He can now tell the difference between adults and children, and may be especially interested in playing with (actually, alongside) kids his own age.
- He recognizes, and reacts differently to, positive and negative tones of voice and happy or sad facial expressions. That means that the way you respond to your baby has a big influence on his behavior. If you seem angry or frightened by something he's done, he senses that he's upset you, and he may cry. At the same time, your smiles and encouraging words could be enough to end his frustration or soothe his tears.
- Shyness or anxiety around strangers continues, and he may fuss or even get really upset if you leave.
- Continuing on his mission to imitate everything you do, your baby now wants to finger-feed himself or hold his own bottle or cup.

WHAT YOU'RE GOING THROUGH

A New and Different Kind of Love

Sooner or later, almost every writer takes a crack at trying to describe love. And for the most part, they fall short. The problem is that there are so many different kinds. The love I feel for my wife, for example, is completely different from the love I feel for my sisters, which is different from the love I feel for my parents. And none of those seems even remotely similar to the love I have for my children.

I usually describe my love for my children in fairly happy terms, but periodically I experience it in a completely different way—one that sometimes frightens me.

Here's how it happens: I'm watching one of my daughters (any one of the three will do) play in the park, her beautiful, innocent face filled with joy. All of a sudden, out of nowhere, I begin to imagine how I would feel if something terrible were to happen to her. What if she fell and broke her neck? What if she got hit by a truck? What if she got horribly sick and died? The loss is almost palpable, and just thinking about these things is enough to depress me for the rest of the day.

And there's more. Sometimes my imagination goes a step further, and I wonder what I would do if someone, anyone, tried to hurt or kidnap or kill one of my children. At the very instant that thought pops into my head, my heart suddenly begins beating faster and so loudly I can almost hear it, my breath quickens, and my teeth and fists clench. I haven't hit another person outside a martial arts class for about thirty years, but during those brief moments when my imagination runs loose, I realize that I would be perfectly capable of killing another human being with my bare hands and without a moment's hesitation.

Feeling Isolated

When my oldest daughter was still quite young, she and her babysitter spent several mornings a week at Totland, a nearby park that had become something of an oasis for caregivers and children. Most afternoons I'd come to pick up my daughter at the park, and I'd stay for an hour or so watching her play with the other kids.

The other caregivers—almost all of whom were women—would be clustered in groups, chatting, sharing information, and learning from each other. Newcomers—as long as they were female—were quickly welcomed into these groups. But despite the nodding relationships I had developed with a few of the women, I was always an outsider, never made completely welcome.

Once in a while another father would come to the park with his child, and we'd nod, smile, or raise our eyebrows at each other. We probably had a lot in common as fathers, and I'm sure we shared many of the same concerns and could have learned a lot from each other. But we didn't. Instead, we sat ten yards apart; if we ever spoke, it was about football or something equally superficial. Each of us was afraid to approach the other for fear of seeming too needy, too ignorant, or not masculine enough. What a couple of idiots.

Over the past few years this has begun to change—a little. As fatherhood comes out of the closet and as stay-at-home dads are becoming more common, contemporary dads are making some tentative steps in each other's direction. But despite the progress, new fathers still tend to steer clear of one another. That approach, however, is often less than completely satisfying. They miss out on the camaraderie and learning they could have had from talking with other guys about parenting, and as a result, many new fathers feel isolated. They have all sorts of concerns, worries, and feelings they don't completely understand, but as far as they know, there's no one else they can share their experience with. Fatherhood, it seems, can be a lonely business at times.

Getting Together with Other Men

One of the best ways to overcome your feelings of isolation or loneliness as a father is to join or start a fathers' group. Even in California, where there are so many support groups that there are support groups for people who belong to too many support groups, the idea of being involved in a fathers' group still sounds a little risky. But it's a risk well worth taking.

I've led a number of groups for new dads, and they almost always start off the same way, with a discussion of sports or politics or almost anything that has nothing to do with parenting. Then, almost by accident, someone will say something about a child, and the floodgates open. Stories tumble out, advice comes in from all sides, and a lot of guys find out that they aren't as alone as they thought they were. The group sessions almost always go on far longer than they were scheduled to.

Joining (or, gulp, starting) a support group for dads offers some wonderful benefits:

- Secrets revealed. Women get a ton of parenting (and other) advice from other women: where to buy the best used children's clothes, places to take the kids on rainy days, surefire cures for illnesses, ways to soothe crying babies, finding and hiring babysitters. You'd be surprised how much you already know, and how much you'll be able to help other men.
- A road map. Although I'm tired of hearing the old cliché about how men don't ask for directions, when it comes to parenting, there's often some truth there. One of the best things about a group setting is finding out quickly that you're not the only one who's feeling a little lost. Fortunately, every dad there has some

"Pass'em, Pop."

directions that may help. And even if they don't, it's better to be lost with some-one else than lost alone.

- Safety. I've found that dads' groups don't work nearly as well when there are women around. It's sometimes a lot easier to talk about sensitive issues with a bunch of guys who're going through (or have already been through or will be going through) what you are.
- Entertainment. Getting together with other men who've made fatherhood a priority in their lives can be a lot of fun. It could be in a park with the kids, or it could be a dads-only event at someone's house or in a bar.

If you want to physically get together with other fathers, there are dads' groups popping up all over the place, and there may be more than one within shouting distance of your home. We've listed several of them in the Resources section. If you'd rather start your own group, finding other fathers to join won't be easy. But if you put the word out, you're sure to get some responses. Here are some likely sources of new (or existing) fathers:

- www.meetup.com and similar websites
- Your church or synagogue
- The hospital where your baby was born, your partner's OB/GYN, or your pediatrician
- Libraries, schools, and daycare centers
- Leaders of mothers' groups

If you're not ready for or interested in face-to-face meetups , or you're just not comfortable joining a group (and there are plenty of us who aren't), it's still important to make regular contact with other fathers—especially if you're a stay-at-home dad or you're raising your children without a partner. So take full advantage of the anonymity of cyberspace and search Twitter, Facebook, Instagram, Google+, and so on, for "new dad," "new father," "dad blogger," and any number of other terms or hashtags that best describe what you're looking for. Once you filter out the "male enhancement" and porn sites and the scammers that want to sell you thousands of Twitter followers or Facebook fans, you're on your way. Whether it's in person or on the Internet, there's plenty of research indicating that fathers who get together with other guys are generally happier. So don't be a hero and try to handle every fatherhood-related matter that comes up by yourself. You can't. And trying to do so will only hurt your kids and yourself.

YOU AND YOUR BABY

A (Very) Brief Introduction to Discipline

"Discipline is the second most important thing you do for a child," says pediatrician T. Berry Brazelton. "Love comes first." There's no question in my mind that Brazelton is absolutely right. But before we go any further, let's clarify one thing: discipline does not mean "punishment"; it means "teaching" and "setting limits." And the goal is to help your child develop impulse control. At this age, though, that's almost impossible, for several reasons.

First, your baby can't make a distinction between a want and a need. Second, he's simply not capable of understanding that he's doing something wrong (or even what "right" and "wrong" mean). If he pokes you in the eye, head-butts you when you're leaning in to give him a kiss, or knocks over the fishbowl, he's not doing it to cause trouble. Finally, babies this age have very short memories. So by the time you've disciplined him, he's already forgotten what he did to get you so upset. But now that your baby's getting more mobile, there's an increased chance that his accidental misbehavior could become dangerous. So it's time to start setting some limits. Nothing rigid—just some basic guidelines to get your baby used to the idea.

At this point, you have only two serious discipline and limit-setting options: minimize danger by baby-proofing the house (see pages 199–205 for more), or distract him and take advantage of his short memory while you still can. Babies this age are very much like cats: if he's gotten hold of that priceless van Gogh you accidentally left on the floor, smile, give him a teddy bear with one hand, and take away the painting with the other; and if he's making a break for the nearest busy

*"Listen up and listen up good,
'cause I'm only going to say this a million times."*

street, pick him up and turn him around the other way. Chances are, he won't even notice. And even if he does, he'll be disappointed for only a few seconds.

Talk to Me, Baby, Give Me a Sign

How many times have you wished your baby could tell you what he's thinking? Well, as it turns out, there's a pretty simple way to find out: teach him sign language.

A few decades ago, researchers began to notice that children whose parents were hearing impaired and taught their children to sign were able to communicate before they were nine months old. Children with two hearing parents don't usually have much to say until after their first birthday. If you think about it, using the hands to communicate makes a lot of sense. After all, babies have a lot more control over their fingers and hands than they do over their tongue and mouth.

Besides giving them a way to communicate earlier, signing improves babies' motor skills, builds vocabulary and language abilities, reduces tantrums and frustration, and has even been linked with an increase in IQ. Signing with your baby is good for you too. When you understand what your baby wants, you'll have fewer tears to deal with, and you (and your partner) will be less frustrated. When you're feeling relaxed and in control, parenting is a lot easier and a lot more fun. That, in turn will bring you and your baby closer.

There are two major baby signing systems. They're similar but there are some important distinctions (there's more information on both in the Resources appendix):

- Joseph Garcia's *Sign with Your Baby* is based solidly on American Sign Language (ASL). Most of the signs your baby will learn are fairly intuitive, such as touching the fingers to the lips for *eat*, and hooking the thumbs together and flapping the hands for *butterfly*. Others are a little tougher to figure out (touching the thumb to the forehead for dad and to the chin for mom) or may be difficult for little hands (putting the thumb between the first and middle fingers of a fist for toilet or holding up your hand as if indicating five and lowering the middle and ring fingers for airplane). Garcia's philosophy is that if you're going to the trouble to teach your baby a language, you might as well go with a real one. A baby who knows some ASL will be able to communicate with other babies who sign (and deaf people of any age) anywhere. And if you're thinking long-term, ASL fulfills the language requirement for admission to a growing number of colleges.
- Linda Acredolo's and Susan Goodwyn's *Baby Signs* is also based on ASL but it's more flexible. Their theory is that since your baby isn't going to be using sign language all that long, it's best to make it as easy to learn as possible. So parents are encouraged to modify the ASL signs as they see fit and to invent their own. This could make communication with people outside the family a little tougher. However, most of the signs you and your baby are likely to come up with will be pretty easy to decipher.

Both systems are excellent, and both give you and your baby an incredible opportunity to communicate with each other. I like Baby Signs a little better, though, because the flexibility appeals to me. If you go this route, try to use as many of the ASL signs as you can and modify them only as necessary.

However, if you prefer a more systematic approach, or if there are any deaf people in your family, Sign with Your Baby is the way to go. And even though, as I mentioned above, some of the signs aren't completely obvious, if you practice them enough, you'll do fine.

WHEN TO START SIGNING AND HOW

Basically, if your baby is at least six months old, points to things on request (where's the kitty-cat?), and waves bye-bye, you're ready to go. Start off with a few (four or five at the most) of the most common signs. My wife and I taught our youngest *milk, food, more,* and *kitty*. Repetition is the key, so make the sign and say the word every chance you get. If you're feeding the baby, ask if he wants more food. If you're giving him a bottle, or your partner is still breastfeeding, tell the baby that he's about to get some milk.

Try to have everyone who has regular contact with the baby use the signs. The more people he sees using them—including babysitters, grandparents, and especially older siblings—the faster he'll learn them.

The big thing here is to be patient—and to keep it fun. You may not get any kind of response from your baby for as long as a month or two. But don't give up. And don't introduce any more signs until your baby starts either mimicking the ones you show him or initiating conversations of his own. As soon as that happens, add new ones as fast as your baby can absorb them.

Your Baby's Teeth

Although your baby's little chompers started forming when your partner was four months pregnant, they probably won't make their first appearance ("eruption," in dental lingo) until about six or seven months. However, plenty of babies start getting teeth as early as three months, and it's not at all uncommon for a child to be toothless until his first birthday. One thing you can count on, though: whenever your baby's teeth show up, they'll be followed immediately by plaque. Yes, the same stuff that your dentist has to chip off your teeth with a chisel a few times a year.

It's a little early to start taking your child to a dentist—six months *after* the first tooth pops in is a good target—but use a washcloth or a small piece of gauze to clean each of his teeth a couple of times a day. If you're feeling more adventurous, you might want to try using a *very* soft toothbrush. Either way, skip the toothpaste for at least another year and keep the tubes far away from your baby for even longer; toothpaste can be poisonous or even lethal in large doses. When he's a year old, use a toothbrush with a very soft bristle. Flossing won't be necessary for a while.

Those first teeth will start falling out by age six or seven. And a lot of parents believe that since they're not going to be around for long, it's okay if they get tooth decay (usually brown or white spots that appear on the teeth) or cavities. Not true. Those baby teeth are there for a reason: to reserve space for the grown-up teeth that will eventually come in. They also help with chewing, speaking, and jawbone development. If your baby's teeth decay or have to be pulled, that could make eating and talking harder and could also make the adult teeth come in crooked.

TEETHING

There are two important things to know about teething. First, your baby's teeth start showing up in a fairly predictable order: first the two lower central incisors, then the two top central incisors, and then the ones on either side. Most kids will

Pacifier Safety

Generally speaking, there's nothing wrong with giving your baby a pacifier. A lot of babies have a need to suck that can't be satisfied by breastfeeding or shoving their own (or even your) fingers into their mouths. Pacifiers are great for soothing most babies (if yours has no interest, don't force the issue), they can help equalize inner-ear pressure on airplanes (the same thing you do by yawning or swallowing), and they may reduce the risk of SIDS, especially during sleep (see pages 103–4). On the other hand, if your baby becomes too dependent on it, he may wake up crying in the middle of the night if it falls out of his mouth.

One thing you don't have to worry about is the pacifier damaging your baby's soon-to-be-dazzling smile. Most dentists agree that sucking on a pacifier isn't a problem until about age four.

Thumbs, however, are a bit more problematic. First of all, because thumbs don't conform to the shape of your baby's mouth as well as pacifiers do, there's a greater chance that thumb sucking will damage your baby's teeth (although that won't be an issue until he's five or so). And if your baby is a constant thumb sucker, there's a small chance it will have an impact on the way he speaks. Finally, most illness-causing germs get into our bodies from our hands. Need I say more?

have all eight incisors by the end of their first year, and a total of twenty teeth by age two.

Second, teething isn't usually much fun for your baby or anyone else nearby. Although some teeth come in without causing any trouble, most kids experience at least some discomfort for a few days before and after a tooth breaks through the gum. Your baby's gums may be sore or tender, and he could be fussier and have trouble falling asleep, which is a real bummer if he just started sleeping through the night. He'll start gnawing with a vengeance, hoping to relieve some of the pressure, and you'll need a bucket to mop up the extra drool. Despite what you may have heard, there's no evidence that symptoms such as headaches, diarrhea, or fever have anything to do with teething. The one exception is a rash that your baby may develop under the chin and on the upper chest. This is usually caused by drool that gets in between your baby's many chins and never has a chance to fully dry. A baby-friendly moisturizer or some of that nipple cream your partner may be using should do the trick.

Fortunately, teething discomfort doesn't last long and is relatively easily dealt

Here are some important guidelines for using pacifiers:

- Never, never, never tie the pacifier around your baby's neck or use string to attach the pacifier to your baby—it can pose a serious strangulation risk. And, don't use tape to keep the pacifier in your baby's mouth. (I actually knew a woman who did this. It's as close as I've ever come to reporting someone to Child Protective Services). If you're tired of picking the pacifier up off the floor thirty-eight times a day, buy yourself a clip-on holder, one that detaches easily.
- Get pacifiers (you'll need more than one, guaranteed) that are dishwasher safe, silicone, and all one piece.
- The shield (the part that stays on the outside of the baby's mouth) should have several holes for saliva.
- Check the nipple for holes, tears, or other signs of wear. If you find any, replace the pacifier immediately—you don't want your baby to chew off pieces and swallow them.
- Don't put sugar or anything else on it to bribe your baby. And, looking ahead, don't even consider putting cayenne pepper or anything similar on it to get your baby to break the habit.

with. Most babies respond quite well to children's acetaminophen (Tylenol) or ibuprofen (Advil), *but only if your pediatrician recommends it.* If so, ask how many drops to give and don't waste your time rubbing it on the baby's gums—it doesn't work. (The gum massage itself may help, though.) Teething rings are also helpful, especially the kind that are bumpy, water-filled, and freezable, and so are teething biscuits, frozen washcloths, and bagels (although if you go the bagel route, you'll be finding mushy crumbs all over your house for a month).

Childproofing Your House

Once your baby realizes that he's able to move around by himself, his mission in life will be to locate—and make you race to—the most dangerous, life-threatening things in your home. So if you haven't already begun the never-ending process of childproofing your house, you'd better start now.

Start by getting down on your hands and knees and looking at the world from your baby's perspective. Don't those lamp cords and speaker wires look like they'd be fun to yank or chew on or wrap around your neck? Don't those outlets seem

Walkers

I had a walker when I was a baby, and my two older kids did too. One might think that something called a walker would help with walking. As it turns out, there's research showing that babies who use walkers actually start walking as much as a month later than kids who don't use walkers. Other studies have shown that walker use may delay mental and physical development. And then there's the actual danger.

Eighty percent of walker-involved accidents are falls down stairs, and most end in a head injury—often the result of the baby pulling something down on top of himself or using the walker as a launching pad so he can lunge after even more dangerous things on higher surfaces. Another common complaint about walkers is that babies can build up some real speed and fly around the house smacking into everything in sight—fun for them (until they get hurt), not so fun for you.

My suggestion? Stay away from walkers (amazingly, they're still being sold) and most of the "safe" alternatives that are out there, unless your pediatrician specifically tells you to get one. Your baby will learn to walk when he's darn good and ready.

to be begging you to stick something metal into them? And those window shade cords look like they'd be perfect for swinging on. Taking care of those enticing wires and cords and covering up your outlets is only the beginning, so let's start with the basics.

ANYWHERE AND EVERYWHERE

- Move all your valuable items out of the baby's reach. It's not too early to try to teach him not to touch, but don't expect much compliance at this age.
- Bolt bookshelves and other freestanding cabinets to the wall (this is especially important if you live in earthquake country). Pulling things down on top of themselves is one of the many ways babies have of scaring the crap out of their parents.
- Don't hang heavy things on the stroller—it can tip over.
- Get special guards for your radiators and raise any space heaters and electric fans off the floor.
- Install a safety gate at the bottom and top of every flight of stairs. After a few months, you can move the bottom gate up a few steps to give the baby a low-risk way to practice climbing.

- Adjust your water heater temperature to 120 degrees. This will reduce the likelihood that your baby will scald himself.
- Get a fire extinguisher and put smoke and carbon monoxide alarms in every bedroom.
- If you have a two-story house (or higher), consider getting a rope escape ladder.
- Take first aid and CPR classes; they're usually offered by the local Red Cross, YMCA, or hospitals.
- Put together a first aid kit (see page 204 for the ingredients).
- Empty your wastebaskets regularly, especially if you've just swept up some broken glass or anything else that might be dangerous.
- Keep the place clean. Coins, paper clips, cat litter (and what's in it), dog food, dust bunnies, and anything else that's reachable is fair game for the baby.

ESPECIALLY IN THE KITCHEN

Ideally, you'd keep your kids out of the kitchen entirely—it's just not possible to make it 100 percent safe. At the very least, put up gates at every entrance to the kitchen to keep your baby out when you're not there. But for those times when you *are* there, keep these points in mind:

- Install safety locks on all but one of your low cabinets and drawers. Most of these locks allow the door to be opened slightly—just enough to accommodate a baby's fingers—so make sure the kind you get also keeps the door from closing completely.
- Stock the one unlocked cabinet with unbreakable pots and pans and encourage your baby to jump right in.
- Your baby's high chair should be sturdy, with a tray that locks into place and a crotch strap to keep him from slipping out.
- Keep baby's high chair away from the walls. His strong little legs can push off the wall and knock the chair over. And never allow him to stand up while in the chair.
- Watch out for irons and ironing boards. The cords are a hazard, and the boards themselves are very easy to knock over.
- Get an oven lock and covers for your oven and stove knobs.
- Use the back burners on the stove whenever possible and keep pot handles turned toward the back of the stove.
- Try to keep the baby out of the kitchen when anyone is cooking. It's too easy to trip over him, drop or spill something on him, or accidentally smack him with something.
- Never hold your baby while you're cooking. Teaching him what steam is or how water boils may seem like a good idea, but bubbling spaghetti sauce or hot oil hurts when it splashes.

- Put mouse and insect traps in places where your baby can't get to them. Better yet, set them after he's asleep and take your kill to the taxidermist before he gets up.
- Use plastic dishes and serving bowls whenever you can—glass breaks, and, at least in my house, the shards seem to show up for weeks, no matter how well I sweep.
- Put knives in the sink or back in the drawer where they belong instead of leaving them on the edge of the counter.
- Post the phone numbers of the nearest poison control agency and your pediatrician near your landline if you have one. If not, make sure they're on your cell's speed dial.

OUTSIDE IN THE SUN

Sunlight and fresh air are fantastic for you and your baby. But remember: no matter how cool you think it might look, when it comes to babies, there's no such thing as a good tan. Babies' skin is a lot thinner than ours and burns much more quickly—especially those with a light complexion. Severe sunburns during childhood have been linked with skin cancers later in life. For that reason, here are some important things to keep in mind if you're planning to be out of the house. Review pages 121–22 for more.

- Don't be fooled by clouds or breeze. UV rays are still getting through and can burn your baby as badly as on a hot day. Be especially careful at high altitude and near water, snow, or sand, all of which can reflect and intensify the sun.
- On sunny days, use the groundhog test: if your shadow is longer than you are tall, it's okay to come out (as long as you follow the other precautions in this section). If your shadow is shorter than you are, though, turn around and go right back into the house.
- Cover up as much skin as possible. Have your baby wear a hat and sunglasses that offer UV protection, and dress him in pants and long sleeves. Tightly woven fabrics (ones that are hard to see through if you hold them up to the light), particularly cotton, are best.
- Make sure any exposed skin is nicely lubed up. Apply sunscreen (SPF 15 or 30) half an hour before going out, and reapply every 60–90 minutes. Once you're outside, try to keep the baby in the shade as much as possible. Try out the sunscreen a few days in advance by applying a small amount to your baby's back or arm. If it gets red or irritated, he may be allergic, so try another brand.
- Set a good example. Let your baby see you wearing a hat and putting sunscreen on yourself.

- If your baby does get sunburned, call your doctor immediately—sooner if there are blisters. He'll probably have you give the baby some infant-strength acetaminophen (Tylenol) or ibuprofen (Advil) for the pain, and may recommend some 0.5 percent hydrocortisone cream. *Do not give your baby aspirin.* Sunburn can be dehydrating, so make sure the baby gets plenty of fluids. Apply a cool washcloth to the burned area and a water-based or aloe vera moisturizer. Stay away from petroleum-based products as well as anything that has benzocaine in it, and don't put butter on it, no matter what your mother says. Finally, stay out of the sun until the burn is completely healed.

ESPECIALLY IN THE LIVING ROOM

- Put decals at baby height on all sliding glass doors and large windows.
- Get your plants off the floor: more than seven hundred species can cause illness or death if eaten, including such common ones as lily of the valley, iris, and poinsettia.
- Pad the corners and edges of low tables, chairs, and fireplace hearths.
- Make sure your fireplace screen and tools can't be pulled down or knocked over.
- Keep furniture away from windows. Babies will climb up whatever they can and may fall through the glass.
- Put gates or protective barriers on all the windows so baby can't throw himself out an open window.

ESPECIALLY IN THE BEDROOM/NURSERY

- No homemade or antique cribs. They almost never conform to today's safety standards. Cribs with protruding corner posts are especially dangerous.
- Crib slats or bars should be no more than 2⅜ inches apart. Anymore than that and your baby may be able to get his head through. And believe me, he'll try.
- Remove all mobiles and hanging toys from the crib. By five months, most kids can push themselves up on their hands and knees and can get tangled up in (and even choke on) strings.
- Keep the crib at least two feet away from blinds, drapes, hanging cords, or wall decorations with ribbons.
- All toys should be washable, large enough so they can't fit in your baby's mouth, nose, or ears, and soft enough so they won't poke out an eye. No strings or detachable parts.
- Toy chest lids should stay up when opened (so they don't slam on tiny fingers). And don't feel that you need to fill the toy chest up. Three or four toys are plenty

What Every Good First Aid Kit Needs

You may want to have one first aid kit for your home and another for each of your vehicles.

- Ace bandages
- acetaminophen (Tylenol) drops and tablets
- adhesive strips
- adhesive tape
- antibiotic ointment
- antibiotic wash
- antiseptic ointment
- butterfly bandages
- clean Popsicle sticks (for splints)
- cleansing agent to clean wounds
- cotton balls (sterile if possible)
- cotton cloth for slings
- disposable hand wipes (individual packets)
- disposable instant ice packs
- emergency telephone numbers
- gauze rolls or pads (sterile if possible)
- mild soap
- syrup of ipecac (to induce vomiting, if necessary)
- tweezers (for splinters and the like)
- pair of clean (surgical) gloves
- scissors with rounded tip
- sterile 4 x 4–inch bandages

It's also a good idea to have an emergency treatment manual around the house. We've got a list of some of the best in the Resources appendix.

for now—more can overwhelm your baby. If you have more, rotate them in and out.

- Don't leave dresser drawers open. From the baby's perspective, they look a lot like stairs.
- Keep crib items to a minimum: a sheet and a few small, soft toys. Babies don't need pillows at this age and large toys or stuffed animals can be climbed on and used to escape from the crib.
- Don't leave your baby alone on the changing table even for a second.

ESPECIALLY IN THE BATHROOM

- If possible, use a gate to keep access restricted to the adults in the house.
- Install a toilet guard.
- Keep bath and shower doors closed.
- Never leave water standing in the bath, the sink, or even a bucket. Drowning is the third most common cause of accidental deaths among young children, and babies can drown in practically no water at all—even an inch or two.

- Keep medication and cosmetics high up.
- Make sure there's nothing your baby can climb up on to gain access to the medicine cabinet.
- Keep razors and hair dryers unplugged and out of reach.
- Never keep electrical appliances near the bathtub.
- Use a bath mat or stick-on safety strips to reduce the risk of slipping in the bathtub.

ESPECIALLY IN THE CAR

- Car seats should be installed in the middle of the back seat (to be away from any air bags) and face backward until your baby's first birthday and until he weighs twenty pounds. If you absolutely have to transport your baby in a car without a back seat, disable the airbags closest to the baby.
- Resist the urge to get a used seat unless you're 110 percent sure that it hasn't been recalled by the manufacturer, isn't missing any parts, comes with all the instructions, and has never been in any kind of accident.
- Get a car seat safety check. According to the National Highway Traffic Safety Administration, 80 percent of infant car seats are installed incorrectly (despite the fact that 90 percent of people think they did the job correctly). Many highway patrols, fire departments, or police departments do them for free.
- Clean up the car. In an accident, anything that's just lying around becomes a dangerous projectile.

Perpetual Motion

WHAT'S GOING ON WITH THE BABY

Physically

- At this stage, your baby is in motion just about every waking minute. She's an excellent crawler and will follow you around for hours.
- Having mastered crawling, she's now working on getting herself upright.
- She'll start by pulling herself up to a half-standing crouch and letting herself drop back down. Sometime in the next few weeks, though, she'll pull herself up to a complete standing position.
- If she's really adventurous, she'll let go with one hand or even lean against something and release both hands. Either way, she'll be shocked to discover that she can't get down. Locking the knees is a skill that comes earlier than unlocking them.
- She now uses a "pincer grip" to pick things up and, because of her increased dexterity, becomes fascinated by tiny things.
- If she's holding a toy and sees something new, she'll drop what she's got and pick up the second. She may even retain the first toy and pick up the second with her other hand.
- Her self-feeding and bottle- or cup-handling skills are improving fast.
- All this activity is so exhausting that she may sleep as long as 10–12 hours at a stretch.

Intellectually

- Your baby's increased mobility has opened a new range of possibilities for exploration and discovery. She now gets into drawers and cabinets and can empty them amazingly quickly.
- Her mobility also lets her get better acquainted with some of the objects that,

until now, she's seen only from afar. Crawling around on the floor, for example, your baby will stop underneath a chair and examine it from every possible angle. Then, writes child psychologist Selma Fraiberg, "Upon leaving the underside of the chair, he pauses to wrestle with one of the legs, gets the feel of its roundness and its slipperiness and sinks his two front teeth into it in order to sample flavor and texture. In a number of circle tours around the chair at various times in the days and weeks to come, he discovers that the various profiles he has been meeting are the several faces of one object, the object we call a chair."

- Slowly, slowly, she's learning that objects exist even when she can't see them, and she'll actively look for toys that she's seen you hide.
- She's been playing fetch with you for a while—dropping things and having you pick them up—and having seen so many things fall, she may start worrying what would happen if she fell. As a result, she may get very frightened at the tops of stairs or other high surfaces.
- Now able to pick up a different object in each hand, your baby will spend a lot of time comparing the capabilities of each side of her body.

Verbally

- She now babbles almost constantly, using your intonation and expression as much as she can.
- She can also use different sounds to express her changing emotions.
- She continues to concentrate on two-syllable "words"; *b*, *p*, and *m* are her favorite consonants. If you haven't yet, you'll be hearing *da-da* very soon.
- Her name is not the only sound she knows. She'll also turn her head in response to other familiar noises, such as a car approaching, the phone ringing, the television "speaking," and the refrigerator opening.

Emotionally/Socially

- With so much to keep her busy during the day, your baby may feel she doesn't have time for naps anymore. The lack of sleep, together with the frustration at not being able to do everything she wants with her body, may make her cranky.
- When she's in a good mood, she really wants to be included in socializing; she may crawl into the middle of a conversation, sit up, and start chattering.
- She smiles at herself in the mirror, and raises her arms when she wants you to pick her up.
- She's smiley and happy with people she knows, but wary and sometimes frightened around strangers. This may make her even clingier than before if she senses that you're going to leave her in an unfamiliar situation or with unfamiliar people.

WHAT YOU'RE GOING THROUGH

Learning Flexibility and Patience

Before my oldest daughter was born, I was incredibly anal-retentive about time. I always showed up wherever I was supposed to be exactly when I was supposed to, and I demanded the same from others. As you now know, going on a simple trip to the store with a baby in tow takes as much planning as an expedition to Mount Everest. And getting anywhere on time is just about impossible.

It took a while, but eventually I learned that trying to be a father and Mr. Prompt at the same time just wasn't going to work. Simply accepting that fact made me a lot more forgiving of other people's lateness as well. Interestingly, this new flexible attitude about time began to rub off on other areas of my life, and it'll probably have the same effect on you.

Besides learning to lighten up a little, most of the new dads in my research said that after six or seven months of fatherhood, they'd become much more accepting of other people's limitations, as well as their own. They'd learned the value of contingency planning, having a backup just in case plan A goes sideways. They thought that caring for a baby had made them more aware of other people's needs and points of view, and more empathetic or "in tune" with other people's feelings and emotions.

Of course, not everyone finds change quite as easy to accept. For some new dads, any sort of deviation from an orderly schedule, or any lack of continuity, can be very discombobulating.

Thinking about How Involved You Are—and What That Means

Being an "involved" dad means different things to different men. Among the most common definitions are:
- Being a teacher, moral guide, and role model for the children.
- Being there physically and emotionally and being available for the children from the very first.
- Doing hands-on things with the children (feeding, bathing, changing, reading, playing, running errands, showing affection, and so on).
- Being an equal partner in parenting.
- Not being stuck in the role of the "wait-till-your-dad-comes-home" disciplinarian.
- Being a good provider (financially) and protector (keeping the family safe).

I realize that throughout this book I may have given you the impression that being an involved dad is wonderful and fantastic and incredible every single minute.

Well, it's not. While it can be the greatest thing you'll ever do, it can also be the most frustrating. It creates opportunities for growth and fun, but it also interferes with others. The table on pages 210–11 summarizes many of the benefits and costs associated with being an involved dad. It's based in part on the work of fatherhood researcher Rob Palkovitz and on interviews I've done with hundreds of new dads.

It's Hard to Make Up for Lost Time

There's nothing like a long day at the office to make you realize just how much you miss your baby. And when you get home, you might be tempted to try to make up for lost time by cramming as much active, physical father-baby contact as you can into the few hours before bedtime (yours or the baby's). That's a pretty tall order, and just about the only way you'll be able to fill it is to be "overly controlling, intrusive, and hyper-stimulating," writes psychiatrist Stanley Greenspan. So, before you start tickling and wrestling and playing with the baby, spend a few minutes reading or cuddling with her, quietly getting to know each other again—even at eight months, a day away from you is a looooong time for your baby. You'll both feel a lot better if you do.

Besides making you miss your baby, a long day at the office can also make you feel guilty about the amount of time you're away from her. A little guilt is probably

"Not the Cape May lump blue-claw crab cake with creme fraiche, fried quail egg, osetra caviar, duck confit, and peach con frutti again?!!"

Benefits

- Satisfaction. As you watch your children grow and develop, you know that your teaching has made a difference in their lives, and you take joy in their accomplishments.
- Sense of pride. You're competent, you know that what you're doing is right and that you've achieved something meaningful by making an investment in your children's development. This feeling comes whether or not you get compliments from others on how great a dad you are or on how great your kids are.
- Love received. In a sense, this is your compensation for being an involved dad. You get to be needed, loved, admired, and appreciated (at least until your child becomes a teenager), and it feels great.
- Personal growth. Maturity, self-discipline, role modeling, and more emotional expression.
- Perceptual shift/expanded self. You're less goal oriented, less driven, more interested in the family. Doing things for kids can be a tremendously satisfying experience.
- Extending the family line—passing on your name, your history. Your children are your legacy.
- Fun. Your kids give you all sorts of excuses to express joy, to experience life as a child again, to play and do things you'd never do without a child (go to a park or the zoo, collect baseball cards, say "poop" in pubic).
- Continued learning. You may learn and develop skills and interests you never had before just to keep up with your kids. You may also relearn some of the subjects you'd forgotten long ago or learn some of the ones you never got around to in the first place.
- Purpose to life. Having kids may give meaning and direction to an otherwise ordinary life. If it doesn't do that, it'll definitely make you reevaluate your current priorities and strive for new ones.
- Enhanced marriage. Some men feel that having kids makes their marriage better, giving Mom and Dad a shared focus in life and in their children's accomplishments.
- Security. You've got someone to care for you in your old age (ha!).

Costs

- Time. For some men time is a metaphor for freedom or the opportunity to focus on themselves. Having kids requires giving up the freedom to do what you want while you're with them. You may have to give up activities that brought you pleasure. (Although the opposite can be true: I rekindled an interest in martial arts when my middle daughter started taking karate.) You also may spend a lot of time thinking about them when you're not with them.
- Sacrifice. You may have to defer satisfying your own goals and dreams or put off career advancement or continued education in order to be the good provider. This tends to be much more common among men who became fathers young.
- Finances. Again, a more common worry among younger dads. It costs a lot to raise a child these days. At some point, you may try to calculate all the things you could have done with the money you've poured into your kids. We'll talk more about this later in this chapter.
- Marital closeness. You'll probably spend less private time with your partner. There'll be less time for physical and/or emotional intimacy or even to talk over important issues.
- Energy. There's the sleep loss of early fatherhood, then the physical exhaustion of chasing a baby around, then more sleep loss when you start worrying about a sick child or drugs and alcohol and sex and friends and grades.
- Potential. All that time and energy you put into being a father is time and energy you could have devoted to writing a book, directing a movie, painting a masterpiece, inventing a cure for cancer, developing the ultimate killer app . . .
- Kids grow up and don't need you as much. A lot of the meaning in your life will come from your relationship with your kids and from feeling loved and needed. If that relationship changes or gets strained, as it is likely to do as your child grows up and seeks independence, you may mourn the loss of meaning.
- You get spread out. All the demands on your time and energy leave you feeling like there isn't enough of you left to be a good dad, friend, spouse, and employee at the same time.

a good thing, but far too many parents let their guilt get out of hand and end up backing away (emotionally) from their children.

Although there's no practical way for you to make up for lost time, it's important that you find some middle ground between being overly controlling and distancing yourself from your baby. The best way to do that is to make sure that whenever you're with your child, you're there 100 percent. Mute the phone, take a break from tweeting or posting to Facebook, turn off the TV, let the dirty dishes pile up in the sink, and eat dinner later. You can do all those things after the baby goes to sleep.

Circumstances may make it impossible for you to make any changes in the actual amount of time you can spend with your family. But if you have any flexibility at all, take another look at the work/family options on pages 152–59. On his deathbed, no father ever wishes he'd spent more time at the office.

YOU AND YOUR BABY

Reading

At eight to nine months of age, children who have been read to regularly can predict and anticipate actions in a familiar book and will mimic gestures and noises. So at this age it's a good idea to involve your baby more actively in the reading process. Talk about the things on the page that aren't described in the text and ask your baby a lot of identification questions. If you can, show your baby real-life examples of the objects pictured in her books.

At around ten months, your baby may be perfectly content to sit with a book and turn pages—probably two or three at a time. Don't worry if she seems not to be paying any attention to what she's "reading"; she's learning a lot about books' structure and feel. And since your baby's most significant interaction with books is trying to eat them, you might also want to pick up a few of the ones that come with teething rings or chewable corners. If you put a book upside down in front of your baby she'll turn it the right way. If you make a mistake in something you're reading to her, she'll correct you.

At eleven months, your baby may be able to follow a character from page to page. This is also the age at which she may start demanding that you read specific stories or that you reread the one you just finished. Board books, cloth books, and sturdy flap books are great for this age.

By the time she's a year old, your baby may be able to turn the pages of her books one at a time. She'll point to specific pictures you ask her to identify and

The Technology of Fatherhood

If you're feeling a little guilty—either about not being able to spend as much time with your baby as you'd like or about your partner having to handle more of the workload at home—you may find yourself eyeing technology as a way to resolve all of those issues. For example:

- If you can't make it home, you could use any one of the many video chat apps to read your baby a story.
- To feel more confident that your family is safe while you're not there, set up video monitoring and have it streamed to your phone or tablet.
- To stay up-to-date on everything your baby is doing at any time of night or day, there are a lot of gadgets that will measure your baby's pulse, temperature, breathing, movement, and more. There are devices that attach to your baby's ankle (like the ankle bracelets that convicts under house arrest wear) or Onesies.
- Concerned about baby safety in the car? There's a car seat that, in case of an accident, inflates a canopy to keep your baby protected from all that stuff you never got around to cleaning up.
- To make sure your baby is healthy, there are diapers that test your baby's urine and send the info to the company for analysis. The idea is to alert you to dehydration or urinary tract infections.
- To help your partner, you could get a power stroller that opens and closes with the push of a button (and no, it won't fold up if the baby's in it).
- Don't know why your baby is crying? Several apps promise to analyze the sobbing and tell you what your baby can't.
- Have your partner, nanny, or daycare provider enter your baby's nap, feeding, and diapering data into an app that you can view from wherever you are. Or they can send you video clips of your baby's newest tricks.

That all sounds really cool, doesn't it? It is. But here's the thing: none of those gizmos can ever come close to replacing the real you. So use these things if you absolutely need to, but relying on technology does *not* count as being involved (unless you're on a military deployment or extended trip and you have no other choice). Oh, and your partner might not be so thrilled about what she may see as your taking the easy way out of getting your hands dirty.

"The weasel represents the forces of evil and the duck the forces of good, a surrogate for American air and naval superiority."

may even make the correct animal sounds when you ask her, "What does a ___ say?" Be sure to respond positively every time your baby makes any attempt to speak—animal noises included.

As you've probably noticed already, reading provides you and your baby with a wonderful opportunity for close physical contact. The best position I've found (it's the one with maximum snuggle potential) is to put the baby on your lap and, with your arms around her, hold the book in front while you read over her shoulder.

When considering the next few months' reading, look for books with bright, big, well-defined illustrations, simple stories, and not too much text. Singing, finger plays, and photographs of babies and very young children are always popular. Keep in mind that what you read isn't as important as how you do it. Because babies prefer rhymed text to unrhymed, Mother Goose stories and other nursery rhymes are great. And don't feel obliged to finish every book you start. Besides your baby's current favorites (which you should keep reading for as long as she's interested), you might want to check out a few selections from our ever-growing list of books for the under-a-year set in the Books for Babies appendix.

As you're reading books to your baby, pay attention to how dads are portrayed. You'll probably find that they aren't present as much as moms, and when fathers *are* there, they aren't as involved with the children as much as moms are. That was the conclusion I reached when I first started researching dads in children's

He Says, She Says

Remember the story about the five blind men and the elephant? Each of them approaches an elephant and bumps into a different part—the leg, the tail, the ear, the trunk, the side—and then authoritatively describes to the others what he thinks an elephant really looks like (a tree trunk, a rope, a fan, a snake, a wall) The moral of the story, of course, is that two (or more) people looking at exactly the same object or situation may see very different things.

The same moral applies when couples are asked to rate the husband's level of involvement in the home. Women tend to compare what their partners do to what they do. Most dads come up short, which leaves the women feeling unhappy and overworked. Men, on the other hand, tend to compare what they do to what their father did or what the guy down the street does. And when they add in being the main or sole bread-winner, men end up feeling pretty proud of themselves and how much they're doing. Unlike with the elephant, the disconnect here isn't the result of blindness. Instead, according to fatherhood researcher Jay Belsky, it's that men and women are using "different yardsticks" to measure.

literature back in the 1990s. In the years since, a number of researchers have done similar studies and reached similar conclusions. The gender disparity will be more and more obvious as your child gets older.

Dealing with Stranger Anxiety

At about seven or eight months, you'll probably notice a marked change in your baby's behavior around strangers. Only a few weeks ago, you could have handed her to just about anyone, and she would have greeted the new person with a huge smile. But now, if a stranger—or even someone the baby has seen a few times before—comes anywhere near her, she'll cling tightly to you and cry.

Welcome to *stranger anxiety*, your baby's first fear. What's happening is that your baby is just beginning to figure out that she and you (and her other primary caretakers) are separate human beings. It's a scary idea, and she's simply afraid that some person she doesn't like very much might take you—and all the goods and services you provide—away. Stranger anxiety affects 50–80 percent of babies. It usually kicks in at around seven or eight months, but sometimes not until a year. It can last anywhere from a few weeks to six months.

Your baby is more likely to experience stranger anxiety if she's Withdrawing, Slow-Adapting, or has a Low Sensory Threshold (see the "Your Baby's Temperament" section on pages 133–41). She'll be less likely to be affected if she's Approaching or Fast-Adapting or if she's been exposed to a steady flow of new people since early infancy.

Here are a few things you can do to help your baby (and yourself) cope with stranger anxiety:

- If you're getting together with friends, try to do it at your own house instead of someplace else. The baby's reaction will be less dramatic in a familiar place.
- Hold your baby closely whenever you enter a new environment or anyplace where there are likely to be other people.
- When you arrive at a new place, don't just hand the baby off to someone she doesn't know. Let her cling to you for a while and use you as a safe haven.
- Warn friends, relatives, and strangers not to be offended by the baby's shyness, crying, screaming, or overall reluctance to have anything to do with them. Tell them to approach the baby as they might any other wild animal: slowly, cautiously, with a big smile, talking quietly, and perhaps even offering a toy.
- Be patient with your baby. Don't pressure her to go to strangers or even to be nice to them. And don't criticize her if she cries or clings to you.
- If you're leaving the baby with a new sitter, have her or him get to your house at least twenty minutes before you have to leave. This will (hopefully) give baby and sitter a few minutes—with you nearby—to get to know each other.
- If your partner stays at home with the baby while you're at work, you need to understand that your baby might lump you in with the people she considers strangers. Don't take it personally. Just follow the steps above on how strangers should approach the baby, and be patient. If you're that at-home parent, understand that your partner will feel horrible when this happens.

FAMILY MATTERS

Money

Without a doubt, money is one of the top two issues couples fight about. Financial squabbles are especially common during the early parenthood years, while both parents are getting settled. Many factors contribute to quarrels over money. Here are some of the most common:

- Lack of communication. Honestly, did you and your partner have a plan for how long she would take off work after the baby came, or how the family's finances were going to be taken care of? Far too many couples put off these discussions (or never have them at all) because they're afraid that it would lead to fights. If you haven't figured these things out yet, it's not too late. Better to have a little fight now than a huge resentment-dripping explosion later.

- Frustration. Women who have put their careers on hold to take a more active role at home may resent having their income (and the associated power) reduced. This goes double for men because of the still-lingering "good provider" pressures.

- Your childhood. The way you were raised can have a big impact—positive or negative—on the way you raise your own kids. If you grew up in a poor family, you may feel weird spending money on anything more than the bare necessities. Or you may feel obliged to give your child all the things you never got—at least the ones that money can buy. If your parents were big spenders, you may be inclined to bury your baby in gifts. Or you might overcorrect by cutting waaay back out of fear that you'll spoil him. Whatever your overall attitude toward money, if your partner's differs considerably from yours, look out.

- Differences in spending habits. You like Cheerios and eating lunch out; your partner wants you to buy the generic brand and bring lunch from home. She burns through your data plan Instagramming and Facebooking every detail about your baby's life—and downloading every detail of her friends' babies' lives, and you want her to start using WiFi instead.

- Differences in definitions. Your partner loves to get things "half off," but in your view, half off of something that costs three times more than it should is still no deal.

- Gender differences. At the risk of slipping into sex stereotypes, when it comes to money, fathers tend to be more concerned than mothers with savings and the family's long-range financial outlook. Mothers tend to be more concerned with the way the children look, partly because they understand that a lot of people see the way a woman's children dress as a reflection of her abilities as a mother. The big problem here is that she may interpret your not wanting to spend money on clothes as a sign that you don't love your baby enough (and, by extension, that you don't love her either).

- Lack of flexibility. As you may have noticed, becoming a mother does funny things to women (see page 111 for more on this). The moral of the story is that even if you do have a plan, build in some wiggle room. Things—and people—change.

Avoiding Money Problems, or at Least Learning to Live with Them

If you and your partner are fighting about money, or if you anticipate that you might, some or all of the following will help:

- Be realistic. Having a baby will have a major impact on your financial life. Food, clothing, medical expenses, and daycare or preschool tuition all add up pretty quickly. (Recent studies estimate that it will cost more than $250,000 to get a child from birth through high school.) If you have a child with disabilities or are caring for an aging parent, you'll have to be even more conscientious.
- Make a budget (there is plenty of good budgeting software, Quicken being among the best). Keep track of everything coming in and going out—especially your cash expenditures, which tend to slip through the cracks but can really add up. Take pictures of every receipt and import them into your budget.
- Hold regular meetings to discuss your financial situation. Listen to each other's concerns and remember that whatever your differences, you both have the best interests of your family at heart. No blaming or yelling, and stay away from discussion-killing phrases like "You always" and "You never."
- Rearrange your priorities. Take care of the absolute necessities—food, clothing, shelter, and paying down your high-interest credit cards—first. If there's anything left over, start saving it for ice cream cones, vacations, summer camps, private school education, and that midlife crisis Porsche (they actually have an SUV).
- Do plenty of comparison shopping. Fifteen minutes on the Internet could save you 15 percent or more.
- Negotiate and compromise. You give up Cheerios and take a brown bag to lunch; she does her social media stuff at home. Remember, there are many ways to cut back without having to skimp. Why pay full price for a pair of pants your child is going to outgrow in a few months when you can get a perfectly good used pair at a local thrift store for just a few bucks?
- Make a plan. Set realistic and achievable savings goals, and make sure you're adequately insured.

And while we're talking about money, I strongly suggest that you do the following as well:

- Max out your 401k or other retirement plan. There's a good chance that Social Security won't be able to cover all of your retirement expenses, especially if your baby moves back home in twenty-five years, so sock away every nickel you're legally allowed to.

- Max out your flexible spending account. If your (or your partner's) employer offers one, you may be able to use pretax dollars to pay for a lot of your child-care and medical expenses. Check with your human resources department and/or financial advisor: exactly how much depends on the plan.
- Start saving for college. Some states offer prepaid tuition plans, which let you pay off your child's tuition at today's rates. Or, open a 529 account. Money you put into the account grows tax-free, as long as you use it for college tuition, books, room and board, and other expenses. The money can be used at nearly any post–high school institution anywhere in the country, including state and private colleges, community colleges, and even vocational schools. You can find out more about 529s from the College Savings Plan Network at www.college savings.org/.
- Get your baby a social security number. Without one you can't open up a 529 account, and perhaps more important, you won't be able to take your child as a deduction or claim the Child Tax Credit.

The Building Blocks of Development

WHAT'S GOING ON WITH THE BABY

Physically

- As if recovering from the frantic developmental pace of the past two months, your baby will probably not add many new skills this month. Instead, he'll spend his time perfecting the old ones.
- By the end of this month he'll be such a confident crawler that he'll be able to buzz around the house grasping a block or other toy in one hand. He'll be able to crawl backward and may even make it up a flight of stairs. When sitting, he can turn his body all the way around without falling over.
- He easily pulls himself to an upright position and can stand for a few seconds while holding your hand. He can cruise (sidestep) along furniture and walls, and when he's done, he no longer has any trouble unlocking his knees and sitting down.
- Now able to move his digits separately, he has discovered that the house is filled with holes and cracks that are just big enough to accommodate his index finger.
- The biggest development this month (and this is pretty important) is that your baby is now coordinated enough to build a "tower" of two or three blocks (which he'll knock down immediately).

Intellectually

- In previous months your baby would learn a new skill and then repeat it endlessly. At this point, though, he'll begin to experiment with new ways of doing things he already know how to do. For example, instead of repeatedly dropping his spoon off his high-chair tray, he may start with the spoon, then drop his bowl off the other side, and finish up by tossing his cup over his shoulder. Besides confirming that the laws of gravity are still in effect, the purpose of the experiment, of course, is to see how many times he can get you to pick things up before you stop.

- He's just beginning to come to terms with the idea that he is not the power behind everything that happens. He may, for example, bring you a wind-up toy to wind up.
- He's also beginning to shake his if-I-can't-see-it-it-doesn't-exist attitude, but just barely. Now if he watches you hide a toy, he will look for it. But if you hide the same toy in a second hiding place, he will continue looking in the first hiding place. In his mind, something out of his sight can exist, but only in one specific place.
- He's also learning about actions and their consequences. If he sees you putting on a coat, he'll know you're going outside, and he may cry.
- As his memory gets better, you'll be able to interrupt him in the middle of an activity and he'll go back to it a few minutes later.

Verbally

- He's developing a distinctive "voice" in his babbling and may identify certain objects by the sound they make (*choo-choo* for train, *moo* for cow).
- Besides recognizing his name, your baby now understands and responds to other words and phrases, such as "No" and "Where's the baby?" He also understands (and might even obey) simple commands such as "Bring me my pipe."
- Although he's several months away from saying anything truly understandable, your baby already has a good grasp of the rhythm and sound of his native language. A German researcher found that even at this young age, babies are sensitive to the structure of words in their own language and can listen to a string of speech and break it down into wordlike units.

Emotionally/Socially

- This baby loves to play. He'll shout if he thinks you should be paying more attention to him. He loves to make you smile and laugh and will do everything he can to get a positive reaction from you. He's also a wonderful mimic and will repeat phrases like "uh-oh" and imitate your facial expressions and such acts as blowing out candles, coughing, sneezing, and pretending to eat with a spoon or drink from a cup.
- He may be able to get you to understand—by pointing, grunting, squealing, or bouncing up and down—that he needs something specific.

- Preferences are becoming more distinct, and he'll push away things (and people) he doesn't want.
- Perhaps a little scared of the new world he's discovering, he clings to you more than ever and cries if you leave him alone; it's the beginning of separation anxiety (different from the stranger anxiety of the past few months). He may also develop fears of things that never used to bother him, such as the vacuum cleaner, dogs, or baths. When my oldest was eight months old, she loved driving over speed bumps in the car, and potholes made her ecstatic. But only a few weeks later, even the slightest change in the surface of the road made her cry hysterically.

WHAT YOU'RE GOING THROUGH

Feeling More Attached to Your Baby

As your baby gets older and becomes more and more responsive and interactive, your attachment and feelings of connection to him will deepen. But the big question is, "When will your baby start feeling that way about you?"

The answer is somewhere between six and nine months. By that time, he's developed the intellectual capacity to associate you with satisfying his needs and wants, and can summon up a mental image of you to keep him company when you're not there.

Don't think that this means you shouldn't bother trying to establish an attachment to your baby from the beginning. On the contrary. Attachment doesn't just happen overnight; it's a gradual process that takes months to develop, and the sooner you get started, the better. Even if you and your baby haven't been able to form a solid attachment to each other (for example, you're in the military and have just come home), it's by no means too late.

As you might imagine, the single most successful strategy for forming lasting, secure attachments with your children is to spend time with them one-on-one, doing everything you possibly can together, from the mundane to the exciting. The way you react and respond to your baby will also have a great influence on the kind of attachment you and he eventually establish.

Attachment theories were first developed in the 1950s by researchers John Bowlby and Mary Ainsworth, who conducted detailed studies of the interactions between several hundred parents and their children. Bowlby and Ainsworth concluded that there are two basic types of attachment: *secure*, meaning that the child feels confident that the parent will respond appropriately to his needs, and *insecure*, meaning that the child is constantly afraid his needs won't be met by the parent. They further divided the insecure category into two subcategories:

avoidant and *ambivalent*. (See the chart on pages 224–25 for a more detailed explanation.)

Based on the information they gathered by observing babies in their first months of life, Bowlby and Ainsworth were able to predict fairly accurately the specific behavior patterns those same babies would exhibit as they grew. Bowlby's and Ainsworth's theories are just as valid today as they were when articulated over fifty years ago.

The Father-Child Connection

Although the vast majority of attachment studies have focused on mothers and children, some researchers are now beginning to study father-child attachment. Their findings confirm what active, involved fathers have known in their hearts for years—that the father-child bond is no less important than the mother-child bond. In fact, over 80 percent of studies that have examined father-child relationships have concluded that there's a strong connection between a father's involvement and his infant's well-being. Here's what the experts say happens to babies who have a strong attachment to their fathers and are "well fathered" as they grow:

- They score higher on intelligence and motor-development tests.
- They're more secure, more confident, and more interested in exploring the world around them.
- They're more independent, extroverted, self-confident, and interested in trying new things.
- They can handle brief periods of separation from Dad or Mom without getting too upset.
- They're more persistent and better at solving problems.

"Really, Howard! You're just like your father."

Attachment Basics

ATTACHMENT	TWELVE-MONTH-OLDS
Secure (about two out of three are securely attached, but that doesn't guarantee that they won't have any problems when they grow up)	• Are confident that their parents will be there when needed. • Know they can depend on their parents to respond to their pain, hunger, and attempts at interaction. • Readily explore their environment using parents as bases. • Don't cry much and are easy to put down after being held.
Avoidant (one out of six)	• May avoid physical contact with parents. • Don't depend on parents as a secure base. • Don't expect to be responded to caringly. • Learn not to act needy no matter how much they may want to be held or loved.
Ambivalent (one out of six)	• Cry a lot but don't know whether their cries will get a response. • Are afraid of being abandoned physically or emotionally. • Are worried, anxious, and easily upset. • Cling to parents, teachers, and other adults. • Tend to be immature and mentally scattered.

• Premature infants whose dads are highly involved have higher IQs at age three than those with less involved dads.

• They're exposed to a wider variety of experiences and will be more well rounded.

• They're more socially responsible.

• They have better verbal and math skills, get better grades in school, participate in more extracurricular activities, are less likely to drop out, and are more likely to graduate from college.

• They're less likely to get pigeonholed by traditional gender stereotypes (things like "Girls aren't good at math").

• They're more affectionate and empathetic.

• Girls enter puberty later and are less likely to become sexually active early or become teen mothers.

• They are more popular with their peers and have fewer behavior problems.

TODDLERS	PARENTS
• Are independent and trusting. • Learn early how people treat other people. • Are open to having their behavior redirected. • Mix well with all age groups. • Become social leaders. • Are curious and eager to learn.	• Respond to children sensitively and consistently. • Pick up the baby when he cries, feed him when he's hungry, hold him when he wants to be held.
• Are less curious. • Are frequently distrustful. • Can be selfish, aggressive, and manipulative. • May have few friends.	• Deny their (and others') feelings and needs. • Believe children should be independent early. • Don't like to cuddle with the baby or pick him up when he cries. • Can be emotionally cold.
• Lack self-confidence. • May experience uncontrolled anger. • May either overreact emotionally or repress feelings. • Are frequently less adaptable.	• Are wildly inconsistent and unpredictable in their parenting. • Are frequently self-involved. • Hope to get from the baby the love that they never had from their own parents and that they may not be able to get from each other.

At the same time, there are a number of factors that may interfere with father-child attachments. Researcher Glen Palm and I have both investigated this issue, and here's a combined list of the top barriers:

- Fathers who are at work most of the week find that "reattaching" with the kids on the weekends takes a lot of time and energy. Not surprisingly, research indicates that having a workable work/family balance promotes father-child attachment.
- A small but significant percentage of fathers feel that their in-laws are overprotective of their adult daughters and get in the way too much.
- Many fathers experience some tension in their relationships with their children because they feel excluded by the mother-infant bond or because they feel that they have to compete with their partners to form a relationship with the child. Some even buy into the notion that women are naturally better parents than men are.

In Case You Thought You Were Alone . . .

There isn't a single animal species in which the female doesn't produce the eggs. But eggs aren't worth much without the male's sperm to fertilize them. In most cases, once the eggs are laid, neither parent sticks around to watch them hatch or to meet their babies. Sometimes, though, eggs need more specialized care, or they'll all perish. In these cases, one or both parents are required to pitch in. Here are just a few examples of some of the dozens of species of animals in which the father plays an important role in carrying, raising, protecting, and educating his young.

Long before the male three-spined stickleback has even met his mate, he sets to work building an attractive little house out of algae. When he's finished, he hangs out in front and makes a pass at the first female who happens by. If she's interested, the male invites her in, but, not being much of a romantic, he asks her to leave after she's laid her eggs, which he quickly fertilizes as soon as she's gone. For the next few weeks, the father guards his nest, keeping it well ventilated and repairing any damage. Until his babies hatch, the father never leaves the nest, even to eat.

Like the stickleback, the male giant water bug does everything he possibly can to attract females. If one is interested, she climbs onto his back and lays nearly a hundred eggs, securing each to his back with a special glue. For the next two weeks the father is completely responsible for the eggs' safety and well-being. When they finally hatch, the babies stick close to Dad until they feel confident enough to swim away.

Unlike the stickleback, a cichlid (pronounced SIK-lid) doesn't need a nest. As soon as the female lays the eggs, the male scoops them up into his mouth. Because his mouth is so full, the father can't eat until the babies hatch—sometimes up to two weeks. And after they're born and can swim by themselves, Dad still protects his children by carrying them in his mouth. He spits them out when it's time to eat, get some air, or just have a little fun. And when playtime is over (or if danger is lurking), he sucks them back in again.

Frogs are famous for being involved fathers. After the eggs of the poison dart frog hatch, the tadpoles crawl onto their father's back, where they hang on with their suckerlike mouths as Dad carries them through the jungle. Darwin's frogs take things one step further. Just as his tiny, jelly-covered eggs are about to hatch, the future father snaps them up with his tongue and slides them into a special pouch inside his body. The eggs hatch, and the tiny tadpoles stay inside the pouch until they lose their tails and jump out of their father's mouth.

Among birds and mammals, there is a high rate of coparenting. For example, male and female geese, gulls, pigeons, woodpeckers, and many other birds work as a team to build their homes, brood (sit on the eggs to keep them warm), and feed and protect the young after they're born. In a similar fashion, the male California mouse is responsible for bringing food into the nest and for huddling with the young to keep them warm (the babies aren't born with the ability to regulate their own body temperatures). These mice have at least two things in common with human parents. First, they are both generally monogamous. Second, the presence of an involved father has a major impact on the babies: pups weigh more, their ears and eyes open earlier, and they have a greater survival rate than pups that are separated from their fathers.

Animal dads, just like their human brothers, make some pretty incredible sacrifices to protect and provide for their families. The male killdeer (a tiny bird named for its "kill-dee" cry and not its big-game hunting skills) protects its eggs and hatchlings from predators by pretending to have a broken wing. The "wounded" bird then flops around on the ground, squawking as if he's about to die, distracting the predator and luring it away from the nest. And several species of desert-dwelling birds, including the sand grouse, fly dozens of miles in a day to soak themselves in water, which they bring back for their parched babies to drink.

"My wife works, and I sit on the eggs. Want to make something of it?"

The emperor penguin is perhaps the most impressive animal father of all. While the missus is out looking for food, Mr. Penguin incubates their single egg, keeping it off the frozen ground by balancing it on the tops of his feet. For two months, he doesn't eat—he just stands there protecting the egg. When the egg hatches, Dad feeds the babies with a milky liquid he secretes from his esophagus. When Mom gets back, Dad—now about twenty-five pounds lighter—can go grab a bite to eat and take a short Arctic vacation.

- The better your relationship with your partner and the more confident she is in your parenting abilities, the more secure the father-child attachment will be.
- In cases of divorce, the quality of the relationship between the former spouses is the biggest predictor of the kind of relationship the father and his children will have.
- If you're not married (or are about to become not married) to your baby's mother, you may hear about how important it is for the baby to have one primary attachment figure—usually the mother. That absurd theory is often used to justify limiting a father's contact with his baby. There is "no basis for rank ordering parents as primary or secondary in their importance to child development," says psychologist Richard Warshak. "Having a relationship with two parents increases children's odds of developing at least one secure attachment." And researcher Linda Nielsen adds that when mom and dad aren't together, "babies who have secure attachments to both parents do just as well as babies in intact families."
- Some fathers say it's hard to form a close relationship because they feel they are unable to comfort their children adequately. A lot of these fathers were able to form close attachments only after their children were weaned.
- Age. Because younger dads are generally less settled in their careers and relationships, they often spend less time with their children than older (over thirty-five) dads.
- Temperament. No matter how much you love your child, you'll find it easier to form an attachment with an "easy" child than with a "difficult" one. (See pages 133–41 for more on temperament.)
- Income. Unwed or unemployed fathers sometimes feel such shame at not being able to live up to society's "good father" image that they back away. Don't.

YOU AND YOUR BABY

Playing Around . . . Again

For the first seven or eight months of your baby's life, he had to be content with staring at things from across the room and waiting for you to bring them to him. But now that he's mobile, he's going to try to make up for lost time. He's incredibly curious about his world, and no obstacle can stand between him and something to touch, squeeze, gum, or grab. (If your baby doesn't seem terribly curious, let your pediatrician know. But don't be alarmed if you catch the baby staring off into space once in a while. Babies this age spend about 20 percent of their waking time soaking up information visually, according to pediatrician Burton White.)

Although our society doesn't value play nearly as highly as some other parent-child pastimes such as feeding and diaper changing, it is nevertheless critical to your baby's development. "Many children who do not have much chance to play and who are only infrequently played with suffer severe intellectual arrest or setbacks," writes developmental psychologist Bruno Bettelheim.

One of your major goals should be to expose your baby to the most varied, enriching play environment possible. But perhaps even more important is your basic philosophy about play. "[T]he way parents feel about play, the importance they give it or their lack of interest in it, is never lost on their child," says Bettelheim. "Only when parents give play not just respect and tolerance but also their personal interest, will the child's play experience provide a solid basis upon which he can develop his relation to them and further to the world."

Brain Builders

These games and exercises can stimulate your baby's capacity to use different skills at the same time (seeing, hearing, thinking, and remembering, for example).

- Get two toys that are nearly identical except that they function in different ways (one might need to be squeezed to make noise, the other shaken). Let the baby play with one of them for a few minutes, then switch. Did he get confused? In the bathtub you could also demonstrate that an empty cup floats, but when you fill the same cup with water, it sinks.
- Ring a bell, squeeze a toy, or shake a rattle. When the baby looks to see what made the sound, put the toy into a group of things he's familiar with. Will he go for the one that made the noise, or will he get sidetracked by the other toys?
- More hiding games. A few months ago you discovered that if you hid a toy under a pillow or towel, your baby would push the obstacle out of the way to "find" the toy. Now that he's a little older and more sophisticated, you can up the ante a little by hiding an interesting toy under three or four towels. The look on his face when he pulls the first towel off and doesn't see what he was expecting will be priceless. Until he's about a year old, he'll probably get confused by the extra obstacles and forget what he was looking for in the first place.
- Imitating and pretend games. When babies imitate us, they're trying to figure out who we are and what we're doing. "When they imitate an older sibling or friend, they're not only trying to understand them, but they're figuring out what it's like to be older," writes Bettelheim. When playing with blocks, for example, be sure to include some nonblock things such as people, cars, trucks, and animals.
- Show him that objects can have more than one function. Envelopes, for example, can be shredded or used to contain other things.

- Encourage him to use tools. For example, tie a string around a toy that is well out of reach. Will he crawl to get the toy, or will he pull the string to bring it closer? What happens if you demonstrate what to do? A word of caution: once your baby has mastered the idea that there are new and exciting ways to get hold of things, watch out for low-hanging tablecloths and other dangling stuff.
- Encourage exploration. Babies who are curious and get lots of time and opportunities to explore end up doing better in school.

Exercises for the Major Muscle Groups

It's taken a while, but your baby is finally discovering that he has control over his feet. And over the next few months, he'll be making more and more use of them by learning to walk. He'll do this all by himself, of course, but helping him build up his muscles and coordination can be great fun for both of you:
- Put some toys near his feet and see if he'll kick them.
- Roll a ball far enough out of your baby's reach so he has to crawl to get it.
- Supervised stair climbing is great. But stay nearby and be extremely careful.

Vive la Différence!

As we've discussed earlier, fathers and mothers have distinctive but complementary styles of playing with their children: fathers tend to be more physical; mothers, less. But besides the physical nature of play, there are some other male/female differences you should be able to see now.

Fathers tend to encourage their children to do things for themselves, take more risks, and experience the consequences of their actions. Mothers, in contrast, tend to want to spare their children disappointment, are more protective, and discourage risk taking. (Keep in mind that I'm talking about *tendencies*. There are plenty of people who don't fit the mold.)

To see how these differences might play out, imagine that your baby is building a tower that is just about to collapse. You'll probably let the tower fall, hoping your baby will learn from his mistakes. Your partner, though, will probably steady the tower as it teeters. And if your baby were a little older and started climbing a tree, your partner would probably tell him to be careful and not to fall, while you'd encourage him to see how high he could go.

Many researchers have found that the differences in father-child and mother-child parenting styles can have a significant impact on the child. "There were indications that children's intellectual functioning was stimulated

This is a good time to start teaching your baby to come down stairs backward. But be prepared to demonstrate yourself and to physically turn your baby around a few dozen times a day.

- Play alternating chasing games: you chase him; he chases you. At the end, "reward" him with a big hug and—if he doesn't protest—a little wrestling. Besides being fun, these kinds of games teach your baby a valuable lesson: when you go away, you always come back. The more that idea is reinforced, the less he'll be impacted by separation anxiety (see page 222). Plus, as it turns out, kids who wrestle with their dads grow up with more highly developed social skills than kids who don't get as much physical play.
- Do some (gentle) baby bouncing. Get one of those big exercise balls and lay your baby on his back across it. Then press him into the ball and let him bounce. If you're feeling adventurous, hold the baby's legs and roll him around a little. Pay close attention to the baby's reaction—he can switch from ecstatic laughter to crying in a heartbeat. And be very careful not to do anything that could snap the baby's neck.

more in families with high father involvement," writes researcher Norma Radin. "We attribute this effect to the fact that fathers appear to have a different way of interacting with children; they tend to be more physical, more provocative, and less stereotyped in their play behavior than mothers."

Mothers and fathers also differ in the way they treat boys and girls. Fathers tend to vocalize more with sons than with daughters; they're more rough-and-tumble with sons than with daughters; and they're a little less likely to hug or snuggle a son than a daughter. They also are more likely to encourage and support sons' quests for independence than daughters'. This plays out in responding a little more quickly to a fussy girl than a fussy boy, or by picking up an infant daughter who's fallen down sooner than an infant son. Mothers do a better job of treating their boys and girls the same, but they, too, make some of the same distinctions.

Interestingly, when it comes to gender roles, mothers and fathers are equally inflexible: both will dress a girl in blue or pink and will encourage her to play with dolls or trucks. But they'd never put a boy in pink, and they give more positive feedback to boys who play with boy toys than to boys who play with girl toys.

Crawling

Although you may be in a hurry to see your baby walk, be patient. Crawling (which includes just about any type of forward movement, such as slithering, hopping along on the butt, or "rowing" forward with one leg) is a major developmental stage, and you should encourage your baby to do it as much as possible. There's some evidence that makes a connection between crawling and later proficiency in math and sciences. Kids who don't crawl apparently don't do as well in those fields.

Getting Those Little Hands and Eyes to Work Together

There are many activities you and your baby can do that stimulate hand-eye coordination:

- Puzzles. The best ones for this age are made of wood and have a separate hole for each piece and a peg for easy lifting.
- Nesting and stacking toys. These help improve gentle placement skills.
- Things to crush, tear, or crinkle—the noisier, the better.
- Weave some string between baby's fingers or tape two of his fingers together. Can he "free" himself?
- Stock your bathtub with toys that squirt or spin.
- Get toys that can be used in the bathtub or a sandbox to pour stuff back and forth. Measuring cups and spoons are also good.
- When you're shopping, have the baby help you put things in the cart.
- If you're brave, let the baby change channels on the TV remote.
- Play hand-clapping games.

More Experiments from the Land of Consequences

The idea that different actions produce different effects is one that can't be reinforced often enough. Here are a few things that are especially appropriate for your nine-to-twelve-month-old:

- Jack-in-the-boxes—especially the kind with four or five doors, each opened by a push, twist, poke, or some other action. These are also good for hand-eye coordination. Be cautious the first few times, though; some babies may be frightened.
- Balls are a big hit. They roll, they bounce off things, and they can knock over other things. For your baby's protection (and to reduce the chance of breaking your good dishes), make sure the balls you use are soft.
- Pots, pans, xylophones, or anything else the baby can bang on. He'll learn that

High-Tech Baby? Not Yet

The Internet is full of adorable videos of five- and six-month-old babies swiping objects on a tablet. I love technology as much as the next guy, but I strongly suggest that you keep your baby tech-free for a while.

First of all, more and more kids are having trouble playing with building blocks and other small toys because they've become so addicted to computers and smartphones (swiping takes a lot less dexterity and coordination than stacking blocks or picking up tiny objects).

Second, screens are not your baby's friend. The American Academy of Pediatrics recommends that babies spend exactly zero time in front of screens (TV, tablet, phone, computer) until age two. And there's good reason. TV watching in particular can disrupt parent-child interaction and is associated with lower cognitive outcomes. Be especially careful around educational videos such as *Baby Einstein* and *Baby Mozart*, which make all sorts of grandiose claims. The reality is that the more time babies spend watching these videos (which are one-way communication instead of the back-and-forth of a person-to-person interaction), the smaller their vocabularies.

Of course, the zero-screen-time rule is not going to be practical 100 percent of the time—you may need to make a phone call or take a shower. If you don't think your baby can entertain himself in a crib, playpen, or other safe place for a few minutes, a tiny bit of screen time won't hurt him. But make sure it's really, really tiny.

different things make different noises when smacked and that hitting something hard sounds different from hitting something soft.
- Doors (and anything else with a hinge)—provided you're there to make sure no one gets pinched. Books operate on the same basic principle.

The bigger your baby's world gets, the more interested he'll become in objects and the less interested in you. And why not? After all, you always seem to be around, but one of those exciting new toys might disappear before he gets a chance to grab it.

Giving up the number-one position in your baby's heart and mind can be tough on the ego, especially if you're being replaced by a stuffed animal or a toy car. But instead of pouting, take a more aggressive, if-you-can't-beat-'em-join-'em attitude: if you're having trouble keeping your baby interested in playing with you, use a toy to get his attention. But don't be in a hurry; wait until the baby

The Building Blocks of Development

There are literally dozens of cutting-edge, high-tech (and expensive) toys and games that claim to be essential to your baby's physical and mental development. Some are worthwhile; others aren't. But there's one toy— just about the least-cutting-edge, lowest-tech, cheapest thing going—that truly is an essential part of every nursery: blocks. Here's why:

- They help your baby develop hand-eye coordination as well as grasping and releasing skills.
- They teach your baby all about patterns, sizes, categories (big ones with the big ones, little ones with the little ones), gravity, balance, and structure. These brief lessons in math and physics lay the foundation for your baby's later understanding of how the world works.
- They teach good thinking skills. "Taken from a psychological view-point," wrote Albert Einstein, "this combinatory play seems to be the essential feature in productive thought—before there is any connection with logical construction in words or other kinds of signs which can be communicated to others."
- They can help your baby grasp the difference between things he has control over, such as which blocks he wants to use and how high he wants to go, and things he doesn't, such as the law of gravity, which keeps pulling down his towers.
- They teach perseverance. Building a tower—or anything else—out of blocks can be an excruciatingly frustrating experience for a baby. But along the way, he'll learn that if he keeps working on something long enough, he'll eventually succeed.

has begun to lose interest in whatever (or whomever) he's playing with before replacing it with something new. And above all, remember that you don't need to engage your baby every second he's awake. He needs some downtime, too, to play on his own or just to think. Really.

FAMILY MATTERS

The Division of Labor

About 90 percent of new parents experience an increase in stress after their babies are born. And the number-one stressor—by a pretty good margin—is the division of labor in the home. Money, which we talked about in the last chapter, is number two.

OH, HOW MUCH WORK COULD A BABY REALLY BE?

Before your baby was born, you and your partner probably anticipated that having a baby would increase the amount of household work you'd both have to do. But I'll bet you were way off on your estimates. Psychologist Jay Belsky found that for most new parents, dishwashing increased from once or twice a day to four times, laundry from one load a week to four or five, shopping from one trip per week to three, meal preparation from two times a day to four, and household cleaning from once a week to once a day.

And that's just the nonbaby areas of your life. When you factor in all the baby-related stuff, things really start to get out of control. "On average, a baby needs to be diapered six or seven times and bathed two or three times per day, soothed two or three times per night and often as many as five times per day," writes Belsky. In addition, the baby's helplessness makes just about every task, from going to the bank to getting dressed in the morning, take five times longer than it used to.

One woman in Belsky's studies summed up the discrepancy between her pre-birth workload estimate and the postbirth reality as essentially the difference between "watching a tornado on TV and having one actually blow the roof off your house."

AND WHO'S GOING TO DO IT?

Another thing you and your partner may have agreed upon before your baby was born was that you'd both be sharing responsibility for all the extra work the baby would require. If so, you're among the estimated 95 percent of people who say that men and women should share equally in child care. And why not? The more equitably domestic tasks are divided up, the happier couples are with their

Success and Failure

Whatever your baby is doing, be sure to praise his efforts as well as his accomplishments. Kids need to learn that trying to do something can often be just as important as actually doing it. Confining your praise and happiness only to the successful completion of a project can make your baby less likely to take risks or try new things for fear of failing.

marriages. Well, that's what conventional wisdom says. But it all depends on how you define "happier."

Several studies have found that couples in "egalitarian" relationships have sex less often than couples with "traditional" housework/child-care arrangements. And when those traditional roles are reversed and Dad does the majority of the housework, sex is even less frequent. That could explain why, as researchers Phil and Carolyn Cowan have found, most couples, despite their good intentions, slip into those traditional roles, with mothers doing more of the stereotypically female jobs and fathers doing more of the guy jobs.

At this point, we need to define another term: *equal*. To be egalitarian, does every job need to be divided right down the middle? Do you and your partner have to change the same number of diapers, soothe the same number of owies, make the same number of trips to the grocery store, give the baby the same number of bottles, and cook the same number of dinners?

In my view, the answer's simple: Nope. We should be going for symmetry rather than equality. In other words, how much time are you and your partner each logging for the benefit of your family? If it takes half an hour to cook dinner and about the same amount of time to give the baby a bath, feed him, put him in PJs, read him a story, and put him to bed, wouldn't those things roughly offset? And what about when one parent works in an office ten hours a day while the other is taking care of the kids (working just as hard) at home for those ten hours? Whose contribution to the family is more important?

The problems arise when one person consistently puts in fewer hours than the other. That's just not fair, and you need to do something pretty quickly to reestablish equilibrium (but not equality).

EVERYONE KNOWS THAT WOMEN DO MORE AROUND THE HOUSE, RIGHT?

Every few months or so, a new study makes the news, announcing that although women are dramatically increasing the hours they work *outside* the home and men are increasing the hours they work *inside* the home, women are still working longer hours than men. Headlines like these are common: "Women Are Still Doing Most of the Housework" and "American Mothers Are Exhausted, Do Far More Child Care and Housework." While technically correct (women are clocking more hours on housework and child care), when you read the actual articles— and the research they're based on (which, sadly, not enough people do)—you find a very different story.

Here's what the data show, as reported in Pew Research Center's 2013 *Modern Parenthood* survey:

TYPE OF WORK	AVERAGE OF ALL MOTHERS AND FATHERS (IN HOURS/WEEK)		AVERAGE OF MOTHERS AND FATHERS IN DUAL-INCOME COUPLES (IN HOURS/WEEK)	
	Fathers	Mothers	Fathers	Mothers
Paid work	37	21	42	31
Housework	10	18	9	16
Child care	7	14	7	12
Totals	54	53	58	59

Other sources, such as the time use surveys from the U.S. Bureau of Labor Statistics, show pretty much the same thing: moms do more housework and child care but dads do more paid work, and when you add up all those hours, it's dead even. This is slowly changing. More women are working outside the home and more are outearning their partners. At the same time, the number of at-home dads is growing.

Despite all that, men's and women's attitudes about who should be the primary breadwinner are still lopsided in favor of traditional gender roles, even among today's young parents (although women are a bit more egalitarian than men). A recent study done at Bentley University's Center for Women and Business found that among Millennials (those born after 1980):

- 68 percent of men expect to be the primary breadwinner in their household over the long term, and 35 percent of women expect that from a spouse or partner.
- 25 percent of men expect their partner to bring in half of the household income, and 44 percent of women expect to be equal contributors.

The numbers get even worse when talking about Millennial parents:

- 71 percent of dads expect to provide the majority of family income, while 46 percent of mothers expect their partner to be the primary earner.
- 20 percent of dads expect their partner to contribute equally, and 32 percent of women expect to be equal contributors.

10 Forming an Identity

MONTHS

WHAT'S GOING ON WITH THE BABY

Physically

- Unless your baby is extremely active, she won't make many big advances in motor skills this month. But not to worry, she's just enjoying a well-deserved break before taking her first real steps toward independence.
- She moves easily from crawling to sitting and may even be able to pull herself upright. Once there, she can stand with very little support and may even try a few seconds without a net at all.
- She can "cruise" (sidestep while holding on to something) just about everywhere, and if you hold both her hands, she'll walk and walk and walk.
- She's getting to be a fairly confident climber as well, getting up and down from couches and chairs almost without fear. Going up stairs is no problem, but coming down is still a challenge.
- She's also much better at manipulating her hands now. She can grasp two objects in one hand, and most of the food she tries to feed herself actually gets into her mouth. Her hand-eye coordination is getting more impressive by the day, and she'll stop to pick up and examine every speck of dirt she crawls or cruises by.
- She is beginning to discover that each side of her body can be used differently. And she may even be exhibiting an early "handedness" preference. She can, for example, use one hand for picking up and manipulating toys, the other for holding.
- If both hands are full, she may put down one object in order to pick up a third.
- Although she's quite graceful in her grasping, her releasing is still fairly clumsy.

239

Intellectually

- Although she still isn't completely convinced that things she can't see do exist, she's starting to suspect as much. Being able to retain an image of you even when you're not in the room will make her a little less upset if you leave her with someone else for a few minutes. This month, she'll look for a toy she sees you hide. If she's seen you move the toy to a second hiding place, she'll look for it there as well.
- She now understands that objects of different sizes need to be treated differently. She'll approach small objects with her fingers, but large ones with both hands.
- She's also intrigued by the idea that objects can exist for several reasons at the same time (they have properties as well as functions). Paper, for example, can be chewed, crumpled, and torn. And crayons can be held, eaten, and, best of all, used to scribble on things. This ability enables your baby to organize things into two categories ("things I can chew on" and "things that are too big to get into my mouth")—a realization that gives her a bit of control and predictability in her life.
- As her memory improves, she's getting more persistent. It's harder to distract her from whatever she's doing, and if you manage to turn her attention to something else, she'll go right back to her original activity as soon as you quit bugging her.
- She's now capable of symbolic thinking (associating something she can see with something she can't). For example, a few months ago, your baby would probably cry when seeing the nurses at her pediatrician's office. She associated nurses with shots. But now she may recognize the doctor's office from the street and will start crying as soon as you pull into the parking lot.

Verbally

- Although she's been saying "dada" and "mama" for a while, she really didn't know what those words meant. But now "dada," "mama," "bye-bye," "no," and possibly a few others have a definite meaning that she uses deliberately. She may even pick a word and repeat it over and over, all day long. (If she's not using words yet, don't worry. Some kids don't start until well after their first birthday.) She's also figured out that she can use certain noises to attract your attention and may deliberately cough, sneeze, yelp, and gasp just to get a rise out of you.
- She now understands a lot of what she hears and may actually cooperate (but probably not in front of friends you're trying to impress) in a brisk game of Identify the Baby's Body Part ("Where's your belly button?").
- She's also able to combine words and gestures: a head shake with "no," a hand wave with "bye-bye."
- She listens actively to adult conversation and will frequently butt in with a few "words" of her own.

Emotionally/Socially

- After a long day of crawling, cruising, babbling, and exploring, your baby really enjoys a nighttime snuggle. Her attention span is much longer than it used to be, and she may want even more stories than before.
- Your baby's mimicking skills are growing by leaps and bounds, and she'll now try to imitate just about everything you do: rubbing her hands together under running water, saying "brr" and shivering after getting out of the bath, and talking on the phone.
- When she cries (which she does much less frequently than a few months ago), it's less to get you to come running and more out of fear—of unfamiliar places or things, or of separation from you.
- She's becoming more sensitive to your emotions and is better able to express her own. If you're happy, she will be too. But if you scold her, she'll pout; if you do something she doesn't like, she's capable of genuine anger; and if you leave her alone for too long (only she knows how long that is), she may "punish" you by clinging and crying at the same time.

WHAT YOU'RE GOING THROUGH

Feeling Irreplaceable

You've been a father for most of a year now, and as we briefly discussed a few months ago (pages 173–74), you should be feeling pretty good about your fathering skills. If you're lucky, your partner, your friends, and your relatives have been telling you what a great dad you are. But there's one person whose opinion of your abilities probably means more to you than anyone else's: the baby.

As a grown man, you'd think you wouldn't need to have your ego stroked by someone who's barely two feet tall and can't walk or talk. But the fact is that there's absolutely nothing in the world that will ever make you feel better, more powerful, or more loved than the feeling of being needed by your own child. Those feelings—that you're irreplaceable and that your life has meaning because of your role as a parent—can do wonders for your self-esteem.

A Sense of Fulfillment

If feeling needed and appreciated by your boss and coworkers can give you a sense of self-worth and security at the office, feeling needed and appreciated as a father has the same result at home. In fact, nearly half the men in researcher Bruce Drobeck's studies, and a similar percentage of men I've interviewed, described fatherhood "as giving them more of a sense of fulfillment and/or purpose in their lives."

*"Can I call you back? I'm creating happy
memories of my childhood for my father."*

For some, becoming a father was the achievement of their fondest dreams and long-term goals. One man said, "I finally feel like I'm where I want to be and doing what I want to be doing." After less than a year of fatherhood, most new dads can hardly remember what it was like to have been childless. Fatherhood seems to have seeped into every aspect of their being.

A New Kind of Feeling Left Out, or Mr. Baby's Father

Becoming a father can wreak havoc on your identity in a lot ways. There's nothing quite like having a kid to make you realize that you're a grown-up. It also makes you realize that besides being a son, you're also a father. Now that may sound rather obvious, but you'd be surprised at how many men have a hard time with the concept. After all, we've spent our whole lives looking at our fathers as fathers and at ourselves as sons.

At the same time, there's nothing like being a dad to put you back in touch with your own childhood and to release some of that childlike behavior you've been suppressing for most of your adult life. Having a child gives you that perfect excuse to coo and giggle and make faces and crawl around on the floor say things like "poop" and "pee." In a way it's liberating.

Strangely, not everyone you come across is going to include "father" in the list of nouns they'd use to describe you. I can't count the number of times that I've been out with my kids in the middle of the day, and someone says something like, "Hey! You babysitting today?" (I've always wanted to shout back, "No, bozo,

I'm not babysitting, I'm taking care of my children!") I've never met a father who hasn't had a similar experience. Too many people see only "man" and not "father."

Sometimes they won't even see "man"—you'll just be Mr. Baby's Father, the invisible guy who's holding the baby. People love to come over and "talk" to babies who aren't nearly old enough to understand what they're hearing, let alone respond. They look the baby right in the eye and ask questions like "And how old are you?" "What's your name, you little cutie?" "Where did you get that darling little outfit you're wearing?" or my favorite, asking my youngest when she was ten months old, "Where did you get that beautiful red hair?" and on and on, in the same way that they might ask a cat whether it's hungry. And if you answer, they seem genuinely startled, as if they hadn't seen you at all.

Still other people—mostly single women—may see "father," but they also see "sensitive guy/potential mate." There's apparently something about a man playing happily with a child that a lot of women find very attractive. A man with a child

It Takes Balls to Be a Dad

Fathers with smaller testicles are generally more involved than their bigger-balled brothers in caring for their children and respond more when looking at pictures of those children. At least that's what researchers at Emory University in Atlanta discovered.

The research project with the brainchild of James Rolling, an anthropologist who was trying to figure out what makes some dads more involved than others. So he and his team did MRIs of the brain and balls of seventy men, all of whom had children one to two years old. They compared their results with surveys—filled out by the dads and the moms—about the dad's level of involvement. They also measured the men's testosterone levels, finding that dads who provided more child care tended to have lower levels.

Testicle size and sperm count are closely linked: the bigger the balls, the more sperm there is. So this team of anthropologists speculated that having more sperm would make a man want to spread it around as far and wide as he could. That would leave less time for—and interest in—child care.

The connection between the round parts of a man's package and his level of involvement with his kids is pretty well known—at least among other primates. Research has found that male chimps, which don't do much to care for their offspring, have testes that are twice as large as a human male's. But gorillas, which are very protective of their babies, have smaller balls.

and a dog is even better. If you're a single dad, this may be kind of fun. If you're married and want to stay that way, watch out.

YOU AND YOUR BABY
Exposing Your Child to Music

By the time your baby started babbling verbally, she had already been babbling musically for several months—cooing happily, adjusting her pitch up or down to match yours. You'd sing or coo back, and the two of you would have a little "duet."

For your baby, there is little if any difference between musical and verbal babbling. But for most parents, the difference is enormous. And the minute parents get even the slightest hint that their babies are beginning to understand language, the cooing and singing stops, and they focus their attention on developing the baby's verbal skills. "Consequently," says Ken Guilmartin, president of the Center for Music and Young Children, "the singing form is not reinforced and becomes developmentally delayed, or even atrophies completely."

Even if you and your partner don't have any particular musical talent, there's no reason why you can't stimulate your baby's musical potential. Now, before you protest that you can't carry a tune to save your life, keep in mind that "potential" and "achievement" are not the same thing. Unfortunately, this is a distinction that far too many parents fail to make.

According to music education researcher Edwin Gordon, every child is born with at least some musical aptitude: 68 percent have perfectly average aptitude; 16 percent well above; and 16 percent well below. "Just as there are no children without intelligence," he says, "there are no children without musical aptitude."

Good, bad, or indifferent, your baby's musical aptitude is greatly affected by the environment you provide. Even if you're so tone-deaf that you're embarrassed to sing in the shower, you can easily provide your baby with a rich musical atmosphere—and you'll probably enjoy yourself in the process. Here's how:

- As you started when your baby was three months old (see pages 117–18), continue exposing her to a wide variety of musical styles. But now try to choose recordings that have frequent changes in rhythm, tempo, and dynamics (loudness/softness). At ten months your baby's attention span is still quite short, and these contrasts will hold her interest longer and more easily, says Guilmartin.
- Never force your baby to listen to music. Your goal here is not to teach her (just like you won't be teaching her how to speak, crawl, or walk); rather, it is to guide and encourage her and let her develop at a natural pace.

- Don't turn off the music if the baby doesn't seem to be paying any attention. "There is little doubt that young children derive as much from listening to music when they appear not to be paying attention as when they appear to be paying attention," says Dr. Gordon.
- Try to avoid songs with words. Because your baby is rapidly developing her language skills, she may pay more attention to the words than to the music.
- Sing. Whenever and wherever you can. And don't worry about being in tune—your baby doesn't care. As above, use nonsense syllables—*dum-dee-dum* kinds of things—instead of real words.
- Listen to music you like. Your baby will be paying close attention to the way you react to the music and will know if you've selected some "good-for-you" piece that you really hate.
- Watch your baby's reaction to the music. She's moving much more actively than a few months ago. Her arm and leg movements may seem (to adults, anyway) to have no connection to the music, but they are actually internally rhythmic.
- Be patient. "The process of learning music is much the same as the process of learning language," write Gordon and his associates Richard Grunow and Christopher Azzara. Here are the steps they've identified:
  - Listening. From birth (and before), you absorbed the rhythm and inflections of your language—without any expectation of response.
  - Imitating. You weren't too successful at first, but you were encouraged to babble even though no one understood a single "word" you said.
  - Thinking (understanding). As you got more proficient with language, you were gradually able to decipher the muddle of sounds coming out of people's mouths into meaningful words and phrases.
  - Improvising. You made up your own words and phrases, and sometimes other people actually understood them.
  - Reading and writing. But not until you'd been listening, imitating, improvising, and thinking for more than five years.

Don't try to mess with the order—it's set in stone. If your parents had insisted on trying to teach you to read before you could speak, you might never have learned to do either.

Talking the Talk

Just because your baby isn't really able to hold up her end of a conversation doesn't mean you should stop talking to her. In fact, the more you talk to her, the more she'll learn.

- Encourage and expand. If your baby says "ba-ba," don't just leave it at that. Instead, respond with a full sentence, something like, "Do you want your bottle?" or "Yes, that's a sheep," depending on what you think she means.
- Identify. Ask, "Where's your tummy?" If she points to it or pats it, praise her and ask another question. If she doesn't answer, point it out for her ("Here's your tummy!") and ask another. Also identify the things your baby is interested in and talk about them.
- Talk about differences. Point to her fingers and then to yours, to her nose and then to an elephant's trunk. Tell her about how hers are smaller, and yours and the elephant's are bigger.
- Explain everything. If you're feeding her, talk about the food, the color, the taste, how messy her face is. If you're outside, talk about the traffic, weather, trees, construction sites. Remember, most of the things you come in contact with during any given day are familiar to you. But to her, it's all brand-new.
- Don't lecture. Just speak in a casual, conversational way, using full sentences and a vocabulary that's a little above where you think your baby is.
- Keep "No" and "Don't" to a minimum. It's incredibly hard, but try. First of all, they're very broad. If you say "No" or "Don't" to your baby, she may not understand exactly what you don't want her to do. All she really knows is that you're not happy with her. Too many Nos and Don'ts will discourage creativity and exploration. Instead, give her some details: "Knives are sharp, and they aren't for babies," or "It's not safe to try to put Mommy's hairpins in the electrical outlets." Of course, all your outlets are safely covered up, but you know what I mean.
- Read. Make stories and books part of your baby's daily routine.
- Keep signing. If you started doing this a few months ago, don't stop now. And if you haven't started yet, it's not too late. Working on spoken language and sign language are not at all contradictory. In fact, babies who've learned to sign usually have larger vocabularies than babies who don't.

Your Role in Molding Your Kids' Sexual Identity

Everyone knows that little girls are sugar and spice and everything nice, while little boys are frogs and snails and puppy-dogs' tails, right? Well, as with most stereotypes, there is, at the core, a kernel of truth there: girls and boys *are* different, and the differences go way beyond anatomy. In fact, they may be present in children's brains before they're born. And after birth, those structural differences may become the basis for behavioral differences. Here's what we know:

- Boys tend to be a little more irritable in their first weeks outside the womb, crying a little more and sleeping a little less than girls. One reason for this may be that mothers spend almost a hundred minutes longer in labor with a son

"I gotta go play with my doll now, so that I'll be a really great dad someday."

than with a daughter—perhaps because boys tend to be physically heavier and longer. This extra time being born leads to increased birth trauma and maternal drug taking, which may account for the difference in behavior.

- Girls are much more interested than boys in people, faces, and dolls (which look like people and have faces). Boys are more interested in objects (like trucks) that move. Boys also seem to prefer looking at a group of objects to just one.
- Boys are a little less discriminating when it comes to food and less sensitive to touch and pain.
- Girls can hear higher-pitched and quieter sounds than boys. But boys aren't as bothered as girls by loud sounds. They also have a dominant ear, which means that they hear less in one ear than the other and can't pick up background noises as well as girls can. Some researchers speculate that this may account for parents' perceptions that boys are less responsive to verbal requests than girls.
- Boys move around a bit more. They may be antsy in their stroller and will try to climb higher or crawl or cruise farther than a girl might. The differences are pretty hard to spot right now, but in a few months, when you take your baby to a park, you'll probably notice that the loudest, most rambunctious kids are boys and the quietest ones are girls.
- Girls may be somewhat more attuned to other people's emotions. Imagine that a baby, a new toy, and a parent are equidistant apart. The vast majority of babies this age will look over to the parent for some guidance as to how to behave. When the parent makes a happy face, both boys and girls will make a move toward the toy. However, when it's a fearful face, girls stay put, but boys move toward to toy anyway.

"We're calling her Fred, after her father."

- Girls start speaking a little younger than boys and have a larger vocabulary. But by age two, the guys have pulled even.
- Boys show fear later than girls do and they're less likely to be startled by loud noises.

Despite their number, the actual biological differences between boys and girls during the first eighteen months of life are so slight that when babies are dressed in nothing but diapers, most adults can't tell a boy from a girl. But that doesn't stop us from treating them quite differently. That raises a very provocative question: Are the differences we see in boys' and girls' behavior—however they got there—real, or are we just imagining them?

Cornell University researchers John and Sandra Condry showed two hundred adults a videotape of a nine-month-old baby playing with various toys. Half were told that they were watching a boy, half that they were watching a girl. Although everyone was viewing the exact same tape, the descriptions the two groups gave of the baby's behavior were startlingly different. The "boy" group overwhelmingly perceived the child's startled reaction to a Jack-in-the-box popping open as anger. The "girl" group saw the reaction as fear.

So do these imagined differences affect the way adults interact with children? Could be. Mothers, for example, respond more quickly to crying girls than to crying boys and breastfeed them longer. And when girls have a difficult disposition, mothers tend to increase their level of affection, holding and comforting the child. But when a boy is similarly fussy, they back off a little. This kind of behavior can have some serious long-term consequences. In one study, for example, boys who received more cuddling were found to have higher IQs than boys who didn't.

It's a Boy Thing

Interestingly, many of our perceptions and prejudices about gender start even before our children are born. "Parents say they don't care what gender their child is as long as it's healthy," says sex researcher Carole Beal. "But the truth is that couples have a definite preference for the sex of their child." That preference is usually for a boy; it's expressed by both men and women, and it's been true for more than sixty years. A 1947 Gallup poll found that 40 percent of Americans would prefer a boy if they could have only one child, and 25 percent preferred a girl. In 2011, those numbers were 40 percent and 28 percent, respectively.

Fathers may prefer boys because they feel more comfortable with them or because they feel that a boy would carry on the family name. Mothers may prefer boys because they know—instinctively or otherwise—how much it means to their husbands. "Boy infants tend to bring fathers into the family more," says Beal. "Fathers of newborn boys visit the nursery more often and stay there longer than fathers of girls."

Preferences like these can have a major impact on everyone in the family. Couples who have girls first often have more children, trying to have a boy. But couples who have boys first often end up with smaller families. Some experts speculate that this is at least in part due to the perception that boys are more "difficult." And two researchers in Stockholm, Sweden, found that men are generally more satisfied with their role as fathers when their babies—boys or girls—are the gender they'd hoped for.

At the same time, there's evidence that children who did not turn out to be the gender their parents preferred had worse relationships with their parents in childhood than preferred-gender kids. That was especially true for kids whose parents had wanted a boy but got a girl. And most interesting (and horrifying), couples who have daughters—especially a first-born daughter—are "significantly more likely" to get divorced than those with a first-born son, according to economists Enrico Moretti and Gordon Dahl. Moretti and Dahl also found that unmarried expectant couples are more likely to get married if they know they're having a boy.

By treating boys and girls differently, we may inadvertently reinforce sex stereotypes. For example, parents tend to react more positively to their daughters' attempts to communicate and more negatively to similar attempts by their sons, thus "confirming" that girls are more verbal than boys. Parents also react more positively when their sons engage in physical play and more negatively when their daughters do, thus "confirming" that boys are more physical than girls. So do boys play with trucks and girls with dolls because they want to or because that's what their *parents* want them to? Think about that the next time you're looking for a gift for your baby.

So here's the big question: Why do we treat boys and girls differently? Some researchers say that parents are simply repeating the socialization they got when they were children. Others say that the differences are rooted in biology. "Boys and girls actually elicit different responses from us," says psychotherapist Michael Gurian. "Primal, visceral, instinctive responses that tell us how to treat them. Because boys are a little bigger and stronger, we tend to play with them more roughly. And because girls are quieter and enjoy eye-to-eye contact, we spend more time talking to them."

Whether it's socialization or biology, the bottom line is the same: boys and girls are different. But be very careful: biology does not have to be destiny. Acknowledging that boys and girls are not the same doesn't imply that one gender is somehow better or worse or smarter or dumber than the other.

The whole point of this section is to get you to see how easy it is to fall into sex-stereotype traps. Sure, you'll still probably treat girls a little differently from boys; that's normal. But hopefully, now that you're a bit more aware of the dynamics, you'll be able to avoid the larger problems and give your kids a richer childhood experience. If you limit your daughter's choices to the soft and cuddly and your son's to the rough and muddy, you could very well end up with a child whose biology has, in fact, become his or her destiny.

If you have a boy, encourage him to communicate as much as he can. Don't discourage him from crying or from playing with dolls, and teach him that asking for help isn't a bad (unmanly) thing. If you have a daughter, wrestle with her, encourage her to play physically, and teach her that assertiveness and independence aren't unfeminine.

But whether you have a boy or a girl, make sure you aren't forcing your child into a type of behavior that doesn't fit his or her character or temperament. The bottom line is that some boys, if you give them a Barbie to play with, will tear her head off and use her legs as a double-barreled shotgun; and some girls are going to want to wear lace everywhere they go.

YOU AND YOUR PARTNER

Communication

One of the most common traps new parents fall into is that they stop—or at least change—the way they communicate. Half the time these changes are permanent. I'll talk more about how this affects the overall couple relationship on pages 283–84. In the meantime, here are some factors that researcher Jay Belsky and others have identified as contributing to the problem:

- "A new child deprives a couple of many of the mechanisms they once used to manage differences," says Belsky. For example, when you used to have disagreements about who did what around the house, you might have solved the problem by getting a housekeeper. But after the baby is born, strained finances might not allow for a cleaning person, which means you'll have to deal with the once painless who-does-what disagreements.
- Lack of spontaneity. Before your baby was born, if you wanted to go see a movie or even just sit around and talk, you could simply do it. But now, as parents, you don't have that luxury. If you want to go out, you have to get a sitter a day or so in advance, make sure the baby is fed, and be back at a certain time.
- Physical exhaustion. Even if you stay home together with your partner, there's a better than even chance that you'll be too tired to stay awake for an entire conversation.
- There's a general decline in intimacy-promoting activities such as sex, hanging out with friends, and so on.
- With so much time, money, and energy focused on your baby, you and your partner don't have as many opportunities to pursue individual interests and activities outside the home. You won't have nearly as many new things to talk about, and you may lose (partially, at least) the ability to hear and understand each other.
- Expectations have changed. The time your partner spends with your baby is time she can't spend with you. She may be feeling pressured to be a fantastic mom, and you may be putting even more pressure on her by reminding her that she's not satisfying your emotional needs as much as she used to.

(11) Planes, Trains, and Automobiles

MONTHS

WHAT'S GOING ON WITH THE BABY

Physically

- Your baby can get himself to a standing position by straightening his legs and pushing off from his hands. He may even be able to stand up from a squatting position and squat back down to pick something up.
- He may also be able to stand without any support and will try to do two activities at the same time, such as standing and waving.
- He can climb up stairs using the railing and can walk holding on to only one of your hands.
- He adores rough play—wrestling, rolling around on the floor, being held upside down, and bouncing on your knees.
- He can clap and turn the pages of a book, but not as accurately as he'd probably like to.
- He can operate a spoon pretty well but prefers to use his hands.
- He can hold on to a crayon and will draw on any surface he can reach. He still has a little trouble releasing objects exactly when and how he wants to.

Intellectually

- One day this month, your newly upright baby will be leaning against a chair, and he'll accidentally make it move a little. He'll immediately understand that he's the one responsible and will do it again. And again. He may, in fact, spend the rest of the day (and the month, for that matter) pushing the chair around the house.
- Imitation reaches new heights this month. But rather than mimicking specific actions, he's now able to imitate concepts, or even a series of actions. He'll hide

things and get you to look for them, feed you, and try to brush his own teeth and get himself dressed.

- He'll spend a lot of time this month dropping small objects into larger containers, learning the difference between big and small, container and contained, "in" and "out."
- He's also expanding his knowledge about symbols. He's fascinated by books but doesn't really know what to make of them. He'll poke at the pictures in a book, intrigued by the idea that he can see something but can't pick it up.
- Although still convinced that he's running the world, he's discovering that his body has limitations. If some precious object is out of reach, he'll push you toward it, trying to get you to reach it for him, thus using you as a tool.

Verbally

- Although his vocabulary is growing, he's nowhere near being able to put together full sentences. But he'll babble in long "paragraphs"—sometimes to himself—and toss in an occasional recognizable word.
- Interestingly, the sounds he uses in his babbling are specific to his native language, and he can no longer produce some of the ones he could even a few months ago.
- Whenever he learns a new word, he'll repeat it to himself dozens of times.
- He recognizes the symbolic use of words: he'll say "yum" if you're talking about ice cream, "meow" if you point out a cat.
- He's developed an incredible ability to hear what he wants to: he'll completely ignore a shouted "Get away from that stove!" just to test out your reaction, but will stop whatever he's doing and rush to your side if you whisper "cookie" from another zip code.

Emotionally/Socially

- Besides happiness and sadness, your baby is now capable of other, more sophisticated emotions. If you play with another baby, for example, he'll become jealous and protest loudly. He's also getting much more demonstrative, and will show genuine tenderness and affection to you as well as to his stuffed animals.
- He now understands approval and disapproval. When he cleans his plate, he'll joyously shout for you to come look, and he'll beam with pride at having done something good. If he's done something he shouldn't have, though, he knows it and will bow his head sheepishly in anticipation of a few sharp words. Generally, he wants to please you, but he also needs to displease you to learn how you'll react.
- He may scream or throw a tantrum if he doesn't get what he wants.

"I did ask her and she said to ask you where I came from."

- He may also be afraid of growing up and may regress emotionally as well as physically to a time when he was a baby and you took care of him.
- Your baby is already beginning to establish his or her own sexual identity. Girls begin to identify with their mother and other females and do what they do, while boys will identify with you and other men and want to do what you do.
- He loves playing alongside other children but isn't ready to play *with* them.

WHAT YOU'RE GOING THROUGH

More Worries about the Baby's Health

For the first few months of your baby's life, you depended on your doctor to keep you informed as to how the baby was doing. And had there been any major problem (neurological defects, Down syndrome, and so on), or anything amiss with your baby's growth or development, you would have heard about it by now.

But most problems that affect children aren't easy to spot. And now that your baby is older and his well-baby checkups are further apart, your pediatrician will rely more on you and your daily observations about your baby's behavior to make any diagnoses. Keeping track of the following and reporting them to your pediatrician will help him or her better assess your child's continuing development:

- Is the baby having trouble manipulating objects or moving around? Delays in developing sensory/motor skills can cause delays in language development as well.

- Is the baby using his body fairly symmetrically? Does he use one hand (or foot, or eye) more than the other?
- Is the baby having trouble eating or swallowing food? Besides resulting in nutritional deficiencies and general health problems, these problems may interfere with your baby's using his jaw, lips, and tongue, and may have an impact on language and cognitive skills.
- Has your baby lost previously attained skills? Did he babble and coo in the past but suddenly stop? Does he no longer react when people come and go? This could be an indication of a hearing problem, which, again, can affect language development.
- Is the baby not achieving, within a month or two, the milestones described in the "What's Going On with the Baby" sections in this book?
- Does the baby seem uninterested in exploring his surroundings?
- Has your baby undergone a major change in temperament? (See pages 133–141.) But remember: difficult temperament by itself is not an indication of any kind of disability.

In most cases, the "problem" behaviors you identify will turn out to be perfectly normal. But that doesn't mean you should stop paying attention. Here are some things you can do to reassure yourself:

- Spend some time reviewing the "What's Going On with the Baby" sections of this book. The more you know about what your baby is and isn't capable of, the less you'll worry.
- Don't worry that your doctor—or your partner—will think you're asking too many questions or becoming overly concerned. You (or your insurance company) are paying your doctor more than enough for him or her to listen respectfully to any questions you might have.
- If, after talking to your doctor, you're still not satisfied (or you think you're being ignored), get another opinion.
- Keep a detailed log of things your child does (or doesn't do) that concern you, when they happen, and under what circumstances.

Men have a tendency to ignore their own health concerns either because they hope whatever's worrying them will go away or because they're afraid the doctor will confirm their worst suspicions. If you want to ignore something that's been bothering you, you're making a big mistake, but that's your prerogative. But don't apply the same standard to your baby. You may not be the most experienced parent in the world, but your gut reactions about what ails your children are usually pretty good and should be acted on. Of course, this doesn't mean bringing the baby into the emergency room every day, but an occasional call to your doctor's advice nurse is fine. If there *is* something to worry about, you're better off knowing sooner than later, when the problem will be much harder to deal with.

YOU AND YOUR BABY

Planes, Trains, and Automobiles

When my oldest daughter was only six months old, my wife and I decided it was about time to take that honeymoon trip we'd been putting off since we'd gotten married. So we redeemed a few years' worth of frequent-flier miles, and the three of us took off on a month-long trip to New York, France, Israel, and Phoenix. All in all, it was a great trip.

Your first trip with your baby is not likely to be as big an expedition as ours, but sooner or later you're going to want to pack up the family and go somewhere.

Planning Your Trip

- Spend some time planning your itinerary. You can take babies under about seven months just about anywhere anytime. After your baby has learned to walk, however, it's best to limit your destinations. Seven cities in four days is hard for even the most seasoned adult traveler. If possible, check out local baby-friendly attractions (zoos, museums, parks, beaches, puppet shows) before you leave.
- Try to pick destinations that won't be terribly crowded. Large groups of unfamiliar people might spook your baby.
- Get tickets or print out your boarding passes (or download them to your phone) in advance. There's no sense standing in lines if you don't have to.
- Travel during off-peak times. Christmas Day, New Year's Day, and Thanksgiving Day (as opposed to the days before or after), for example, are good. If you're driving, there'll be less traffic on the road; if you're traveling some other way, you'll find a lot more empty seats, meaning more room to stretch out or run around.
- Consider red-eye flights. They may increase the chances your baby will sleep on the plane, and can also help get the jet-lag-acclimation process under way.
- Prepare for jet lag/time differences before you leave. You can keep the baby up late, put him to bed early, and so forth. Also adjust meal times.
- Prepare your child for the upcoming trip by talking about it regularly. Make it sound like it's going to be the most fun anyone has ever had.
- Schedule a doctor's appointment (for your child) for a few weeks before you leave. Tell your pediatrician where you're going and ask for the names of a few good local doctors. Also ask her to suggest any medical supplies you should

bring along. If your child is taking any medication and will come anywhere near running out while you're on the road, get an extra prescription.

What to Bring

No matter where you go, the trick to making things run smoothly on a trip away from home is to surround your baby with as many familiar things as possible. This will help minimize the shock of the new routine and scenery. Whatever your destination, then, you'll probably need most of the following:

- Eating utensils and bibs.
- Bottles and formula, if you're using it. If you're traveling overseas and will be using powdered formula, plan on bringing some bottled water.
- Car seat. Doubles nicely as a high chair if there isn't one around and you really need to restrain your baby while she's eating.
- A good backpack. It'll free up your arms so you can schlep the six tons of other baby-related stuff you'll be needing.
- Extra pacifiers, especially if your baby sucks on one a lot during the day or needs one to get to sleep.
- A portable crib. Or, if you'll be staying in a hotel, call ahead to reserve one.
- A first aid kit (see page 204 for the ingredients).
- Baby shampoo and diaper cream.
- The all-purpose travel bag (see below).
- Lots of familiar toys, stuffed animals, favorite foods, and a nightlight. These will help the baby adjust more quickly to the new surroundings.
- Try not to overpack. If you aren't going trekking in the Himalayas, you don't really need to take along three weeks' worth of disposable diapers—they're

The All-Purpose Travel Bag

If there's ever any danger of getting separated from your luggage (even if most of it is just in the trunk of your car), you should have a well-stocked bag with the necessary "emergency" supplies:

- Diapers, lots of wipes, and a few extra outfits.
- New toys (one for each hour of travel time); mirrors and suction-cup rattles are big hits with babies.
- Food, including extra formula if needed.
- Something to suck on (pacifiers, teething rings, and so forth).
- A few books.
- Some favorite comfort items (blankets, teddy bears, and so on).

available just about anywhere. The first thing my wife and I did when we arrived in New York was get a huge cardboard box and ship home about half of the stuff we'd brought.

Once You Get There

- Keep up the routines you've established at home. Read, sing, and play at the same times if you can. This is especially important for Predictable babies (see page 135).
- Don't overbook activities. One or two excursions a day is plenty.
- Keep a sharp eye on baby/relative contact. If friends and relatives haven't seen the baby for a while or are meeting him for the first time, they'll all want to hold, squeeze, cuddle, and entertain him. This can freak out even the calmest of babies. Be especially sensitive if your baby is going through a period of stranger or separation anxiety.
- If you're planning to leave the baby with a sitter or a relative, have her come early so the two of them can get to know each other for a few minutes before you head out.
- Stay away from meats, fish, eggs, and dairy products. If you're going to get food poisoning on the road, it'll probably come from one of those food groups. And if you're traveling overseas, stay away from water, milk, juice, raw foods, and anything served by street vendors unless you know for sure it's safe. This is especially important if your partner is still nursing.

Traveling by Car

- For short trips, try to leave an hour or so before your baby's usual nap time and, once he falls asleep, drive as far as you can while his nap lasts.
- For longer trips, consider doing your driving from 4 P.M. to midnight. That way, you'll only have a few hours of entertainment and stops for feedings before baby goes to sleep for the night.
- If you need to drive during the day, you or your partner should ride in the back seat with the baby in one- or two-hour shifts to keep him amused and awake. Car travel tends to knock babies out and can really screw up their sleep schedules.
- Take lots of breaks and make sure everyone has plenty of opportunity to stretch, unwind, and relax. Stop at interesting places, pet the cows (be sure to wash your hands afterward), watch the road-repair crews, point out new sights (forests, cloud shapes, and so forth), sing songs, read stories. Going through an automatic car wash can be a thrill for some kids, but for others it can be terrifying. Whatever you do, have fun.

Eating Out with Your Baby

One day, when you and your partner are feeling very brave, you may decide to take your baby to a restaurant. If so, keep the following in mind:

- Call ahead to see whether babies are welcome and to make sure they have enough high chairs.
- Don't stay out past your baby's bedtime. Being in a new place can be stressful enough.
- Stay away from crowded, noisy places unless you know your baby loves that kind of environment.
- Keep it casual. White tablecloths and crystal wineglasses are to babies what red flags are to bulls.
- Sit near an exit. You may need to take an upset baby out of the restaurant at a moment's notice.
- If the baby will be eating with you, don't forget his food and a few extra spoons, just in case one (or two) ends up on the floor.
- If your baby is walking, don't let him visit other tables unless you're absolutely sure that the people there really want to be visited. It may be cute to you but annoying to others. Also, wandering (and crawling) babies are tripping hazards to waiters.
- If you're holding the baby on your lap, be very, very careful. Babies are born with a sixth sense about restaurants, and they will lunge for whatever's hottest and sharpest and will make the biggest mess when it's spilled.
- Don't expect the restaurant staff to entertain your baby.
- Don't be embarrassed if you have to leave suddenly. Babies melt down, have blowups, and get sick.

- Put the car seat in the middle of the back seat; it's safest there. The seat should still be facing backward, and you need to make absolutely sure it's installed properly. As I mentioned earlier, you can probably get this done for free by your local police department or highway patrol.
- Lock car doors from the inside.
- Never, never leave your child alone in a car—especially in the summer. Babies can suffocate a lot faster than you might think. Every year you hear tragic stories of people who didn't follow this advice and killed their child.
- If your baby is nursing and gets hungry while you're on the road, stop the car and let your partner feed the baby. Every few years there's another story about a mom who's arrested for breastfeeding while driving (my favorite is the woman

in China who was nursing her baby while riding a moped). It's simply not safe to do that while driving—for you, your partner, your baby, or the truckers who may be distracted by the sight of your partner's exposed breast.

GOOD THINGS TO BRING IN THE CAR

- Lots of food and drink.
- Lots and lots of books, toys, blankies, and stuffies.
- An older child, if you happen to have one. This will make entertaining the baby a lot easier.
- Your iPod or music player and a good selection of music. Make sure to bring some you like as well. One warning: if you have to slam on your brakes at sixty miles an hour, every object you have in your car is a potential projectile. So before you bring anything along, think about whether you'd like to be hit in the head by it.

Traveling by Plane

- Get to the airport early. Going through security with a baby can be a real adventure. You'll have to fold up the stroller to put it through the X-ray machine, and in most cases you'll have to carry the baby through the metal detectors. And be prepared: if you set off any alarms, the security people may pat your baby down too.
- Use your stroller to haul your carry-ons, car seat, and other stuff, and carry the baby in a front pack or sling. Most airlines will let you check the stroller at the gate.
- Try to get bulkhead seats (usually the first row). They generally offer a little more room, and you won't have to worry that your child will kick the seat of the people in front of you. Also, ask to be seated next to an empty seat if possible. Be sure to hold your absolutely adorable baby in your arms while you're asking—this can improve your chances of getting what you want.
- Don't board early. Instead, send your partner on with the carry-on stuff while you stay out in the lounge, letting the kids run themselves ragged until the last minute. Why spend any more time cooped up in the airplane than you absolutely have to?
- If you're going on a long trip, and your child is particularly restless or active, schedule a stopover or two to give you all a chance to get off the plane, stretch, and run around.
- Every child under two years old should suck on something—breast, bottle, or pacifier—on the way up and the way down. This will counteract the pressurization and reduce the chances of painful earaches. It may also make your baby a little drowsier.
- Make sure your child drinks a lot on board and try to keep his nasal passages

moist. Airplane travel can dry out your baby's (and your) mucous membranes, making him more susceptible to colds or sinus infections.

- Buy your baby his own seat. Yes, it's more expensive, but holding a baby on your lap for a few hours, especially in a packed plane, can be a real pain. It's also not nearly as safe as having the baby neatly secured in a car seat.
- Check as many bags as you can, but carry on the all-purpose travel bag (see page 257).

WHAT TO BRING ON THE PLANE

- Same as for cars (see page 260).
- Some extra food—for the adults and the baby. The meals you ordered might not show up, or if you're taking a short flight, there might not be any food at all.
- A rear-facing car seat. Check with the manufacturer to make sure that it's approved for airline use and that it will actually fit in the seat.
- Pacifiers. This is not the time to break your child of his sucking habit (I actually sat next to a woman whose baby was screaming and who refused to give him the pacifier she was holding. That was just plain cruel. And it wasn't very nice to the baby either). Your fellow passengers will thank you.
- If your partner is nursing, bring a light blanket that she can throw over her shoulder for privacy.

DEALING WITH JET LAG

- If you're traveling for only a few days, keep the baby doing things at the time he would be doing them at home. This will make it easier to return to your regular schedule when you get back home.
- Spend time outside. Natural light helps acclimate people to new time zones more quickly.

FAMILY MATTERS

Insurance

Becoming a parent does some interesting things to your mind and to your outlook on life. On the one hand, having a child makes you want to live forever and not miss a single second with your child. On the other hand, watching your child grow older is like a hard slap in the face; it makes you realize that no matter how much you want to, you're not going to live forever.

Unfortunately, there really aren't any hard-and-fast rules or secret formulas

"Greetings, stockholders."

to help you determine how much insurance you and/or your partner need. But spending some time thinking about the following questions will help you clarify your needs:

- If something were to happen to either you or your partner, how much income would you (or she) need to maintain your current lifestyle? Could you or your partner take care of all the family's expenses alone? Life insurance is not a get-rich-quick scheme, and it's not a forced savings plan; it's a way to make sure expenses are covered so that you or your partner wouldn't have to sell your house or change jobs if, God forbid, the other should die unexpectedly.
- Do you need or want to pay off your mortgage, car, credit cards, or other debts?
- Do you need or want to leave an estate large enough to pay fully for your kids' college education?
- How many years of your income do you want your insurance to replace?
- What other expenses need to be covered? For example, if one parent dies, the surviving one would probably need additional child care.
- What do you expect your tax situation to be? If you have a huge estate, your heirs will have to come up with a tidy sum to cover inheritance taxes.
- How much coverage do you already have? You may already be covered under a policy provided by your employer, the military, your union, or some organization you belong to.
- Do you or your partner have children from a previous relationship? Have either of you adopted the other's children? If not, and one of you dies, will the

children live with the stepparent or with the other biological parent? How much of the children's expenses is the stepparent legally (and morally) required to pay?

- How much does Social Security provide? Most insurance salespeople never bring this up to their clients. But here's the deal: If you and/or your partner have been working for any length of time, your survivors are eligible for certain Social Security benefits (some of the money you pay into Social Security actually goes toward survivors' insurance). The Social Security Administration (SSA) estimates that about 98 percent of children with working parents would get some benefits if one of them died. The amount of the payment will depend on how old you are, how long you've been working, and how much you've earned over your lifetime. Social Security benefits may be taxable, and since they're paid monthly, they can't be counted on to help with estate taxes. The SSA has two websites that can help you sort through this: www.ssa.gov/pubs/EN-05-10084.pdf or www.ssa.gov/pubs/EN-05-10024.pdf.

There are two basic ways to make sure your insurance needs are properly taken care of:

- Read a few good personal finance guides (or at least sections of them). Despite what you might think, it's not all that complicated.
- Get yourself a financial planner (see pages 264–65 for some helpful tips).

Either way, you should at least be aware of your insurance options. Basically, there are two types of life insurance on the market: term and cash value; each is further divided into several subcategories. Here's a brief overview:

TERM

There are three types of term insurance, and they all share these features:
- Fairly low cost, especially in the early years.
- Premiums increase over time as your odds of dying go up.
- Policies are in effect only for a specified period of time.
- No cash value accumulation.
- Benefits may be taxed.

HERE ARE YOUR BASIC TERM INSURANCE CHOICES:
- Renewable term. If you keep your death benefit the same, the premiums will rise. But if you develop a health problem, you may get canceled altogether.
- Level premium. The death benefit and the premium remain the same for a specified period of time, sometimes for as long as thirty years.

Picking a Financial Planner

Many financial planners are paid on a commission basis, based on your insurance purchases, stock trades, and/or the total value of your portfolio. So whether or not your investments do well, the financial planner gets his commission. Others are paid on a fee basis and typically charge from $50 to $250 per hour.

This doesn't mean, of course, that fee-based planners are inherently better than their commission-based colleagues (although many experts believe that you'll be happier, and possibly richer, with someone who charges a fee and not a commission). Your goal is to find someone you like and who you believe will have your best interests at heart. Here are a few things you can do to help you weed out the losers:

- Get references from friends, business associates, and so forth. Alternatively, the Financial Planning Association (www.plannersearch.org) will give you references to some local certified financial planners. The National Association of Personal Financial Advisors, (napfa.org) makes referrals to fee-only (as opposed to commission-based) planners.
- Select at least three potential candidates and set up initial consultations (which shouldn't cost you anything). Then conduct tough interviews. Here's what you want to know:
  - Educational background. Not to be snobby here, but the more formal the education—especially in financial management—the better.
  - Certifications. Certified financial planners (CFPs) go through a rigorous training program, do continuing education to stay current, and must have a minimum amount of experience before they can use the CFP certification. That designation can help you differentiate between someone who's really a planner from someone who just sells stocks and insurance.
  - Licenses. Is he or she legally able to buy and sell financial products such as stocks, bonds, mutual funds, and insurance?

- Decreasing term. The death benefit decreases each year, but premiums remain the same. In other words, each year you get less insurance for the same cost.

CASH VALUE

There are an increasing number of cash value insurance products available. Despite their differences, they all share the following features:

- Level of experience. Unless you've got money to burn, let your niece break in her MBA on someone else. Stick to experienced professionals with at least three years in the business.
- Profile of the typical client. What you're looking for is a planner who has experience working with people whose income level, family situation, and financial goals are similar to yours. If a planner you're interviewing deals mostly with rich people and you're just getting started, you may not get the attention you need.
- Compensation. If fee-based, how is the fee calculated? Is it hourly? A flat fee for preparing a detailed plan? A percentage of the assets the planner is advising you on? If commission, what are the percentages on each product offered? Any hesitation to show you a commission schedule is a red flag.
- Sample financial plan. You want to see what you're going to be getting for your money. Be careful, though: fancy graphics, incomprehensible boilerplate language, and expensive leather binders may be used to distract you from a report's lack of substance.
- References. How long have customers been with the planner? Are they happy? Better off? Any complaints or weaknesses?
- Check your prospective planner's complaint record and credentials. This is super important. Financial planners are regulated by two organizations, and your future planner should be regulated by either (or possibly both) the Financial Industry Regulatory Authority (FINRA, which regulates financial products such as insurance and stocks) and the Securities and Exchange Commission (SEC, which regulates financial advice). Also check with your state's securities regulator. The North American Securities Administrators Association has a list of state agencies at www.nasaa.org/; click on Contact Your Regulator.

- These policies are essentially a combination of term insurance and a savings plan. A portion of your premium pays for pure term insurance, while the rest goes into some kind of side fund. Depending on the plan, you'll have more or less control over how the fund is invested.
- These policies tend to offer—initially—very competitive interest rates. The rate is usually guaranteed for a year but then drops to whatever the market is paying.

- You can pay pretty much whatever you want to. But because the cost of the underlying term insurance is rising every year, you may reach a point where your payment isn't enough to cover the cost of the insurance. If that happens, the shortfall will be taken out of your investment fund, which will reduce your cash value.
- The cash benefit accumulates tax-free, and you can borrow against it—usually at pretty competitive rates—or withdraw from it during your lifetime. Unless they're repaid, withdrawals and loans reduce the face amount of the policy.
- If properly placed in trust, the entire cash and accumulated savings can go to your heirs free of income tax.
- The fees can kill you, so to speak. Commissions—which are built into your costs—routinely run as much as 100 percent of the first year's premium. For that reason, if you cancel your policy within ten years or so, you could lose most or all of the value you've accumulated. In addition, management fees for the investment funds are often much higher than the industry average.

HERE ARE YOUR CASH VALUE CHOICES:
- Whole life. Locks in a death benefit, cash values, and premium. The side fund is invested by the insurance company.
- Universal life. Similar to Whole life, except that you can change the premium payment and death benefits anytime. And since the side fund is invested in fixed-income home securities (bonds and so forth), your cash values can fluctuate.
- Variable life. Similar to Universal, except that you have a bit more input into how your side fund is invested. Your choices usually include money markets, government securities, corporate bonds, growth, fixed-income, or total-return portfolios.

MAKING THE CHOICE

If you've decided that you need or want life insurance, the big question is whether to go with term or cash value. I've had long discussions with a number of insurance people and financial advisers, and here's what I think: get yourself a guaranteed renewable policy with level premiums for at least ten years. That way your policy can't be canceled if you get sick, and you won't need a physical exam every year. Then set up a good savings, investment, and retirement plan for your family. If you've got enough knowledge and expertise to do it on your own, great. If not, get an expert to help you (see pages 264–65).

There is one exception to this rule: if you expect your estate to be worth more than the current estate-tax exemption, a cash value policy is a good way to leave your heirs something to pay off federal estate taxes. Estates below the exemption level pass tax-free.

WHERE TO GET IT

If you or your partner work for a big company or belong to a union, you probably already have at least some life and/or disability insurance. And you may even be able to get additional coverage for great rates and without having to have a physical examination.

Even if you are covered, you might want to consider getting some additional, independent insurance. If you ever leave your job, you'll probably be leaving your life insurance policy behind.

If you have a broker you work with, start there. But don't be shy about shopping around. Costs for the very same policy can vary by as much as 200–300 percent. There are a number of online services that can help you compare policies and get the one that's best for you.

Whether you opt for term or cash value, be sure to go with a carrier you can count on being around when the time comes to pay up. The traditional way to do this was to go with a company that's top rated by one of the big ratings agencies: A.M. Best (ambest.com), Fitch (www.fitchratings.com), Moody's (moodys.com), and Standard & Poor's (www.standardandpoors.com). Unfortunately, in recent years, those agencies have lost some of their credibility by receiving money from the insurance companies whose financial strength they rate. Nevertheless, companies that receive the ratings agencies' top marks are generally pretty safe bets.

DISABILITY

As long as you've got insurance on your mind, I'd suggest that you take a long, hard look at disability coverage. If your employer offers a long-term disability policy, sign up now. If not, or if you are self-employed, talk to your broker about getting one. A long-term disability can sometimes be more devastating to your family's finances than death.

There Now, That Wasn't So Bad, Was It?

WHAT'S GOING ON WITH THE BABY

Physically

- Still building toward walking, your baby can now get to a standing position from a squat and can lower herself gracefully from standing to sitting.
- She's also getting more confident about combining standing and walking. She can turn 90 degrees, stoop to pick things up, and walk holding on to you with one hand while clutching a favorite toy (or two or three) in the other. She might even experiment with taking a few backward steps or do a little dance if there's music on.
- Even if your baby does take a few unassisted steps this month, she'll still use crawling or creeping as her main means of transportation, mostly because it's faster.
- However, she's so excited by the prospect of finally being able to walk on her own that she may not want to sleep or eat. Expect her to bounce up and down in her crib instead of napping and to refuse any kind of new food. And since she may be able to climb out of her crib, make sure you've lowered the crib mattress as far down as it will go (if you have a crib where the side goes up and down, you should replace it: "drop-side" cribs were banned several years ago). And be sure there's something soft on the floor for her to land on, just in case . . .
- She can take simple covers off containers (but probably not screw tops), lift latches, and open doors. And she'll help you dress and undress her (well, at least she thinks she's helping . . .). What she really likes to do, though, is yank off hats, socks, mittens, and anything else she can get hold of—especially just after you've put it on her.

- She's finally mastered her opposable thumb and can now pick up tiny objects between her thumb and pointing finger. More important, she can release them whenever she feels like it.
- She's also expressing a strong preference for "handedness," using one hand for grasping, the other for manipulating. If you put an object in her "passive" hand, she'll transfer it to the "active" one.
- She's now learned to store objects. If she's holding one thing in each hand and you offer her a third, she wants to get control of all three; she'll transfer the contents of one hand to her mouth or armpit and then pick up the third object with the free hand.

Intellectually

- One of the most important intellectual accomplishments of your baby's first year is her ability to retain a visual image of an object she has seen before but that is currently out of sight. By the end of this month, she'll be able to demonstrate this ability by searching—in more than one place—for objects she knows are out there but didn't actually see you hide.
- In another major intellectual leap, your baby will begin to use trial and error to solve her problems and overcome obstacles.
- She loves putting objects inside other objects and imitating anything anyone does: sweeping the floor, typing on the computer, talking on the phone, or howling in pain if you hurt yourself.
- As annoying as it may get, it's important to recognize that your baby's constant banging, building and knocking over, and putting things in and dumping them out are important learning activities that are teaching her more about the multiple properties of the objects in her world. Adding water to sand changes the way the sand feels (and tastes); dropping marbles into a metal can produces a much different sound than dropping them into a plastic box; and dumping them onto the living room rug isn't nearly as much fun as watching them bounce and roll around after dumping them on the vinyl kitchen floor or down the stairs.

Verbally

- She probably has a vocabulary of six to eight real words, as well as five or six more sound words, such as *moo, woof,* or *boom,* which she'll practice over and over and over.
- Her passive vocabulary is significantly larger, and she'll gleefully identify quite a few of her body parts, as well as such familiar objects as you and your partner, her bottle, a favorite stuffie, and her crib.

- She loves to try to imitate what you say, so watch your mouth. She's developing an amazing capacity to pick out the one swear word you use in a five-minute conversation, and she'll repeat it back to you twenty or thirty times a minute for the next few days.
- She'll also babble in phrases that have the same rhythm and intonation as her native language, and may make up words for people or objects.
- She still hasn't mastered the symbolic use of words. If you point to a book at a friend's house and say, "Look at the book," your baby may be confused. In her world, the word *book* applies only to the ones at home.
- She knows exactly what "No" means, but she doesn't always pay attention. And she's discovered that it can be fun to make you repeat "No" again and again.

Emotionally/Socially

- She actively tries to avoid doing things she knows you don't like and loves your applause, laughter, and approval.
- She's not always cooperative and will regularly test your limits (and your patience). She's also developing a basic sense of right and wrong and shows guilt when she does something she knows she shouldn't.
- She's developing a sense of humor and finds incongruities most entertaining. If you tell her a dog says "moo," or if you crawl or pretend to cry, she'll laugh hysterically.
- In her home, where she feels most secure, your baby will play with other kids and may share some of her toys with them. In less secure environments, however, she's not nearly as sociable and may not stray far from you.
- She's got some pretty firm ideas of what she wants and will do everything she can (cry, have a tantrum, smile sweetly) to influence your decisions.
- All in all, she's a real person now, with a distinct personality all her own.

WHAT YOU'RE GOING THROUGH

Anger

While my wife was pregnant with our first child, I spent a lot of time thinking about the things I would never do once I became a father. First on my list was No Hitting the Kids. Then I thought about all those parents (including my own) I'd seen over the years scream at their children in the grocery store or the post office. "How weak," I remember thinking to myself. "If people can't control themselves any better than that, they really shouldn't be parents." I quickly and rather smugly added No Yelling at the Kids to my list.

One afternoon my oldest daughter woke up from her nap crying like she never had before. I knew she wasn't tired, so I checked to see if her diaper was full (it wasn't), whether her clothes were binding her (they weren't), and even took her temperature (normal). She didn't respond to my comforting words or my requests to stop crying and tell me what was wrong (at six months, why should she?), and she continued howling. I was alone in the house, and after half an hour I'd had enough. I was frustrated and angry.

For months I'd been telling everyone in sight how perfect and well behaved my baby was and how I love her so much that I'd throw myself in front of a steamroller for her. But at that moment I felt tempted to throw her under the steamroller.

Almost immediately, I was nearly overcome with feelings of embarrassment and guilt and shame. I also felt like a complete failure as a father. What kind of father would have such horrible thoughts about his own baby? Well, the truth is that sooner or later, *every* dad (and mom) has flashes of intense anger toward his child. And anyone who claims to never have felt like choking his or her kids is either lying to you or isn't a parent at all.

COPING WITH ANGER

Besides the baby's actual behavior, things like job pressures, financial difficulties, health problems, sleep deprivation, or even car trouble can be redirected toward our kids and make us lash out at them. Whatever you're angry about, remember

If You Lose Control . . .

Because anger can completely take over your mind and body in a heartbeat, it's easy to understand how even parents with the best intentions accidentally lose control. If you do:

- Apologize. Explain to your child that you lost your temper. Make sure she knows that it was her behavior you didn't like, not her as a person, that you love her, and that you'll never hit her again. She may not understand everything you're saying, but she'll definitely understand your calm, loving voice.
- Don't go overboard, though. Resist the urge to punish yourself for your mistakes by being extra lenient with your child. You're only human, so lighten up.

Remember, anger can be just the first step in a vicious circle: something angers you enough that you lose control; feeling out of control makes you angrier; and feeling angry makes you feel even more out of control, which . . .

Unchecked, this process can escalate into physical and emotional abuse (which, besides screaming, can include insulting, humiliating, or withholding love). Hitting a child of any age—but especially one this young—is absolutely unacceptable. So if you have even the tiniest suspicion that you might lose control again, get some help immediately: call a friend, a therapist, your child's pediatrician, or even a local parental-stress hotline (we've got some suggestions in the Resources appendix. You might also want to review the strategies for dealing with crying on pages 66–70). And if you're worried that your partner might prove to be violent, suggest she do the same.

that there's nothing wrong with feeling it—even when it's directed at your kids. It's what you do with your anger, however, that can be a problem. Trying to deny it or imagine that it never happened doesn't work. Here are some suggestions that will help you understand, and better deal with, your anger.

- Change your perspective. Although your child may periodically do something deliberately to annoy you, many of her actions are really beyond her control. In fact, being able to make you angry is actually a normal part of your child's development—she's learning about actions and reactions.
- Be your own shrink. Do you find yourself getting angry at your child for the same thing over and over? Do you get angry at certain times of day or while you're doing certain kinds of activities? Some of your anger could be triggered

by your baby reminding you of particularly painful memories of when you were a child. So try to figure out what your baby is doing and why it makes you so angry. At the very least, knowing what sets you off may help you avoid those situations as much as possible.

- Laugh. It may be a pain to clean up, but drawing on the walls with lipstick can be funny—if you let it—and makes for a great Instagram post.
- Take a break. It's perfectly fine to leave the room, even if your child is screaming her head off. Just make sure she's in a place (like a crib) where she can't hurt herself or anyone (or anything) else. Ideally, your partner will take over for you while you regain your composure. But if she's not there, your baby will be fine without you for a few minutes. Continuing to try to soothe your screaming baby when you're furious will just make things worse. Babies can pick up on tension and will react to it by crying even more, which is not the result you're hoping for.
- Have a plan. Since it's a given that you're going to get angry at some point(s), think now, while you're calm, about a few techniques you might use to diffuse some of your anger. You could clench and unclench your fists, close your eyes, count to ten, take deep breaths, remove yourself from the situation, or anything else that can distract you long enough that you won't do something you'll regret for a long, long time.
- Watch what you say. Don't insult or humiliate your child. If you must criticize her, do it in private. Contrary to the old adage "Sticks and stones may break my bones, but names will never hurt me," calling your baby names can, in fact, have a greater long-term negative impact than hitting.
  - Use "I" messages: "I don't like it when you scratch me—it hurts" is a much more effective message than "You're a bad girl because you scratched me."
  - Saying things like "You always . . ." or "You never . . ." can fill a child with a sense of futility, a conviction that she'll fail no matter what she does or how hard she tries.
  - Avoid mixed messages. Yelling at your child to stop yelling will probably not do you a lot of good.
- Watch what you do. Children learn more about how to express anger from watching how you do it than from punishment. So don't let your baby see you vent steam in a physical way; she won't be able to understand your anger and might even be afraid that you'll turn on her. Or, she could also try to imitate you, and might hurt herself, someone else, or someone's property.
- Get physical. Taking a long jog, swimming, jumping rope, punching a pillow, and taking a boxing class are good ways to let off some steam. If there are any batting cages nearby, try them out—if you squint, slow-moving softballs can look an awful lot like a human head . . .

YOU AND YOUR BABY

Discipline Update

When I was a kid, one of my dad's favorite sayings was, "You're free to swing your arms around any way you want. But that freedom ends right where someone else's nose begins." In a nutshell, teaching your child this lesson—to be respectful of other people's noses—is the primary goal of discipline.

A few months ago this was a concept your baby couldn't possibly have grasped. And the only way for you to control her evil impulses was to distract her with a toy and hope she'd forget about whatever it was she shouldn't have been doing in the first place. But your baby's memory has been improving every day, and by the time she's a year old, one toy just won't do the trick anymore; now you'll need two or three. And pretty soon, toys or any other attempts to distract her won't work at all.

At this point, expect your baby to move things up a notch or two, behaving in ways she knows she shouldn't just to trigger a reaction. For example, she'll wait until you're looking right at her before making a move for the stairs or taking a swipe at your fine crystal. As annoying and frustrating as her parent baiting will seem, try to remember that it's actually a healthy part of her development. In order to feel secure, she needs to have limits. And the only way to grasp where the limits are is to see how far she can push before they kick in.

The big question now—one that will come up again and again as your baby gets older—is: How much independence do you allow before drawing the line? For me, it gets back to my dad's line about swinging arms. Let her have plenty of room to explore, but stop her before she hurts anyone or anything, including herself. Here's how:

- Limit potential risks and give her a safe place to explore. Basically, this means childproofing the hell out of your house and keeping anything you really want to stay in one piece as far away from the baby as possible. (To minimize problems elsewhere, ask your parents and in-laws to take similar preventive measures.)
- Put her in situations where you won't have to correct her as much.
- Have plenty of substitutes available. Old phones and remote controls, spare computer keyboards, and so on. But be prepared: some kids can tell instinctively that what you're giving them isn't the real thing, and they won't be amused.
- Stop dangerous behavior immediately, but calmly. If your baby is pounding on a plate-glass window with her toy hammer and you scream, drop your coffee, and leap across the room to wrestle her to the ground, she'll find your reaction so much fun that she'll be sure to repeat exactly the behavior that provoked it the first time. Instead, tell her firmly to stop (one time only). If that doesn't work, calmly walk over and disarm her.

- Be consistent. Don't allow certain kinds of behavior some days and forbid it on others. That just confuses babies (and plenty of adults too).
- Don't have too many rules. Saying something like, "You can shred any section of the newspaper you want except for the comics," is too complicated for your baby to understand.
- Limit the number of warnings. If you tell your baby "No!" five times, give two "If you do that one more time" warnings and three final warnings, you're telling your baby that she can ignore you at least nine times before you man up and do something about it.
- Give plenty of positive feedback when your baby does something right. Children receive far more negative comments ("Stop that," "Put down that Samurai sword!") from their parents than positive ones (estimates vary from 1:3 to 1:48!).
- Be a Yes man. Telling a baby "No!" to something often makes her want to do it even more. Plus, "No!" can be awfully specific. For example, if you tell her "No poking the dog," she may stop poking the dog for a minute, but what about the cat? You didn't say anything about the cat, so it must be okay, right? So instead of surrounding your baby with things she can't do, show her how to do alternative things correctly: "Animals don't like it when we poke them." Then take her hand and pet the dog with her, while saying, "Nice doggie. This is how we pet animals."
- Be realistic. Babies are hardwired to explore. And sometimes, even though your baby really wants to listen to you, her urges to touch, grab, toss, squish, or drop are too strong.

- Be tolerant of your baby's "negativity." Your baby's "no"s are an important part of her developing identity. Giving your baby some decision-making control will help her accept the limits you set.
- Spend some serious time trying to figure out what the baby needs. Research shows that early obedience (in nine- to twelve-month-olds) is related to the sensitivity of responsiveness to infant signals, not to the frequency of commands or forcible interventions.
- Be a good model. While setting limits is important, it's really only half the battle. Your baby is learning a huge amount from watching and imitating you. So don't do anything you don't want the baby to do.

Dealing with Temper Tantrums

As you've seen, the end of the first year is packed with developmental milestones. Some, like walking and talking, are wonderful to see. Others, like temper tantrums, are a little less pleasant.

In some cases, your baby's tantrums may be the result of frustration at not being able to get you to understand something. More likely, though, her tantrums will be triggered by your not letting her have or do something she wanted to have or do. It's slowly dawning on her that she's not in control of as much of the world as she thought, and she's not happy about it. Here are a few ways you can deal with the inevitable:

1. If you know what she wants and you don't want to give it to her, try redirecting her or offering an option.
2. If you don't know what she wants, make a real effort to find out. Asking direct questions may help you straighten things out. Hunger and exhaustion are responsible for a lot of tantrums. Taking your baby into the grocery store during one of her regular nap times and expecting her to stay awake is a mistake you won't want to make again.
3. If she can't or won't tell you, do a quick check to make sure there's nothing physically wrong—no cuts, bruises, or assorted owies, no fever, no clothing that's too tight, and so on.
4. If your baby doesn't respond to your words, stop talking. You can't reason with an irrational wild animal, and during a tantrum, that's exactly what your child is.
5. Now, here's the tough part: If she's not hungry, tired, sick, or in pain and the tantrum continues, make sure she's in a place where she can't hurt herself or do any damage and ignore her. Yes, just turn away and go about your

Biting, Pinching, and Hitting

For some strange reason, right around their first birthdays, almost all babies go through a phase when they bite and/or hit and/or pinch people—strangers, loved ones, and even animals. (This may be old news to your partner, who may have felt your baby's teeth on her nipples months ago.) If (when) your baby starts, the first thing you need to do is find out why. Your baby may be acting this way because she's:

- Trying to express affection (you probably nibble gently on her, and she may simply be trying to imitate you).
- Trying to communicate a particular need.

business. This is one of the rare times when I think it's okay to check your email—but only for a minute—on your phone when you're with your child. Nothing makes a tantrum disappear faster than the realization that it isn't having the desired effect.

6. If the tantrum happens in a public place—every parent's worst nightmare— quickly go through 1 through 3 above. If that doesn't work, immediately get her and yourself out of there. Just pick her up and carry her away. If you have to leave an almost-full shopping cart behind or walk out of a restaurant, do it.

7. Do not spank or yell at your child. Yes, this may be the most embarrassing moment of your life, and you may be worried that people are staring at you (some of them may be), thinking you're a horrible parent, but the sooner you get out, the sooner they'll stop staring at you. And hitting or screaming at your child will only make even more people stare at you.

8. Don't imitate your child. Throwing yourself on the floor and having a tantrum of your own, complete with kicking legs and flailing arms, might be enough to shock your baby into stopping. However, keep in mind that your baby is learning a lot by imitating you. Pitching your own fit could inadvertently give your baby some new ideas to try next time.

9. Don't give in, no matter what. If you do, you'll be proving to your baby that she's discovered a great way to get Mom and Dad to do what she wants.

Finally, consider yourself lucky. Any meltdowns your baby has now are nothing compared to the ones you'll be seeing in another year or so. And those are nothing compared to the ones she'll throw when she becomes a teenager. Enjoy the relative calm while you can.

- Frustrated that she can't express herself verbally.
- Teething and trying to relieve her discomfort.
- Simply conducting an experiment to see how others will react.
- Tired, overstimulated, or frustrated.
- Trying to defend herself, her property, or her territory.
- Imitating an older friend or sibling.

Fortunately, the hitting-and-pinching-and-biting phase doesn't usually last longer than a few months (although, when you're getting bitten a few times a day, that can seem like a very long time). Here, however, are a few dos and don'ts that may make this painful period a little shorter:

- Don't get angry; it will only make her defensive.
- Don't slap or spank.
- Don't bite back or have the baby bite herself "to show her what it feels like"; this sets a rotten example and will only reinforce the behavior by implying that it's really okay.
- Do remove the baby promptly. If she's sitting on your lap and bites you, put her down for a minute (no longer) and take a few steps away. If she's hit or bitten someone else, take her away from that person for a minute.
- Don't say, "You're bad," or any variation on that theme. Instead say, "Biting is bad."
- Don't insist on an apology. There's almost no chance that your baby has any idea what regret is or that biting really hurts (babies this age are completely incapable of imagining anything from any perspective but their own).
- Don't overreact. The baby might find your reaction so amusing that she'll bite or hit again just to get your attention.
- Do look for patterns or triggers. Is it happening at certain times of the day (right before nap time, for example)? Does she do it only to certain people or when she's playing with certain toys?
- Do rethink your discipline policies. You may be setting so many limits that your baby may be trying to bite her way to freedom.
- Do acknowledge good behavior. If your baby doesn't pinch or bite or hit, tell her what a good job she did and reward her with a huge smile, a hug, and anything else she might like.

Weaning Your Baby from Breast or Bottle

Most pediatricians today agree that mothers should breastfeed their babies for as long as possible—generally between six months and a year. What to do after that, however, is the source of far less agreement.

So should your partner stop breastfeeding completely now or gradually phase it out? Should you transition your baby from breast to bottle, or skip the bottle and go directly to cups? And if you've been bottle-feeding from the start, when should you stop? The answers, of course, are up to you, your partner, and your baby.

We're assuming here that your baby is eating at least some solid foods in addition to her breast- or bottle-feeding. Eventually, she'll get all her food via cup and utensils, but the process of weaning her completely can take months or even years.

WHY TO WEAN YOUR BABY FROM THE BREAST (OR AT LEAST CUT BACK SOME)

- By the time she turns one, your baby will have gotten most of the long-term health benefits from breastfeeding. At this point, she's getting far more emotional nourishment than gastronomic nourishment from nursing. Your partner may decide to nurse for longer, which is fine as long as she realizes that breast milk alone can't satisfy all the baby's needs and may, in fact, suppress her appetite for solids.
- The baby may start (or may already be) using the breast as a comfort or sleep aid, thus delaying development of the ability to soothe herself or fall asleep on her own.
- A small number of dads feel that enough is enough: their partner's breasts may have been at least partially off-limits for a year, and they feel that it's time to unlatch that baby. They may see their partner's refusal to do so as a kind of slap in the face.

WHY TO WEAN THE BABY FROM THE BOTTLE (OR START CUTTING BACK)

- Your baby may fill herself up on liquids so much that she will lose interest in all those solid foods she needs for a well-balanced diet.
- Babies who feed from bottles are more susceptible to ear infections and/or tooth decay. Babies usually use bottles when on their backs. In addition, when coming from a bottle, the milk can drip even when the baby isn't sucking. Those two factors can combine to leave a pool of liquid in the baby's mouth that could back up into the Eustachian tubes and cause an ear infection. If the baby's teeth slosh around in that pool long enough, they could rot. Nursing babies are rarely on their backs. Plus, since milk flows into the baby's mouth only when she sucks, the mouth is usually emptied completely with each swallow, thereby reducing the chance of developing either an ear infection or a cavity.

From the Baby's Point of View, the Whole Thing Just Sucks

Babies are born with an intense desire to suck. It's what enables them to get milk out of a breast or bottle when they're only hours or days old. Some babies outgrow their need to suck very early on and will do their sucking only when they're eating. These babies may not have much trouble with the whole weaning process. Others, though, also suck to calm themselves or when they're feeling tired, overwhelmed, lonely, stressed, unloved, or even bored. So if your baby seems to want to suck something, let her—especially if you're taking away the breast or the bottle that has been the source of so much comfort. And don't worry: as I discussed earlier, there's no danger that sucking a pacifier or thumb at this age will hurt your child's teeth in any way.

- By about fifteen months, your baby may begin forming an emotional attachment to her bottle (just as she might to a blanket, thumb, or favorite stuffed animal). Emotional attachments are nice, but breaking an attachment to a bottle will be a lot easier now than in a few months, when the baby starts getting stubborn and contrary.
- Some experts believe that overdependence on the bottle can interfere with physical and mental developmental milestones and recommend giving it up entirely by eighteen months.
- A hint for easing the process of giving up the bottle: If the baby demands her usual drink, offer some solid food first. If she's full before starting the bottle, she probably won't be as interested in it and will miss it less when it's gone.

PERFECTLY GOOD REASONS TO CONTINUE LIMITED BREASTFEEDING

- The baby likes it.
- Your partner likes it. The contact and connection with the baby may be hard to give up.
- It's more natural, cheaper, and more convenient than prepared food. Although remember, your baby should be moving toward getting most of her nutrition from sources other than your partner's breasts.
- Just because. Whether and how long to nurse can become a very political issue. But the decisions you make regarding your baby should be made with only *her* best interests in mind. You and your partner know your baby better than anyone, and if the two of you decide that you want the baby to nurse until she's three, go ahead and do it.

MAKING THE SWITCH

On one occasion while my wife was still nursing, she got held up in meetings and couldn't get home to feed the baby. If our daughter had been used to taking a bottle, this wouldn't have been a problem. But I'd only tried once or twice to get her to take a bottle and hadn't put up much of a fight when she'd spit it out. My punishment for having been so lax was that I had to drive twenty miles to my wife's office—with the baby screaming at the top of her lungs—so she could nurse. The moral of the story is: get the baby used to taking a bottle as early as possible (but not before she's completely comfortable with the breast). Here are some things you can do to get even the most committed breastfeeder to give the bottle a try:

- Use smaller bottles and nipples. Keep experimenting until you find a size and style the baby likes. If she's got a pacifier, try a bottle nipple that is shaped like the one on her pacifier.

Temperament Tidbits

How well your baby makes the transition from breastfeeding to bottle-feeding or cups may depend more on her temperament than on any other factor. According to temperament researcher Jim Cameron:

- Extremely active toddlers with high frustration tolerance (they aren't easily frustrated) usually wean themselves. They prefer bottles to breast because of the convenience.
- High-Activity, Slow-Adapting kids also like the independence and convenience of a bottle or cup during the day. But they'll still want to nurse in the morning and at night.
- Active kids who don't tolerate frustration as well, however, know that parents are quite helpful in overcoming frustration. To them, giving up nursing means giving up support and help from parents, and they won't be in any hurry to do it.
- Slow-Adapting kids see the breast as security and won't give it up without a fight, especially at night. A gradual phase-out is particularly important for these kids.
- Moderately high-energy, Fast-Adapting kids wean themselves on their own.
- Kids who are moderately High-Activity and moderately low in frustration tolerance are fairly ambivalent about weaning. They'll generally take their direction from you and your partner.

- When introducing the bottle, hold the baby in the position she's in for breastfeeding.
- Ease the transition by filling bottles or cups with pumped breast milk, if that's what your partner does.
- Go slow. Introduce the bottle for a few minutes at first, then add a minute or two every day.
- Phase the breasts out gradually. Kids tend to be more attached to the morning and evening feedings, so start by eliminating your baby's midday meal(s) first and replace it with a bottle, some solid food, or both. If that goes well for a few days, drop the morning feeding next. Of course, exceptions can be made: we dropped the evening feeding first because our daughters were getting up at five in the morning to eat anyway. But do what works best for your partner and your baby. A lot of moms have trouble giving up the last evening feeding because it's been a special time for her and the baby to bond. And if nursing has been part of the bedtime routine, your baby may not want to give up that last feeding quite yet.
- A tip: make sure your partner is out of the house (or at least out of sight in another room) when you're trying to give the baby a bottle. If your partner (actually, her breasts) are within smelling distance, your baby may refuse the bottle.
- A warning: the American Academy of Pediatrics suggests not starting your baby on cow's milk until after her first birthday. When you do finally switch to milk, start with whole milk. Your baby needs the fat in it for healthy brain development.
- A final note: don't try to wean your baby in one day—it could be traumatic to both your partner and the baby. So take your time and do it over the course of a few weeks or months.

WHEN NOT TO WEAN YOUR BABY

No matter how old your baby is or how long she's been breast- or bottle-feeding, there are a few really rotten times to try to wean her:
- When any impending or recent major transition might make the baby feel vulnerable, out of control, and in need of extra parental support. Moving to a new home, the birth of a younger sibling or the announcement of pregnancy, a new babysitter, and starting daycare are good examples.
- If the baby has been sick.
- If you or your partner are under some kind of extreme pressure.
- If the baby is teething.

FAMILY MATTERS

Ch-Ch-Ch-Changing Relationships

Considering how small and helpless babies are, it's sometimes surprising just how much of an impact they can have on the lives of the adults around them. Just think, for example, about how different things are for you now compared to your prefatherhood life.

Babies create new relationships in people's lives simply by being born: you and your partner have gone from being children to being parents, your parents are now grandparents, your brothers and sisters are uncles and aunts, and so on. And naturally, those relationships (as well as the rights and responsibilities that go with them) will take some getting used to.

But perhaps babies' greatest power is their ability to profoundly change relationships that had existed long before they were born. They can reunite families and mend old wounds, or they can open new ones. They can even change the nature of your friendships. Here are a few ways this might play out.

Your Changing Relationship with Your Partner

A lot of couples imagine that having and raising children together will make their relationship stronger, and a lot of times they're right—especially if the pregnancy was planned, the baby was conceived through "artificial" means (insemination, donor sperm, donor eggs, or surrogacy), or the child was adopted. But as we've discussed, having a baby creates all sorts of challenges: sleep deprivation, little or no sex, less money, less free time, more work and responsibility, and so on. As researcher Jay Belsky puts it, in the early stages of parenthood a new baby "tends to push his mother and father apart by revealing the hidden and half-hidden differences in their relationship."

In previous chapters I've talked a lot about the ways that having a baby might strain your relationship with your partner. So let's spend a little time focusing on some of the very *positive* ways the baby can affect your life and your relationship with your partner.

- The support you gave your partner during the pregnancy and birth, and seeing what an amazing dad you are may make her fall in love with you all over again.
- You may feel a sense of gratitude to the baby for enabling you to feel what it's like to be loved and to love more deeply than you ever have before.
- The baby may give you and your partner a sense of tremendous pride at having jointly created something absolutely amazing.
- You're probably pretty proud of yourself right now—and you should be. You're confident in your own abilities and you've experienced how incredible it is to be

loved and needed by a little creature who wants nothing more in life than to be with you (her teddy bear is a close second). That makes you love her even more. And the love you have for your baby can make you love the one who helped make that baby possible even more.

- Having faced, worked through, and overcome the challenges of the first year of parenthood may make you and your partner feel more deeply committed to your relationship and to making it work. You now also have someone to pass along new and old family traditions to.
- For some men, having a baby is like having a great new toy and may give you a chance to relive certain parts of your childhood.

Parent/Grandparent Relationships

THE GOOD . . .

- After their first child is born, most men feel closer to their parents, especially their fathers. Even those who don't feel closer are usually at least willing to end, or put behind them, long-running family disputes.
- Seeing your parents in action with your child may bring back happy memories of your own childhood. You may also be pleasantly surprised at how your parents have changed since you were young. The father who may not have had much time for you, for example, may now spend hours with his grandchild. And the mother who limited your junk food intake to half a stick of sugarless gum a week may be a little more relaxed now.
- Now that you know exactly how much work it is to be a parent, you may be a bit more appreciative of what your own parents did—and sacrificed—for you. Some day, decades from now, your own children will have the same epiphany about you.
- After all these years of being a child, you're in charge now; if they want to be with the baby, they'll have to do things your way.
- You'll develop a closer relationship with your in-laws.

THE BAD . . .

- Seeing your parents in action with your child may bring back unhappy memories of your own childhood. And if your parents are treating the baby differently (i.e., better) than they treated you, you may be jealous, wondering where all that love was when you were a kid.
- Your parents may not be supportive or accepting of your increased role in your child's life.
- They may want to assume a role in your child's life—either too involved or not involved enough—that you aren't happy with. Grandparents are free to love

Introduction to Potty Training

Have you heard the one about the kid who was toilet trained at eight months? If you haven't, you will soon. But prepare yourself: it isn't a joke—or at least, it's not supposed to be. People will tell you all sorts of things about the babies they knew who were out of diapers before they could walk. But no matter what anyone says, or how much you might want to believe the stories, they're really just urban nursery legends.

First of all, there's really no such thing as potty training; your child will learn to use the toilet on her own only when she's ready. And at eight months or even a year, she's simply incapable of controlling her bowels or bladder. Sure, she may grunt and groan while producing a bowel movement, and everyone in the house (except her, of course) will be able to smell it, but she has no idea there's any connection between the feeling she gets when she's filling a diaper and the actual contents. If anybody's being "trained" at this age, it's the parents, who may have learned to recognize their baby's signals and rush her to the toilet. But rest assured, the baby can't do it on her own.

At about fifteen months your baby will begin associating what's in her diaper with herself and may announce from time to time that she's produced something. But only after the fact. At eighteen months she may occasionally announce that she is about to do something, but she still hasn't learned how to hold it in long enough to make it to a toilet. For the best results, unless your child is extremely interested, wait until she's at least two before seriously starting to "train" her.

In the meantime, however, you can help increase your child's awareness of what's going on in her diapers by talking about the process as it's happening. As you're changing her, show the baby what she's done, but don't emphasize the yuckiness of it. Instead, say something admiring, like, "Hey, that's a pretty impressive load—someday you'll do this in the toilet like me and Mommy."

their grandchildren without any of the restrictions of parenthood, says psychologist Brad Sachs.

- There may be some friction between your parenting style and that of your parents, between the way you react to the baby's needs and the way they do. It's not uncommon to hear from parents statements such as, "I seem to have done a pretty good job raising you and your siblings, so don't tell me how to . . ." or "Don't you think it's time she (your partner) stopped nursing that child?"

Screening Your Baby's Entertainment

I've talked throughout this book about the fantastic benefits of reading to your child. But as your baby gets older, she'll get more and more of her information from other sources, in particular, television, videos, computers, tablets, and phones. As we discussed earlier, the American Academy of Pediatrics recommends zero screen time for children under two. But plenty of parents (and child-care workers) disregard that advice, which, given our hectic schedules and the expansion of technology into every area of our lives, just isn't realistic for everyone. If you're a single or at-home parent of a colicky or difficult child, putting her in front of video for a few minutes or letting her play a game on your tablet might be the only break you get all day. The key is to not go overboard, which, sadly, way too many parents do. A few examples from recent studies by Common Sense Media (www.commonsensemedia.org) and the Kaiser Family Foundation:

- Thirty percent of babies 0–12 months have a TV in their bedroom.
- On a typical day, 47 percent of those infants and babies under one year watch TV or DVDs, and those who do watch spend an average of nearly two hours (1:54) doing so.
- Thirty-five percent of children live in a home where the TV is on all the time, even if no one is watching.

This kind of media consumption by children who are barely verbal and mobile is causing real problems.

- Most of the programming babies are exposed to on television is not age appropriate. Instead, they're watching something with their parents or an older sibling. A significant amount of recent research has shown that even

- If you think they did a lousy job as parents, you may be afraid that you're doomed to repeat their mistakes, or that they'll repeat them with your child.
- If your parents live nearby, they may always be "in the neighborhood," and you might be seeing them more than you really care to. At the same time, they might resent it if you're too dependent on them for child care.
- There may be disputes and power struggles between your parents and your partner's about their grandparental roles.

However your relationship with your parents and/or in-laws changes, remember this: "A loving and vigorous bond between the grandparent and grandchild," babies as young as ten to twelve months are influenced by the behavior of the characters they see on television.

- When kids are engrossed in some kind of screen, they aren't getting one-on-one, face-to-face contact with their parents. It's no surprise that TV watching before age two is linked with smaller vocabularies and lower cognitive performance.
- Background TV is associated with distracted parents, disengaged parent-child relationships, and the same negative verbal and intellectual effects mentioned above.
- Screen time for kids this age can interrupt children's sleep cycles.

The solution? There are several:
- If there's a television in your baby's room, take it out.
- If you absolutely need to put your baby in front of a screen, at least make sure she's watching something appropriate. You may love Hitchcock films but watch them after your baby is down for the night. BabyFirst (www.babyfirst tv.com) is a network aimed at six- to eighteen-month-olds. They have an advisory board full of child development experts who vet all the programming.
- Again, if you absolutely need to put your baby in front of a screen, try to spend some of the time watching *with* your baby. Use the time to cuddle and to talk about what's on the screen—that kind of active engagement can counteract some of the negatives associated with media. Common Sense Media has extensive listings and reviews of every kind of media, from apps to movies and everything in between.

writes Sachs, "is not just related to, but essential to, the emotional health and stability of all three generations."

Other Relationships

You may not realize it at first, but you and your partner will gradually find that your relationships with friends and other non-immediate family members have changed.

- You may be interested (or at least more interested than you were before becoming a parent) in getting together with relatives your own age, especially those with kids, so that the next generation can get to know their cousins.

"Do you remember any of those things people said we'd tell our grandkids someday?"

- Similarly, your circle of close friends will gradually change to include more couples, especially couples with kids.
- You and your partner aren't going to be nearly as available for last-minute movies or double dates, and you might not be quite as happy to have friends drop by unannounced.
- Your new, less spontaneous lifestyle may affect your relationships with your single male friends most of all. Having a new baby probably means fewer all-night poker games. Your buddies may stop calling you because they think you're too busy or not interested in hanging out with them anymore. Or you might stop calling them because seeing their relatively carefree and obligation-free lives may make you jealous or depress the hell out of you.
- While your child is young, she'll be happy to play with whomever you introduce her to, and her first friends are most likely going to be your friends' kids. But as she gets older and starts showing an interest in other children and making friends of her own, she'll take on a more active role on the family social committee. And all of a sudden you'll find yourself socializing with her friends' parents.
- Relationships between you and other adults may continue longer than they otherwise might because the kids like playing together.
- Relationships can be subtly—or not so subtly—affected by competition. Let's face it: we all want our children to be the biggest, smartest, fastest, cutest, and funniest, and it's only natural (especially for guys) to get a little competitive.

- Friends or relatives with children who are older than yours might start getting on your nerves by insisting on telling you every single thing they think you're doing wrong as a parent.
- As with your parents and in-laws, some friends or relatives may be disdainful or unsupportive of your taking an active, involved role in your baby's life, falling back on the old stereotype that men should leave the parenting stuff up to their wives or that putting your family first could have a negative impact on your career.

Here are a few things you can do to smooth out some of the bumps in your changing relationships with friends and family:

- Watch what you say. No matter how much people without kids pretend, there's a limit to how much they really want to hear about all the exciting things (to you, anyway) that your baby can do or how many times she filled her diaper today.
- Learn to accept change. It may seem harsh, but the fact is that you may lose some friends (and they'll lose you) now that you're a parent. But you'll gain plenty of new ones in the process.
- Don't listen to everything everyone else tells you. Whatever they know about taking care of children they learned on the job. And that's how you're learning too.
- Watch the competition. If your friend's baby crawls, walks, talks, sings, says "da-da," or gets a modeling contract or an early-admissions preschool acceptance letter before your baby does, you may find yourself more than a little envious. But you know that your baby is the best one in the world. Go ahead and let them delude themselves into thinking that theirs is. Why burst their bubble?

Going Public with Fatherhood

In the concluding chapter of *The Expectant Father*, I painted a rather gloomy portrait of the ways men and women—both individually and collectively as a society—actively discourage men from getting involved with their children. Things have begun to change: at hospitals around the country, almost as many men as women are attending new-parent classes with their partner or dad-only classes where they're available. The number of dad bloggers is staggering, as are the number of at-home dads and dads' groups. And you can't go outside these days without seeing a dad pushing a stroller or carrying a baby in a front pack.

But we've got a long way to go. Men still don't get enough of the support and encouragement they so sorely need to assume a greater nurturing role. Fortunately, though, more and more men are expressing their dissatisfaction with this

Baby's First Birthday Party

Let's get one thing straight: your baby's first birthday party is really more for you than for her. She won't help you put together the guest list, she's too little to play Pin the Tail on the Donkey or to bob for apples, she'll probably be more interested in the wrapping paper than what's inside it, and she won't write any of the thank-you notes. Still, it's a major event for the whole family. Here are some first birthday dos and don'ts:

- Don't knock yourself out planning special activities. At this age your baby will prefer the familiar to the new almost every time. Save the piñatas for a few years on—the last thing you want is a bunch of kids running around your house swinging broom handles or baseball bats.
- Don't invite too many kids—two or three is plenty. And limit the adults to six or seven. Any more and you run the risk of overwhelming the baby. If you're inviting other adults with children, make sure they stay to take care of their own.
- Do a quick childproofing sweep of the area where the party will take place. The house may be perfectly safe for your baby, but not safe enough to stand up to the invasion of a horde of toddlers.
- Don't make a huge cake (unless the adults plan to eat it). And don't serve any choking foods—popcorn, peanuts, small candies, hot dogs, even carrot sticks.
- Do save the clowns, magicians, and masks for next year. Your one-year-old is more likely to be scared by masks and magic than entertained.
- Do keep the party short (no more than an hour and a half) and try not to have it overlap with nap or sleep times or any other time when your baby tends to be cranky.
- Don't go overboard on gifts. And don't demand or even expect your baby to make wild declarations of thanks or any other great performances for the cameras. It's just not going to happen.
- Do give identical party favors to any other child guests. Make sure your baby gets one as well.
- If you have older children, do include them as much as you can. Even though your baby doesn't know what's going on, your other children do, and they can get very jealous. So have them help you design the birthday cake, put together the menu, and select the music. Also, let each of them invite a special guest of their own.

- Do get special presents for your older children. Their world has changed a lot over the past year, and you should acknowledge it.
- Do keep a list (or have someone else do it) of who gave what so you can send thank-yous later.

After the party, try to devote some time to reminiscing—and taking notes—about your baby's first year. When you think about it, she's come a tremendously long way—so long that it's hard to remember how things were twelve short months ago. To start with, she's about 50 percent longer and three times as heavy as she was at birth. She's gone from crying as her only means of communication to being able to make specific requests with words or gestures. She's progressed from being a collection of almost random twitches and jerks to being able to move around wherever she wants. All in all, she's just like a real person, only smaller.

Do you remember when your baby made her first noncrying noise and her first nongas smile? When did you first feel that she loved you? When did she first look at you with true recognition? When did she start using a spoon, crawling, taking her first steps, sleeping through the night? You probably chronicled a lot of this on Facebook or Instagram, but I'm sure there were moments when you couldn't get to your phone quickly enough. Write down as many as you and your partner can think of, and try to collect some baby-related anecdotes from friends and family. Turn it all into a slide show or, if you're a little old-school, put it on a flash drive that your baby can open when she's older (assuming flash drives haven't gone the way of the floppy disc). If you're even older-school, there are always baby books—made of, gasp, actual paper—that you can write in and attach pictures to, and so on. Honestly, there's something really nice about holding something tangible in your hand that another person held in his or hers.

Once all the guests have gone home, the mess is cleaned up, and the baby is down for the night, pop open a bottle of champagne with your partner and drink a toast to each other. You've got plenty to celebrate too! In a lot of ways you've grown and developed as much as your baby has. You've found child care and endured sleepless nights, sibling rivalries, and work/family conflicts. And you've gone from being tentative and worried that you wouldn't know what to do, to confident and competent.

"My father wakes up the sun every morning. What does your father do?"

Neanderthal status quo and are taking a far more active role in their children's lives anyway. Of course, some of this may be happening because of economic necessity: more and more mothers are entering the workplace, and someone else has to step in to share the child-care burden. But in my view, the more significant reason for the nurturing-father revolution has to do with men themselves.

Most men, especially those whose fathers were physically or emotionally absent, instinctively know what they missed when they were young. And just as they know they were deprived of a relationship with their fathers, they know that their fathers were deprived of relationships with them. The real measure of a man's commitment to a new kind of relationship with his kids is how he feels about being a father and about the impact fatherhood is having on his life.

Dads these days are consistently saying that they see fathering as an important and satisfying experience. They disagree that only mothers should be responsible for discipline or for caring for a sick child; instead, they consider parenting a partnership experience to be shared equally with their partner.

Still, far too many men continue to undervalue the importance of the role they play in their children's lives. Too many children have missed having a relationship with their fathers, and too many fathers have missed having relationships with their children.

I've spent the better part of my career trying to break that cycle, and I'm delighted that you're joining me. As a new dad, you're in a unique position to be a role model for other dads as well as for guys who aren't even thinking about fatherhood yet. Together, we can make the word *fatherhood* as synonymous with child-rearing and nurturing as *motherhood*. And there's no better time to start than right now.

For most new fathers, the last few months of their first year as parents are a time of relative calm. They've dealt with the big emotional, professional, and personal hurdles of fatherhood and are now comfortably juggling their roles as husband, father, provider, and son. In short, they're finally feeling "like a family" and are entering what my colleague Bruce Linton calls the "community phase" of fatherhood.

This is a time when many new dads feel ready to socialize—along with their partners and children—with other families and use their fatherhood as a way to participate more actively in the public domain. They typically take on a more active role in their churches or synagogues, and they experience a heightened sense of public responsibility. Issues such as the quality of schools, city planning and zoning, the environment, and public safety become much more pressing than before.

In the introduction to this book, I quoted author Michael Levine, who said that "having children makes you no more a parent than having a piano makes you a pianist." Well, at this point you may not be any closer to being a pianist than you were a year ago. But there's no doubt that you're a father. And a pretty good one at that.

Appendixes

Resources

To paraphrase Dorothy in *The Wizard of Oz*: "My! Resources for new dads come and go so quickly here." And because they do, this is by no means a comprehensive list. But I'd really like to create one—and you can help. If you know of a resource that can benefit dads and their families, let us know. You can see the full, constantly updated list at www.resourcesfordads.com or www.mrdad.com/resources.

Adoption

Adoption.com provides information on all aspects of adoption for those who wish to place a child for adoption; for those who want to adopt; for adoptees and birth parents who are searching; and for those who want to adopt internationally; support information; and much more.
adoption.com

Adoptuskids.org offers a national photo listing of children from across the nation and provides links to a variety of websites throughout the U.S.
Tel: (888) 200-4005
email: info@adoptuskids.org
www.adoptuskids.org/

American Adoption Congress (AAC) is composed of individuals, families, and organizations committed to adoption reform and is committed to achieving changes in attitudes, policies, and legislation that will guarantee access to identifying information for all adoptees and their birth and adoptive families.
www.americanadoptioncongress.org/index.php

National Adoption Center offers a great list of questions to ask adoption agencies; addresses single-parent, tax, and legal issues; provides photos of kids waiting to be adopted, book reviews, lists of state and local contacts, and links to other adoption-related organizations.
Tel.: (800) TO-ADOPT
email: nac@adopt.org

Advice, General

There are literally dozens of parenting resources out there for new parents. Among my favorites are:

Kidsinthehouse.com features 8,000 videos (including several dozen of mine) from more than 400 experts that can help answer all your questions on pregnancy and parenting.
www.kidsinthehouse.com

Mr. Dad is my website, where you'll find advice, blogs, columns, podcasts, interviews, and a whole lot more.
www.mrdad.com

The National Parenting Center offers advice from a variety of parenting authorities (doctors, psychologists, and parenting experts/authors). Based on age-specific groups, the articles provide a great deal of information on children in each stage of development.
www.tnpc.com/

Parenting 24/7 was developed by the University of Illinois to be a "one-stop" source of news, information, and advice on parenting. It includes recent news articles on a wide variety of topics, as well as a large number of video clips of parents and professionals discussing parenting challenges and strategies.
Tel: (217) 333-2912
email: parenting247@uiuc.edu
parenting247.org

African American Fathers

African American Male Leadership Institute
Tel: (803) 822-3510
email: aamli@midlandstech.edu
www.midlandstech.edu/aamli/default.html

Black Dads
blackdadconnection.org/

At-Home Dads

National At-Home Dad Network has great resources on how to find/register/start a dads group. They also have links to stay-at-home dad bloggers, statistics, resources, and a lot more.
athomedad.org/

Babies, Behavioral Health and Special Needs

The American Academy of Child & Adolescent Psychiatry is a comprehensive resource with articles ranging from separation anxiety to behavioral disorders.
www.aacap.org

Autism Speaks has substantial resources for parents who want information or support for children on the autistic spectrum.
www.autismspeaks.org

Parent to Parent USA matches parents of children with special needs with trained volunteer support parents who provide emotional support, resources, and guidance.
www.p2pusa.org/p2pusa/sitepages/p2p-home.aspx

Babies, General Health Issues

Healthy Children is sponsored by the American Academy of Pediatrics for parents. It provides information on topics including child development, health, safety, and family issues.
www.healthychildren.org

Immunization Action Coalition provides the nation's premier source of child, teen, and adult immunization information for health professionals and their patients.
Tel: (651) 647-9009
email: admin@immunize.org
www.immunize.org/

Babies, Safety

American Red Cross
www.redcross.org/

Children's Safety Network provides a national resource center for the prevention of childhood injuries and violence.
www.childrenssafetynetwork.org/

National Child Safety Council. Its goal is to prevent needless childhood accidents and help save lives through meaningful safety education.
www.nationalchildsafetycouncil.org/

BOOKS ON SAFETY

Mitchell J. Einzig, ed. *Baby & Child Emergency First Aid: Simple Step-By-Step Instructions for the Most Common Childhood Emergencies.* New York: Meadowbrook Press, 2011.

Christopher M. Johnson. *Keeping Your Kids Out of the Emergency Room: A Guide to Childhood Injuries and Illnesses.* Lanham, MD: Rowman & Littlefield Publishers, 2013.

Lawrence E. Shapiro, Richard L. Jablow, and Julia Holmes. *The Baby Emergency Handbook: Lifesaving Information Every Parent Needs to Know.* Oakland, CA: New Harbinger, 2008.

See also *Advice, General.* Most of those websites have information on just about any child-safety question you may have.

Babies, Premature

Preemieparents.com is a well-stocked collection of articles, books, links, and resources for parents of preemies.
www.preemieparents.com

Preemie Voices offers resources for all those who touch and impact the lives of one of America's most fragile patient population; provided by MedImmune.
preemievoices.com/

Prematurity provides a wealth of support and information on the long-term effects of prematurity for parents of children born premature.
www.prematurity.org/index.html

Breastfeeding

Kelly Mom is a very nice site that includes information on breastfeeding and some excellent resources on medication safety during breastfeeding.
kellymom.com/

La Leche League International Inc. provides information and mother-to-mother support through La Leche League's network of lay leaders and professional experts.
www.lalecheleague.org/

United States Breastfeeding Committee. Its goal is to improve the nation's health by working collaboratively to protect, promote, and support breastfeeding.
Tel: (202) 367-1132
email: office@usbreastfeeding.org
www.usbreastfeeding.org/

Child Care

Care.com
www.care.com/

Child Care Aware is a nationwide organization created to help parents identify quality child care in their communities.
Tel.: (800) 424-2246
www.childcareaware.org/

Home Pay will take care of all your payroll needs for nannies and sitters.
Tel.: (888) 273-3356
www.myhomepay.com/

International Nanny Association
www.nanny.org

Nanny Tax Inc. is another payroll service.
Tel.: (888) NANNYTAX/888-626-6982
www.nannytax.com/

Children and Media

American Academy of Pediatrics Media Matters Campaign includes policy statements, articles, and public education brochures created by pediatricians.
www2.aap.org/advocacy/mediamatters.htm

Common Sense Media features reviews of movies, music, books, games, and other websites intended to help families make decisions about what they watch, hear, read, and play.
www.commonsensemedia.org/

Just Think Foundation offers resources for parents, teachers, and youth.
https://www.change.org/o/just_think_foundation

Death and Grief

First Candle offers resources on how to survive stillbirth and SIDS and also guides you through decisions you need to make during this difficult time.
www.firstcandle.org/

MISS Foundation is a nonprofit organization that provides immediate and ongoing support to grieving families.
Tel: (888) 455-MISS
email: info@missfoundation.org
www.misschildren.org/

Now I Lay Me Down to Sleep provides the gift of remembrance photography for parents suffering the loss of a baby.
www.nowilaymedowntosleep.org/

Tears Foundation assists newly bereaved families who have lost an infant by providing financial support for funeral expenses and emotional support services.
www.thetearsfoundation.org/

Fatherhood, General

Greatdad.com is great website that features voices of different dad writers and experts. Because dads don't always think like moms, GreatDad has the only dad-written, week-by-week newsletters covering pregnancy and baby, as well as a city-by-city resource guide of fun things to do with your kids based on interest and age level.
www.greatdad.com

Mr. Dad has many of my articles and columns on all aspects of fatherhood.
www.mrdad.com

The National Center for Fathering has resources designed to help men become more aware of their own fathering style and then work toward improving their skills.
Tel.: (800) 593-DADS
email: dads@fathers.com
www.fathers.com

National Fatherhood Initiative offers membership that includes the quarterly newsletter *Fatherhood Today*; updates on family issues and political/legislative developments; the Fatherhood Resource Catalog of books, videos, and audio tapes, offering a discount on all items; and updates on activities and events.
Tel.: (301) 948-0599
email: info@fatherhood.org
www.fatherhood.org

National Responsible Fatherhood Clearinghouse supports the efforts of the U.S. Department of Health and Human Services (HHS) to assist states and communities to promote and support Responsible Fatherhood and Healthy Marriage. Primarily a resource for professionals operating Responsible Fatherhood programs.
www.fatherhood.gov/

Fathers, Divorced or Single

American Coalition for Fathers and Children is dedicated to promoting equal rights for all parties affected by divorce or the breakup of a family. Chapters nationwide.
Tel.: (800) 978-3237
email: info@acfc.org
www.acfc.org

Singlefather.org
www.singlefather.org/index.php

Single Fathers Due to Cancer is dedicated to the thousands of fathers who lose their spouses each year to cancer and must adjust to being sole parents.
email: singlefathersduetocancer @unc.edu
www.singlefathersduetocancer.org/ home.do

Fathers, Donor Insemination, Artificial Insemination, Donor Eggs, etc.

Donor Conception Network is a supportive network of 1,700 mainly U.K.-based families with children conceived with donated sperm, eggs, or embryos, those considering or undergoing donor conception procedures; and donor-conceived people.
mchlibrary.jhmi.edu

Life as a Dad to Donor-Insemination Kids is a thoughtful blog about raising children conceived by artificial means.
di-dad.blogspot.com/

MCH Library is a service provided by Georgetown University's National Center for Education in Maternal Child Health. Despite the name, it lists a lot of resources that focus on psychological and social impacts of Assisted Reproductive Technologies (ART) on children conceived via ART and on their families—including dads.
www.mchlibrary.jhmi.edu

Fathers, Groups

City Dads Group is a growing national organization dedicated to helping fathers socialize and support one another.
www.citydadsgroup.com/

Just a Dad 247 has an amazingly comprehensive map of dads groups all around the world—not just at-home-dad groups, but all of them.
justadad247.com/map-of-dad-groups/ or goo.gl/bUIC9i

Fathers, Older

Older Fathers Blog
olderfathers.blogspot.com/

Seasoned Sires
seasonedsires.com/

Gay Parents

Gayfamilysupport.com is a website with an abundance of information and resources dedicated to assisting families support their LGBT children.
www.Gayfamilysupport.com

Gay Parent Magazine is a magazine for gay and lesbian parents and those hoping to become gay and lesbian parents.
www.gayparentmag.com/

PFLAG is the largest organization in the nation offering support to parents, families, and friends of LGBT persons. pflag-chapter-map.herokuapp.com/

Grandparents

Grandparents Raising Grandchildren www.usa.gov/Topics/Grandparents. shtml

Grandparents Rights Organization. Its purpose is to educate and support grandparents and grandchildren and to advocate for their desire to continue a relationship that may be threatened with loss of contact, usually following: family acrimony; a grandchild being born out of wedlock; the death of one of the grandchild's parents; or the divorce of the grandchild's parents. www.grandparentsrights.org/

National Kinship Alliance for Children is a nationwide network of grandparents, community members, and professionals working together to provide education and support, advocacy, and thought leadership for children, grandparents, and kinship families. Tel: (888) 659-3745 (Warmline) email: info@kinshipalliance.org kinshipalliance.org

Healthy Living

Greenhome offers a full range of healthy, eco-friendly products for home and nursery, from paints that don't give off toxic gases to nontoxic insecticides and cleaning products. www.greenhome.com

Holistic Moms Network www.holisticmoms.org/

The Nourishing Home thenourishinghome.com/ kids-in-the-kitchen/

Latino and/or Spanish-Speaking Fathers

National Latino Fatherhood and Family Institute offers consulting, seminars, and training. Its goal is to address the multifaceted needs of Latino men and foster a positive approach toward working with Latino populations, building on the strengths of cultural traditions. Tel: (408) 676-8215 www.nationalcompadresnetwork.com/ nlffi/nlffi.html

Men, General

Man Therapy is a really great resource giving therapy to men the way men would do it. mantherapy.org/

Men's Health Network is a national education organization that recognizes men's health as a specific social concern. It has a fantastic database of articles, resources, and links on every conceivable fatherhood issue. www.menshealthnetwork.org

Men's Resources International mensresourcesinternational.org/

Menstuff offers a huge collection of resources on men, men's health, fatherhood, parenting, relationships, and more. www.menstuff.org/frameindex.html

Music

Kindermusik www.kindermusik.com

Musikgarten www.musikgarten.org/

Music Together www.musictogether.com

Each of these companies offers music and movement programs for infants and their parents. CDs and songbooks are available. Classes in each method are offered throughout the United States. Listings of classes and teachers are available on the websites.

Native American Fathers

National Indian Parent Information Center provides support, education, and encouragement for the families of Native American tribal children with disabilities or learning challenges.
Tel: (855) 720-2910
email: indian.info@nipic.org
www.nipic.org/

Native American Fatherhood and Families Association is dedicated to strengthening families by responsibly involving fathers in the lives of their children, families, and communities and partnering with mothers to provide happy and safe families.
Tel: (480) 833-5007
email: info@aznaffa.org
www.nativeamericanfathers.org

Native American Professional Parent Resources empowers, educates, and provides supportive services to build healthy Native American children and families.
Tel: (505) 345-6289
nappr.org/

Reading

The American Library Association provides reviews of children's books and lists of award winners.
www.ala.org

Children's Literature provides a searchable database of reviews of the latest kids' books.
www.childrenslit.com

The Children's Picture Book Database at Miami University offers a bibliography of books for preschoolers to third graders that can be used to design literature-based thematic units. It is searchable by topics, concepts, and skills. Though the database is particularly useful for teachers and librarians, it can also greatly benefit parents eager to find picture books on specific topics for their children.
dlp.lib.miamioh.edu/

Sign Language

Babysigns offers videos and books based on the work of Linda Acredolo and Susan Goodwyn.
www.babysigns.com

My Smart Hands is a group of baby sign language instructors that use 100 percent ASL signs to teach parents how to communicate with their hearing babies.
mysmarthands.com/

Sign2Me offers videos and books based on the work of Joseph Garcia.
sign2me.com

Social Media Dads

There are tons of dad bloggers out there, as well as some great fatherhood-related groups on Facebook, Google+, and elsewhere. Listing them all would be impossible, but they're pretty easy to find.

Stress

Child Development Info: Stress Management for Parents
childdevelopmentinfo.com/
family-living/stress/

National Parent Helpline
Tel: (855) 4A PARENT
email: info@nationalparenthelpline.org
www.nationalparenthelpline.org/

Parents Helping Parents supports caregivers by offering a parental stress line and parent support groups.
Tel: (800) 632-8188
e-mail: info@parentshelpingparents.org
www.parentshelpingparents.org/

Toys and Games

Babyscholars.com offers a large selection of toys and games, from classic wooden blocks to the latest computer games.
www.babyscholars.com

Mr. Dad Seal of Approval is the program I created to recognize products and services that will get dads and kids playing together and improve father-child relationships.
www.mrdad.com/seal

Parents@Play is a nationally syndicated newspaper column that reviews toys and games that get parents and kids playing together.
parentsatplay.com/

Travel

Familytravelfiles.com
www.thefamilytravelfiles.com

Kids World Travel Guide
www.kids-world-travel-guide.com/index.html

Travel for Kids
travelforkids.com/

All three sites offer tips and recommendations for family vacations, from where to go to what to do when you get there.

Twins and More

Preemietwins.com is a nice resource for parents of twins born prematurely.
preemietwins.com

The Twins Foundation is a great source for research on twins.
www.twinsfoundation.com

Twins Magazine has print and online versions. Both offer advice, anecdotes, facts, support, and resources for parents of twins.
www.twinsmagazine.com

Work/Family Balance

1 Million for Work Flexibility is an organization that advocates for telecommuting and other forms of flexibility.
www.workflexibility.org/

Fathers, Work and Family Blog
fathersworkandfamily.com/

Third Path Institute provides resources, information, and consulting to help people find a "third path" to better balance work and family. They advocate for shared care at home and flexible, supportive approaches at work.
www.thirdpath.org/

We're constantly revising and updating this book and are always looking for ways to improve it. So if you have any comments or suggestions, please send an email to:
   armin@mrdad.com

Please also connect with us on social media:

- •Twitter: @mrdad
- •Pinterest.com/mrdad
- •plus.google.com/+Mrdad
- •Facebook.com/mrdad
- •Linkedin.com/in/mrdad

Books for Babies

This list is by no means definitive. With about five thousand new children's titles published each year, the pool of good books never stops growing. I strongly urge you to get to know your local librarians, who are always up-to-date.

FOR THE FIRST 6–8 MONTHS

Babies this age don't really care what you read to them. Your baby's most interested in simple, bright images, the sound of your voice, the rhythm and rhyme of the words, and, most of all, being held by you. Here are some of the best books for babies this age (some are a little "ahead" of your baby's development, but that's okay).

High Contrast

Baby Animals and *Black and White*, Phyllis Limbacher Tildes

Black on White and *Black & White*, Tana Hoban

Hello, Animals! and *Hello, Bugs!*, Smriti Prasadam

I Kissed the Baby!, Mary Murphy

I Like Black and White, Barbara Jean Hicks

Look, Look! and *Look at the Animals!*, Peter Linenthal

Quiet Loud; *Tickle*; *No, No, Yes* (and others), Leslie Patricelli

What Does Baby See?, Begin Smart Books

Touch and Feel

Bright Baby Touch and Feel Shapes, Roger Priddy

Colors and *Counting*, Emily Bolam

Pat the Bunny, Dorothy Kunhardt

Pat the Cat, Edith Kunhardt Davis

Textures, Joanne Barker

Rhythm and Rhyme

These are great for kids of all ages. Start now and find some favorites.

The Baby's Bedtime Book, Kay Chorao

Eyes, Nose, Fingers, and Toes, Judy Hindley

The House That Jack Built, Janet Stevens

The Mother Goose Treasury, Raymond Briggs

My Mother Goose: A Collection of Favorite Rhymes, Songs, and Concepts, David McPhail

Ring a Ring O'Roses, Flint Public Library

Three Little Kittens, Lorinda Bryan Cauley

Trot Trot to Boston: Play Rhymes for Baby, Carol F. Ra

Singing Bee! A Collection of Favorite Children's Songs, Jane Hart

A Week of Lullabies, Helen Plotz

Other Good Books

All Fall Down, Helen Oxenbury

The Baby (and others), John Burningham

Baby Bear, Baby Bear, What Do You See?, Bill Martin Jr.

Baby Farm Animals, Garth Williams

Baby's Animal Friends, Phoebe Dunn

Chugga-Chugga Choo-Choo, Kevin Lewis

First Things First: A Baby's Companion, Charlotte Voake

Funny Faces: A Very First Picture Book, Nicola Tuxworth

Hello, Day!, Anita Lobel

How Big Is a Pig?, Clare Beaton

I See (and others), Rachel Isadora

Spot's Toys, Eric Hill

This Is Me, Lenore Blegvad

Welcome, Little Baby (and others), Aliki

FOR 8–12 MONTHS

At this age, babies still like bright colors and photographs, especially of other babies. They also love touching books, and either try to turn pages or eat the whole thing—sometimes both at the same time. If your baby has favorite books, there's no reason to give them up. But here are some more books he or she may enjoy.

Bright Colors and Photographs

Animal Time!; Baby Bugs (and many others), Tom Arma

Baby's Day and *Off to Bed*, Michel Blake

Counting Kisses, Karen Katz

I Love Baby Animals: Fun Children's Picture Book with Amazing Photos of Baby Animals, David Chuka

I Love Colors, Margaret Miller

My Car, Byron Barton

The Okay Book, Todd Parr

Touch and Feel/Lift-the-Flap

Animal Play: A Touch and Feel Cloth Book, Harriet Ziefert

Animals Talk (Touch, Look, and Learn), Emily Bolam

Bathtime (Baby Touch and Feel), DK Publishing

Bowbeard Walks the Plank (Playmobil Playfeet), Paul Flemming

Daddy's Scratchy Face, Edith Kunhardt Davis

I Like Bugs, Lorena Siminovich

Max's Snowsuit, Rosemary Wells

Peek-a-Moo, Marie Torres Cimarusti

Peek-a Who?, Nina Laden

That's not My Puppy: Its Coat Is Too Hairy and *That's Not My Tractor!*, Fiona Watt

Where Is Baby's Puppy?, Karen Katz

Where Is Maisy?, Lucy Cousins

Concepts (Numbers, Letters, Words, Shapes, Sizes, etc.)

The ABC Bunny, Wanda Gag

ABC Dogs, Kathy Darling

Baby's First Words, Vic Heatherton

Big and Little, Margaret Miller

Clap Hands (and many others), Helen Oxenbury

First Words, Katie Cox

First Words for Babies and Toddlers, Jane Salt

Flaptastic: Sizes (and others), DK Publishing

Freight Train, Donald Crews

I Can Eat a Rainbow: A Fun Look at Healthy Fruits and Vegetables, Annabel Karmel

Kids Like Me Learn ABCs and *Kids Like Me Learn Colors*, Laura Ronay

My Shapes/Mis Formas, Rebecca Emberley

Sparkly Day; *Twinkly Night* (and other *Baby Dazzlers* books), Helen Stephens

Ten Little Fingers and Ten Little Toes, Mem Fox

Ten, Nine, Eight, Molly Bang

The Very Hungry Caterpillar, Eric Carle

Rhythm and Rhyme

The Baby's Lap Book, Kay Chorao

Hey Diddle Diddle, Moira Kemp

Humpty Dumpty, Annie Kubler

Mother Goose Picture Puzzles, Will Hillenbrand

The Neighborhood Mother Goose, Nina Crews

Read-Aloud Rhymes for the Very Young, selected by Jack Prelutsky

Sylvia Long's Mother Goose Block Books, Sylvia Long

The Three Bears Rhyme Book, Jane Yolen

Twinkle, Twinkle: An Animal Lover's Mother Goose, Bobbi Fabian

The Wheels on the Bus and *Knick-Knack Paddywhack!*, Paul O. Zelinsky

Other Excellent Books

Baby Animals (and many others), Gyo Fujikawa

The Baby's Catalogue, Janet and Allan Ahlberg

Baby Signs for Animals; *Baby Signs for Bedtime* (and others), Linda Acredolo and Susan Goodwyn

The Ball Bounced (and many others), Nancy Tafuri

Bears, Ruth Krauss

The Book of Baths, Karen Gray Ruelle

Brown Bear, Brown Bear, What Do You See?, Bill Martin Jr.

But Not the Hippopotamus; *Opposites*; *Moo, Baa, La La La!*; and anything else ever written by Sandra Boynton

Chicka Chicka Boom Boom, Bill Martin Jr. and John Archambault

Daddy, Play with Me (and many others), Shigeo Watanabe

Dr. Seuss's Sleep Book, Dr. Seuss

Goodnight Moon, Margaret Wise Brown

How a Baby Grows, Nora Buck

"More, More, More," Said the Baby: 3 Love Stories, Vera B. Williams

One Hot Summer Day, Nina Crews

Pretty Brown Face and *Watch Me Dance*, Andrea Pinkney

The Seals on the Bus, Lenny Hort

Sleepy Book, Charlotte Zolotow

Spot Goes Splash (and many other *Spot books*), Eric Hill

Tickle; *All Fall Down*; *Say Goodnight*; *Dad's Back* (and many others), Jan Ormerod

Time for Bed (and others), Mem Fox

Who Said Meow?, Maria Polushkin

Height and Weight Charts

The charts on pages 308 and 309 are very similar to the ones used by your child's pediatrician. Please remember that "normal" is something of a sliding scale, so use these charts for reference only. Many factors, including your baby's birth weight, nutrition, and genetics (such as your height and weight) will influence your child's measurements. Don't focus on a single entry: squirming babies are hard to weigh and measure. What's most important is consistency over time. If you and your partner are short and thin and your six-month-old has been in the 10th percentile since birth, that's probably perfectly normal. However, if your baby was in the 50th percentile in height and weight at one month and drops to the 10th or zooms up to the 90th at three months, there could be a problem. As always, if you're worried about your child's growth, be sure to discuss your concerns with your child's doctor.

BIRTH TO 36 MONTHS: BOYS

Length-for-age and Weight-for-age percentiles

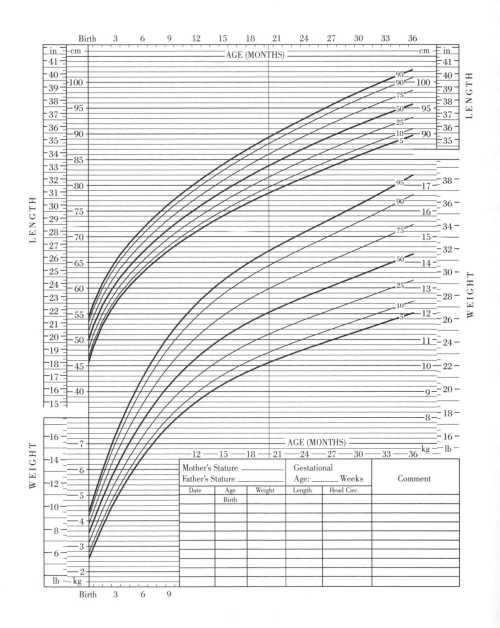

BIRTH TO 36 MONTHS: GIRLS

Length-for-age and Weight-for-age percentiles

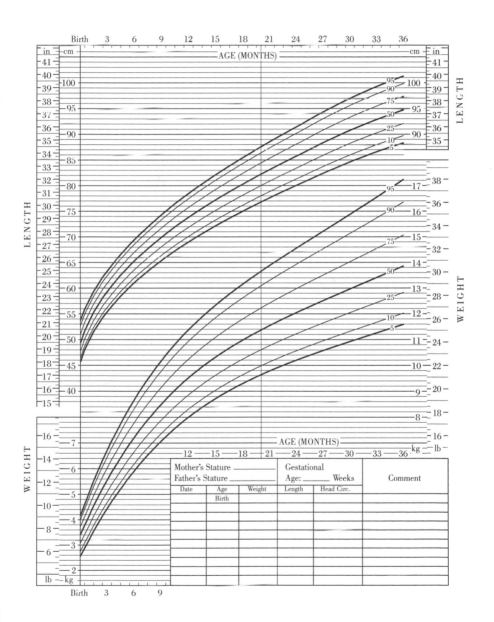

309

Selected Bibliography

BOOKS

Acredolo, Linda, and Susan Goodwyn. *Baby Signs: How to Talk with Your Baby Before Your Baby Can Talk.* 3rd edition. New York: McGraw-Hill, 2009.

Ambert, Anne-Marie. *The Effect of Children on Parents.* New York: Haworth Press, 2001.

Ames, Louise Bates, Frances L. Ilg, and Carol Chase Haber. *Your One-Year-Old: The Fun-Loving, Fussy 12- to 24-Month-Old.* New York: Delacorte Press, 1982.

Austrian, Sonia G., ed. *Developmental Theories Through the Life Cycle.* New York: Columbia University Press, 2002.

Barry, Dave. *Dave Barry's Bad Habits: A 100% Fact-Free Book.* New York: Holt Paperbacks, 1993.

Batten, Mary. *Hey, Daddy!: Animal Fathers and Their Babies.* Atlanta: Peachtree, 2002.

Belsky, Jay, and John Kelly. *The Transition to Parenthood: How a First Child Changes a Marriage; Why Some Couples Grow Closer and Others Apart.* New York: Delacorte Press, 1994.

Bettelheim, Bruno. *A Good Enough Parent: A Book on Child-Rearing.* New York: Vintage, 1988.

Biller, Henry B., and Robert J. Trotter. *The Father Factor: What You Need to Know to Make a Difference.* New York: Pocket Books, 1994.

Bluestine, Eric. *The Ways Children Learn Music: An Introduction and Practical Guide to Music Learning Theory.* Revised edition. Chicago: GIA Publications, 2000.

Brazelton, T. Berry, and Bertrand Cramer. *The Earliest Relationship: Parents, Infants, and the Drama of Early Attachment.* Reading, MA: Addison-Wesley, 1990.

Britton, James. *Language and Learning: The Importance of Speech in Children's Development.* New York: Penguin, 1970.

Bronstein, Phyllis, and Carolyn Pape Cowan, eds. *Fatherhood Today: Men's Changing Role in the Family.* New York: John Wiley & Sons, 1988.

Brott, Armin. *Father for Life: A Journey of Joy, Challenge, and Change.* New York: Abbeville Press, 2003.

Brott, Armin, and Jennifer Ash. *The Expectant Father: The Ultimate Guide for Dads-to-Be.* 4th edition. New York: Abbeville Press, 2015.

Caplan, Frank, ed. *The First Twelve Months of Life.* New York: Grosset & Dunlap, 1973.

Carnoy, Martin, and David Carnoy. *Fathers of a Certain Age: The Joys and Problems of Middle-Aged Fatherhood.* Minneapolis: Fairview Press, 1997.

Cath, Stanley H., Alan R. Gurwitt, and John Munder Ross, eds. *Father and Child: Developmental and Clinical Perspectives.* Hillsdale, NJ: Analytic Press, 1994.

Cowan, Carolyn Pape, and Philip A. Cowan. *When Partners Become Parents: The Big Life Change for Couples.* Revised edition. Mahwah, NJ: Lawrence Erlbaum Associates, 1999.

Daniels, Marilyn. *Dancing with Words: Signing for Hearing Children's Literacy.* South Hadley, MA: Bergin & Garvey, 2001.

Dewar, Gwen. *The Social World of Newborns: A Guide for the Science-Minded Parent.* http://www.parentingscience .com/newborns-and-the-social-world .html.

Drobeck, Bruce. "The Impact on Men of the Transition to Fatherhood: A Phenomenological Investigation." Ph.D. diss., Texas Woman's University, 1990.

Finley, G. E. *Adoptive and Biological Fathers' Enjoyment of First-Time Fathering.* Minneapolis: National Council on Family Relations, 1999.

Flannery-Quinn, Suzanne Marie, "The Portrayals of Male Parents in Caldecott Award-Winning American Picture Books (1938–2002): Examining the Culture of Fatherhood Presented to Young People." Ph.D. diss., Child and Family Studies, Syracuse University, 2003.

Fox, Mem. *Reading Magic: Why Reading Aloud to Our Children Will Change Their Lives Forever.* 2nd edition. Orlando, FL: Mariner Books, 2008.

Fraiberg, Selma H. *The Magic Years: Understanding and Handling the Problems of Early Childhood.* New York: Charles Scribner's Sons, 1959.

Garcia, Joseph. *Sign with Your Baby: How to Communicate with Infants before They Can Speak.* Seattle: Northlight, 2002.

Gordon, Edwin E. *Music Learning Theory for Newborn and Young Children.* Chicago: GIA Publications, 2013.

Greenspan, Stanley, and Nancy Thorndike Greenspan. *First Feelings: Milestones in the Emotional Development of Your Baby and Child.* New York: Penguin, 1989.

Grossmann, K., K. E. Grossmann, H. Kindler, and P. Zimmermann. "A Wider View of Attachment and Exploration: The Influence of Mothers and Fathers on the Development of Psychological Security from Infancy to Young Adulthood." In *Handbook of Attachment: Theory, Research, and Clinical Applications*, edited by J. Cassidy and P. R. Shaver. 2nd edition, 857–79. New York: Guilford Press, 2010.

Harrington, Brad, Fred Van Deusen, Jennifer Sabatini Fraone, and Samantha Eddy. *The New Dad: Take Your Leave; Perspectives on Paternity Leave from*

Fathers, Leading Organizations, and Global Policies. Chestnut Hill, MA: Boston College Center for Work and Family, 2014.

Hass, Aaron. *The Gift of Fatherhood: How Men's Lives Are Transformed by Their Children.* New York: Fireside, 1994.

Hoare, Carol Hren. *Erikson on Development in Adulthood: New Insights from the Unpublished Papers.* Oxford, UK, and New York: Oxford University Press, 2002.

Jassey, Lewis, and Jonathan Jassey. *The Newborn Sleep Book: A Simple, Proven Method for Training Your New Baby to Sleep Through the Night.* New York: Perigee, 2014.

Jordan, Pamela L. "The Mother's Role in Promoting Fathering Behavior." In *Becoming a Father: Contemporary Social, Developmental, and Clinical Perspectives*, edited by J. L. Shapiro et al., 61–71. New York: Springer, 1995.

Kitzinger, Sheila. *The Experience of Breastfeeding.* Middlesex, UK: Penguin, 1987.

Lamb, Michael E., ed. *The Role of the Father in Child Development.* 5th edition. Hoboken, NJ: Wiley, 2010.

Linton, Bruce. "The Phases of Paternal Development: Pregnancy Through Twelve Months Postpartum." Ph.D. diss., Columbia Pacific University, San Rafael, CA, 1991.

Meyer, Donald J. *Uncommon Fathers: Reflections on Raising a Child with a Disability.* Bethesda, MD: Woodbine House, 1995.

Minnesota Fathering Alliance. *Working with Fathers: Methods and Perspectives.* Stillwater, MN: Nu Ink Unlimited, 1992.

Moser, Franziska. "Social Construction of Gender-(un)fairness: An Analysis of Educational Material and Individual Language Use." Ph.D. diss., Freie Universität Berlin, 2013.

The New American Father. Washington, DC: Pew Research Center, June 14, 2013, http://www.pewsocialtrends.org/files/2013/06/FINAL_Fathers_report.pdf.

Newman, Barbara M., and Philip R. Newman. *Development Through Life: A Psychosocial Approach.* 12th edition. Independence, KY: Cengage Learning, 2015.

Noller, Patricia, Judith A. Feeney, and Candida Peterson. *Personal Relationships across the Lifespan.* Hove, UK: Psychology Press; New York: Taylor & Francis, 2001.

Palkovitz, Rob. *Involved Fathering and Men's Adult Development: Provisional Balances.* Mahwah, NJ: Lawrence Erlbaum, 2002.

Parke, Ross D. *Fatherhood.* Cambridge, MA: Harvard University Press, 1996.

Parker, Kim, and Wendy Wang. *Modern Parenthood: Roles of Moms and Dads Converge as They Balance Work and Family.* Washington, DC: Pew Research Center, March 14, 2013, http://www.pewsocialtrends.org/files/2013/03/FINAL_modern_parenthood_03-2013.pdf.

Pleck, Joseph H. "Are 'Family Supportive' Employer Policies Relevant to Men?" In *Men, Work, and Family*, edited by Jane C. Hood, 217–37. Newbury Park, CA.: Sage, 1993.

Pruett, Kyle D. *Fatherneed: Why Father Care Is as Essential as Mother Care for Your Child.* New York: Free Press, 2000.

Raeburn, Paul. *Do Fathers Matter? What Science Is Telling Us About the Parent We've Overlooked*. New York: Scientific American and Farrar, Straus and Giroux, 2014.

Sachs, Brad E. *Things Just Haven't Been the Same: Making the Transition from Marriage to Parenthood*. New York: William Morrow, 1992.

Snarey, John. *How Fathers Care for the Next Generation: A Four-Decade Study*. Cambridge, MA: Harvard University Press, 1993.

Spangler, Doug. *Fatherhood: An Owner's Manual*. Richmond, CA: Fabus, 1994.

Trelease, Jim. *The Read-Aloud Handbook*. 7th edition. New York: Penguin, 2013.

White, Burton L. *The New First Three Years of Life*. New York: Fireside, 1995.

Zero to Eight: Children's Media Use in America. Common Sense Media, fall 2011, https://www.commonsense media.org/research/zero-to-eight-childrens-media-use-in-america.

ARTICLES AND PAPERS

Adams, M., C. Walker, and P. O'Connell. "Invisible or Involved Fathers? A Content Analysis of Representations of Parenting in Young Children's Picture Books in the UK." *Sex Roles* 65, no. 3–4 (2011): 259–70.

Alexander, Gerianne M., T. Wilcox, and R. Woods. "Sex Differences in Infants' Visual Interest in Toys." *Archives of Sexual Behavior* 38 (2009): 427–33.

Appelbaum, E., and R. Milkman. "Leaves That Pay: Employer and Worker Experiences with Paid Family Leave in California." Center for Economic and Policy Research, January 2011, http://www.cepr.net/index.php/publications/reports/leaves-that-pay.

Baumrind, Diana. "Current Patterns of Parental Authority." *Developmental Psychology* 4, no. 1, part 2 (January 1971): 1–103.

Bettany, Shona, Ben Kerrane, and Margaret Hogg. "The Material-Semiotics of Fatherhood: The Co-Emergence of Technology and Contemporary Fatherhood." *Journal of Business Research* 67, no. 7 (2014): 1544–51.

Boushey, Heather, and Sarah Jane Glynn. "There Are Significant Business Costs to Replacing Employees." Center for American Progress, November 16, 2012, http://cdn.americanprogress.org/wp-content/uploads/2012/11/CostofTurnover.pdf.

Burn, Katherine F., Victor W. Henderson, David Ames, Lorraine Dennerstein, and Cassandra Szoeke. "Role of Grandparenting in Postmenopausal Women's Cognitive Health." *Menopause* 21, no. 10 (2014): 1069–74.

Condry, John, and Sandra Condry. "Sex Differences: A Study of the Eye of the Beholder." *Child Development* 47, no. 3 (1976): 812–19.

Condry, John, and David F. Ross. "Sex and Aggression: The Influence of Gender Label on the Perception of Aggression in Children." *Child Development* 56, no. 1 (February 1985): 225–33.

Davis, R. N., M. M. Davis, G. L. Freed, and S. J. Clark. "Father's Depression Related to Positive and Negative Parenting Behaviors with 1-Year-Old Children." *Pediatrics* 127, no. 4 (2011): 612–18.

DeLuccie, Mary F. "Mothers as Gatekeepers: A Model of Maternal Mediators of Father Involvement." *Journal of*

Genetic Psychology 156, no. 1 (1994): 115–31.

De Pisapia, N., M. H. Bornstein, P. Rigo, G. Esposito, S. de Falco, and P. Venuti. "Gender Differences in Directional Brain Responses to Infant Hunger Cries." *Neuroreport* 24, no. 3 (2013): 142–46.

Dickstein, Susan, and Ross D. Parke. "Social Referencing in Infancy: A Glance at Fathers and Marriage." *Child Development* 59, no. 2 (April 1988): 506–11.

Dionne, G., E. Touchette, J. Montplaisir, N. Forget-Duboir, M. Boivin, D. Petit, and R. Tremblay. "Association between Sleep-Wake Consolidation and Language Development in Early Childhood: A Longitudinal Twin Study." *Sleep* 34, no. 8 (2011): 987–95.

Dondi, M., F. Simion, and G. Caltran. "Can Newborns Discriminate between Their Own Cry and the Cry of Another Newborn Infant?" *Developmental Psychology* 35, no. 2 (March 1999): 418–26.

Draghi-Lorenz, Riccardo. "Jealousy in the First Year: Evidence of Early Interpersonal Awareness." Paper presented at the British Psychological Society Developmental Section annual conference, September 1997.

Dunn, M., A. Rochlen, and K. O'Brien. "Employee, Partner, Mother: An Exploratory Investigation of Working Women with Stay at Home Fathers." *Journal of Career Development* 40 (2013): 3–22.

Fagot, Beverly, and Richard Hagan. "Observations of Parent Reactions to Sex-Stereotyped Behaviors: Age and Sex Effects." *Child Development* 62, no. 3 (June 1991): 617–28.

Feldman, R., E. Bamberger, and Y. Kanat-Maymon. "Parent-Specific Reciprocity from Infancy to Adolescence Shapes Children's Social Competence and Dialogical Skills." *Attachment & Human Development* 15, no. 4 (2013): 407–23.

Field, Tiffany, S. Schanberg, et al. "Tactile/Kinesthetic Stimulation Effects on Preterm Neonates." *Pediatrics* 77, no. 5 (1986): 654–58.

Fishman, Elizabeth A., and Steven A. Meyers. "Marital Satisfaction and Child Adjustment: Direct and Mediated Pathways." *Contemporary Family Therapy* 22, no. 4 (2000): 437–52.

Geangu, E., O. Benga, D. Stahl, and T. Striano. "Contagious Crying beyond the First Days of Life." *Infant Behavior and Development*. 33, no. 3 (June 2010): 279–88.

Geiger, A., P. Achermann, and O. G. Jenni. "Association between Sleep Duration and Intelligence Scores in Healthy Children." *Developmental Psychology* 46, no. 4 (July 2010): 949–54.

Gentry, James, and Robert Harrison. "Is Advertising a Barrier to Male Movement toward Gender Change?" *Marketing Theory* 10, no. 1 (March 2010): 74–96.

Goodman, J. H. "Paternal Postpartum Depression, Its Relationship to Maternal Postpartum Depression, and Implications for Family Health." *Journal of Advanced Nursing* 45, no. 1 (January 2004): 26–35.

Goux, Darshan. "Millennials in the Workplace." Bentley University Center for Women and Business, 2012, https://www.bentley.edu/centers/sites/www.bentley.edu.centers/files/centers/cwb/millennials-report.pdf.

Hall, Wendy A. "New Fatherhood: Myths and Realities." *Public Health Nursing* 11, no. 4 (August 1994): 219–28.

Han, W.-J., C. Ruhm, J. Waldfogel, and E. Washbrook. "The Timing of Mothers' Employment after Childbirth." *Monthly Labor Review* 131, no. 6 (June 2008): 15–27.

Jadva, Melissa Hines, and Susan Golombok. "Infants' Preferences for Toys, Colors, and Shapes: Sex Differences and Similarities." *Archives of Sexual Behavior* 39, no. 6 (March 2010): 1261–73.

Jordan, Pamela L. "Laboring for Relevance: Expectant and New Fatherhood." *Nursing Research* 39, no. 1 (January–February 1990): 11–16.

Jordan, Pamela L., et al. "Breastfeeding and Fathers: Illuminating the Darker Side." *Birth* 17, no. 4 (March 1990): 210–13.

Kim, P., L. C. Mayes, J. F. Leckman, R. Feldman, and J. E. Swain. "Early Postpartum Parental Preoccupation and Positive Parenting Thoughts: Relationship with Parent-Infant Interaction." *Infant Mental Health Journal* 34, no. 2 (2013): 104–16.

Kirkorian, H. L., T. A. Pempek, L. A. Murphy, M. E. Schmidt, and D. R. Anderson. "The Impact of Background Television on Parent-Child Interaction." *Child Development* 80, no. 5 (September–October 2009): 1350–59.

Leckman, James. "Early Parental Preoccupations and Behaviors and Their Possible Relationship to the Symptoms of Obsessive-Compulsive Disorder." *Acta Psychiatrica Scandinavica* 100, Supplement 396 (1999): 1–26.

MacDonald, Kevin, and Ross D. Parke. "Parent-Child Physical Play: The Effects of Sex and Age of Children and Parents." *Sex Roles* 15, no. 7–8 (October 1986): 367–78.

Martin, G. B., and R. D. Clark. "Distress Crying in Neonates: Species and Peer Specificity." *Developmental Psychology* 18 (1987): 3–9.

Mascaro, J. S., P. D. Hackett, and J. K. Rilling. "Testicular Volume Is Inversely Correlated with Nurturing-Related Brain Activity in Human Fathers." *Proceedings of the National Academy of Sciences* 110, no. 39 (September 2013): 15746–51.

McBride, B. A., G. L. Brown, K. K. Bost, N. Shin, B. Vaughn, and B. Korth. "Paternal Identity, Maternal Gatekeeping, and Father Involvement." *Family Relations* 54, no. 3 (2005): 360–72.

McKenna, James J., and Sara Mosko. "Evolution and Infant Sleep: An Experimental Study of Infant-Parent Co-Sleeping and Its Implications for SIDS." *ACTA Paediatrica: An International Journal of Paediatrics* 82, supplement 389 (June 1993): 31–35.

McLaughlin, Katrina, and Orla Muldoon. "Father Identity, Involvement and Work–Family Balance: An In-Depth Interview Study." *Journal of Community and Applied Social Psychology* 24, no. 5 (September–October 2014): 439–52.

Mesman J., M. H. van IJzendoorn, and M. J. Bakermans-Kranenburg. "The Many Faces of the Still-Face Paradigm: A Review and Meta-Analysis." *Developmental Review* 29 (2009): 120–62.

Moormann, Sara M., and Jeffrey E. Stokes. "Solidarity in the Grandparent–Adult Grandchild Relationship and Trajectories of Depressive Symptoms." *The Gerontologist* (June 2014).

Musser, Anna K., Azza H. Ahmed, Karen J. Foli, and Jennifer A. Coddington.

315

"Paternal Postpartum Depression: What Health Care Providers Should Know." *Journal of Pediatric Health Care* 27, no. 6 (November–December 2013): 479–85.

Nicolson, P. "A Brief Report of Women's Expectations of Men's Behaviour in the Transition to Parenthood: Contradictions and Conflicts for Counselling Psychology Practice." *Counselling Psychology Quarterly* 3, no. 4 (1990): 353–61.

Nielsen, Linda. "Parenting Plans for Infants, Toddlers, and Preschoolers: Research and Issues." *Journal of Divorce & Remarriage* 55, no. 4 (2014): 315–33.

Odom, Erika C., Ruowei Li, Kelley S. Scanlon, Cria G. Perrine, and Laurence Grummer-Strawn. "Reasons for Earlier Than Desired Cessation of Breastfeeding." *Pediatrics* 131, no. 3 (2013): e726–32.

O'Leary, Joann, and Clare Thorwick. "Fathers' Perspectives During Pregnancy, Postperinatal Loss." *Journal of Obstetric, Gynecologic, & Neonatal Nursing* 35, no. 1 (January 2006): 78–86.

Palkovitz, Rob, Marcella A. Copes, and Tara N. Woolfolk. "'Its Like . . . You Discover a New Sense of Being': Involved Fathering as an Evoker of Adult Development." *Men and Masculinities* 4, no. 1 (2001): 49–69.

Palm, G. "Involved Fatherhood: A Second Chance." *Journal of Men's Studies* 2 (1993): 139–55.

Palm, Glen, and Bill Joyce. "Attachment from a Father's Perspective." Typescript, 1994.

Paulson, J. F., Heather A. Keefe, and Jenn A. Leiferman. "Early Parental Depression and Child Language Development." *Journal of Child Psychology and Psychiatry* 50, no. 3 (March 2009): 254–62.

Pluess, M., and J. Belsky. "Differential Susceptibility to Parenting and Quality Child Care." *Developmental Psychology* 46, no. 2 (2010): 379–90.

Ramchandani, Paul, T. O. O'Connor, J. Evans, J. Heron, L. Murray, and A. Stein. "The Effects of Pre- and Postnatal Depression in Fathers: A Natural Experiment Comparing the Effects of Exposure to Depression in Offspring." *Journal of Child Psychology and Psychiatry* 49, no. 10 (2008): 1069–78.

Rauscher, Frances, et al. "Music Training Causes Long-Term Enhancement of Preschool Children's Spatial-Temporal Reasoning." *Neurological Research* 19, no. 1 (February 1997): 2–8.

Rochlen, A. B., M. Suizzo, R. A. McKelley, and V. Scaringi. "'I'm Just Providing for My Family': A Qualitative Study of Stay-at-Home Fathers." *Psychology of Men & Masculinity* 9, no. 4 (2008): 193–206.

Rosenthal, David G., Nicole Learned, Ying-Hua Liu, and Michael Weitzman. "Characteristics of Fathers with Depressive Symptoms." *Maternal and Child Health Journal* 17, no. 1 (January 2013): 119–28.

Schmidt, M. E., T. A. Pempek, H. L. Kirkorian, A. F. Lund, and D. R. Anderson. "The Effects of Background Television on the Toy Play Behavior of Very Young Children." *Child Development* 79, no. 4 (July–August 2008): 1137–51.

Schoppe-Sullivan, S. J., G. L. Brown, E. A. Cannon, S. C. Mangelsdorf, and M. S. Sokolowski. "Maternal Gatekeeping, Coparenting Quality, and Fathering Behavior in Families with Infants." *Journal of Family Psychology* 22, no. 3 (June 2008): 389–98.

Stright A. D., K. C. Gallagher, and K. Kelley. "Infant Temperament Moderates Relations between Maternal Parenting in Early Childhood and Children's Adjustment in First Grade." *Child Development* 79, no. 1 (January–February 2008): 186–200.

Thach, Bradley T., George W. Rutherford Jr., and Kathleen Harris. "Deaths and Injuries Attributed to Infant Crib Bumper Pads." *The Journal of Pediatrics* 151, no. 3 (September 2007): 271–74.e3.

Tikotzky, Liat, Sadeh, A., and T. Glickman-Gavrieli. "Infant Sleep and Paternal Involvement in Infant Caregiving During the First 6 Months of Life." *Journal of Pediatric Psychology* 36, no. 1 (2011): 36–46.

Washbrook, E., C. Ruhm, J. Waldfogel, and W.-J. Han. (2011). "Public Policies, Women's Employment after Childbirth, and Child Well-Being." *The B.E. Journal of Economic Analysis and Policy* 11, no. 1 (2011).

Whitehurst, G. J., et al. "Accelerating Language Development through Picture Book Reading." *Developmental Psychology* 24, no. 4 (July 1988): 552–59.

Wilson, Andrea C., et al. "Relation of Infant Diet to Childhood Health: Seven Year Follow Up of Cohort of Children in Dundee Infant Feeding Study." *British Medical Journal* 316, no. 21 (1998): 21–25.

Wleklinski, Barbara, LEAD Center Subject Matter Expert, and Elizabeth Jennings, LEAD Center Assistant Project Director. "The Business Case for Workplace Flexibility." Workshop at the Annual National Association of Workforce Development Professionals (NAWDP) Conference, Minneapolis, MN, May 2013.

Acknowledgments

I'd like to thank the following people (roughly in alphabetical order), whose help has made this book far better—and far more accurate—than it otherwise might have been. Some helped with the first edition, some with the second, some with the third, some with all three.

Bob Abrams for his confidence and support; Justin Anderson for everything having to do with teeth; Jim Cameron and the folks at Temperament Talk, whose work on temperament changed my life; Susan Costello for her support, encouragement, patience, and editing skills; Phil and Carolyn Cowan and Ross Parke for their inspiration and suggestions, and for having paved the road; Jackie Decter, for her continued wisdom, insight, patience, sense of humor, and, above all, her sharp eye and firm-but-deft touch; Bruce Drobeck, Bruce Linton, Rob Palkovitz, and Glen Palm, who, completely independently of each other, have made major contributions to the literature on fatherhood and freely shared their research with me; Celia Fuller, Misha Beletsky, and Ada Rodriguez for their design contributions; Ken Guilmartin and Edward Gordon for their valuable contributions to the sections on music; Amy Handy for her constructive criticism and for smoothing out the rough edges; Seth Himmelhoch, who more than once magically pulled out from his files precisely what I needed; Pam Jordan for her wisdom, guts, and encouragement; Louise Kurtz for supervising the production of this book; Nicole Lanctot for keeping everything running smoothly; Jim Levine for getting everyone together with a minimum of bloodshed; the wonderful, compassionate, and completely selfless folks at the SIDS Alliance; Dawn Swanson, the incredible children's librarian at the Berkeley Public Library, for her help selecting the best kids' books;

my parents for their hospitality, careful editing, and for not getting too upset when I griped about their parenting techniques—a few decades too late for them to do anything about it; Liz for her careful eye and for helping to create Zoë; and the hundreds of dads—new, expecting, and experienced—I've relied on over the years who bravely and openly shared their insights, thoughts, fears, worries, advice, and wisdom. Last, but certainly not least, are all the dad bloggers and non-blogger dads who reviewed chapters, made suggestions, and a lot more, including Eric Bennion (@DiaryDad; diarydad.com), Larry Bernstein (memyselfandkids.com), Michael Bryant (@purposefulpappy; thepurposefulpappy.com), Neal Call (raisedby mydaughter.blogspot.com/), Doug French (@mrdougfrench; mrdougfrench .com), Michael Mocbes (@dadcation; dadcation.com) Ron Reardon (@RonReardon; fullyinvesteddads.com), Spike Zelenka (@doubletrbldaddy; doubletroubledaddy .com), and especially Pat Jacobs and David Keply (both @justadad247; justadad 247.com).

Index

B

ILLUSTRATION CREDITS

George Abbott/The Cartoon Bank: p. 17; Harry Bliss/The Cartoon Bank: p. 209; Roz Chast/The Cartoon Bank: p. 271; Frank Cotham/The Cartoon Bank: pp. 39, 57; Chon Day/The Cartoon Bank: p. 227; Joseph Farris/The Cartoon Bank: p. 154; Ed Frascino/The Cartoon Bank: pp. 247, 252, 258, 288, 292; Anne Gibbons/The Cartoon Bank: p. 236; William Haefeli/The Cartoon Bank: pp. 43, 80, 195, 242; John Jonik/The Cartoon Bank: p. 177; Arnie Levin/The Cartoon Bank: p. 223; Robert Mankoff/The Cartoon Bank: p. 193; Peter Mueller/The Cartoon Bank: pp. 140, 275; J. P. Rini/The Cartoon Bank: p. 128; David Sipress/The Cartoon Bank: pp. 2, 108, 130, 152, 173; Mick Stevens/The Cartoon Bank: p. 248; Jack Ziegler/The Cartoon Bank: pp. 70, 146, 214

ABOUT THE AUTHOR

A nationally recognized parenting expert, Armin A. Brott is also the author of nine critically acclaimed books for fathers. Titles include *The Expectant Father: The Ultimate Guide for Dads-to-Be* and *The New Father: A Dad's Guide to the Toddler Years.* He has written on fatherhood for hundreds of newspapers and magazines and is a frequent guest on such television programs as the *Today* show. He also writes a nationally syndicated newspaper column ("Ask Mr. Dad"), and hosts a syndicated radio show (*Positive Parenting*). He lives with his family in Oakland, California. To learn more, please visit his website, **mrdad.com**.

**FATHERING YOUR
SCHOOL-AGE CHILD**
*A Dad's Guide to the Wonder
Years: 3 to 9*
By Armin A. Brott
Paper · **$12.95**
ISBN 978-0-7892-0924-5
Hardcover · **$24.95**
ISBN 978-0-7892-0923-8

THE MILITARY FATHER
*A Hands-on Guide for
Deployed Dads*
By Armin A. Brott
Hardcover · **$24.95**
ISBN 978-0-7892-1030-2

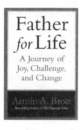

FATHER FOR LIFE
*A Journey of Joy, Challenge,
and Change*
By Armin A. Brott
Hardcover · **$24.95**
ISBN 978-0-7892-0784-5

**THE EXPECTANT AND
FIRST YEAR FATHER**
2-BOOK BOXED SET
THE EXPECTANT FATHER
The Ultimate Guide for Dads-to-Be
THE NEW FATHER
A Dad's Guide to the First Year
$29.95 · ISBN 978-0-7892-1221-4

FAQ FOR EXPECTANT FATHERS
By Armin A. Brott
Paper · **$9.95**
ISBN 978-0-7892-1269-6

FAQ FOR NEW FATIIERS
By Armin A. Brott
Paper · **$9.95**
ISBN 978-0-7892-1270-2

For more information on the *New Father* series and a complete list of titles,
visit **www.abbeville.com/newfather**

*Available from your favorite bookstore or online retailer,
or by calling* 1-800-ARTBOOK

OVER 2,000,000 FATHERHOOD BOOKS IN PRINT!

An information-packed, month-by-month guide to all the emotional, financial, and yes, even physical changes the father-to-be may experience during the course of his partner's pregnancy—now significantly updated and expanded. Incorporating the wisdom of top experts in the field, from obstetricians and birth-class instructors to psychologists and sociologists, the fourth edition of *The Expectant Father* includes the latest research about assisted reproductive technologies (ART) and many other topics, and is filled with sound advice and practical tips for men, such as:

THE EXPECTANT FATHER
FOURTH EDITION
The Ultimate Guide for Dads-to-Be
By Armin A. Brott and
Jennifer Ash

Paper · $13.95
ISBN 978-0-7892-1213-9
Hardcover · $24.95
978-0-7892-1212-2

- Ways to support and encourage your partner throughout pregnancy
- Overcoming infertility
- What childbirth classes don't teach you
- How to make sense of your conflicting emotions
- How to juggle your work and family roles
- Special ways to prepare if you're adopting a baby
- How to become the father you really want to be

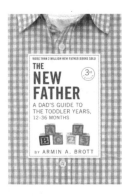

Learn how to make a positive impact in these milestone years of your child's development, when he or she goes from crawling to walking, and from knowing just a few words to speaking in complete sentences. Armin Brott guides you through this crucial phase of fatherhood three months at a time, in the third volume of the New Father series trusted by millions of dads nationwide. Each chapter covers:

THE NEW FATHER
*A Dad's Guide to the Toddler Years,
12–36 Months*
THIRD EDITION
By Armin A. Brott

Paper · $15.95
ISBN 978-0-7892-1323-5
Hardcover · $24.95
ISBN 978-0-7892-1324-2

- Your child's physical, intellectual, verbal, and emotional/social development
- What you're experiencing as a father
- Age-appropriate activities you and your child can enjoy together
- Family matters, including your relationship with your partner, sibling relationships, and more

For more information on the *New Father* series and a complete list of titles,
visit **www.abbeville.com/newfather**

*Available from your favorite bookstore or online retailer,
or by calling* 1-800-ARTBOOK